CONTENTS

INTRODUCTION

This book is for those who are interested in the Christian ministry of healing. In the pages that follow I include material which will be a resource and research tool for those who seek to expand their personal horizons within Christian healing.

Healing Broader and Deeper is set within two distinct halves. The first contains a series of reflective essays. Each of these essays seeks to unfold new dimensions in the ministry of healing. The second half of the book is a sweep of healing narratives from the New Testament accompanied by my own expository notes.

How might this book be used? The individual reader will find much suggestive material in the first six chapters not often addressed elsewhere and approached in a manner which is I believe quite distinctive. For the reader who comes to these pages as part of a personal spiritual discipline the material in the expository notes will aid bible study as well as offer background material upon the healing miracles for purposes of reflection and meditation. The person who is charged with the task of leading a study group will be able to delve into the first six chapters and select from within them any number of topics that might be adapted for use in shorter or longer study sessions. To these study sessions could be added appropriately connected biblical material from the range of expository notes which form the second half of this book. I am very happy for study groups to use examples I offer, though courtesy suggests and copyright requires that if they are reprinted my authorship is acknowledged!

A number of factors have led me to write this book. First and foremost is my own absolute conviction that the ministry of healing should form part and parcel of the regular life of a worshipping Christian community. As will be seen from the pages that follow I am convinced beyond measure that whilst some are called to exercise a specific or particular gift of healing, all Christians should be involved in it through their prayers, through their compassion for others and crucially in their open and warm dealings with others. This is especially so when Christians find themselves responding to people in their hours of need and being with them through the difficulty. A ministry of healing is being exercised when, additionally the situation is held privately or publicly in prayer.

A second factor which has brought me to write this book is the need to share insights with any others who might find themselves drawn to these pages. What I have written does not comprise a single treatise with one line of developing argument throughout. For this reason the reader with the disciplined mind of a scholar might find me an annoying author in that I range around the subjects I tackle in somewhat buccaneering manner. But I have not been slack or casual in my approach. My intention throughout the preparation of this book has been to acknowledge the breadth and wide-ranging complexity of the task facing all those who come to exercise a ministry of healing. Accordingly I have not offered a comprehensive *vade mecum* sufficient for all occasions and purposes. More deliberately I offer insights relating both to practice and study which I have found to be important. Far more is left out than included.

And then, third, I must be autobiographical and, I confess, urbane. In my memory I can still see the look of unspoken disapproval on the face of my director of studies when, during my early undergraduate days in Edinburgh I told him I did not intend to pursue language options for the Old and New Testament courses. It was perhaps the correct decision at the time. For example, the larger range of texts to be studied in English gave me new and immense horizons. Furthermore I was able to focus my studies towards competing philosophical options. But as my commitment to the ministry of healing has increased in the way it has these last few years, I have found myself unable to avoid New Testament Greek any longer! An understanding of what the Bible means when it variously talks about curing, healing, making whole, cleansing, driving out and so on can only be gained by an awareness of what these terms mean within the Greek text of scripture.

Accordingly I seek to open a window looking out towards an overview of the Biblical text in its references to healing. I do so as someone with no specialist knowledge of biblical studies - a factor only too obvious to those who do have such expertise! What I say however, will I hope encourage others similarly lacking in biblical languages to delve more deeply into the original text. To aid this process I have included in the biblical excerpts the relevant Greek words for healing. The chapter on 'Healing Words' offers a theologically based prelude to the biblical study notes.

Any respectable author must acknowledge the generosity of those who have assisted the production of a book. My own list could be endless for I have relied heavily upon others to compensate for my deficiencies. Richard Bauckham, Professor of Biblical Studies at the

University of St Andrews has proved a very valued friend by responding patiently to my ponderous questions on various points of interpretation and exegesis. My father in law, the Revd Douglas Tucker has painstakingly traced the course of my expository notes cross referencing what I say against his copy of 'Liddell and Scott'. His meticulous reading has ensured that many errors were removed at an early stage in the writing.

Others have read this book in manuscript form; Naomi Higham a promising young theologian has given valuable comment as has also Richard Bauckham to whom I clearly owe a double debt. Michael Keeling, also of St Andrews, has a keen eye in the reading of manuscripts. When University duties press ever more deeply into people's outside reading time, I am especially privileged for commitment given to my writing in spite of administrative chores and scholarly demands. In this respect also I am further indebted to Stephen Pattison of the Open University. He is an international authority on matters associated with health and healing, not least as a critic of much for what passes as a Christian ministry of healing. He too has proved a friendship of years can survive a reading of this work.

Alison Naylor has helped with editorial checking, clerical backup and greatly assisted with preparation of the text. All these have enabled me shape this book to its betterment; that residual inadequacies will remain is the inevitable by-product of my authorship rather than their counsel.

I have three sons. The elder two are used to seeing me sitting in front of a keyboard for hours on end typing the material which hopefully you will soon be reading. My wife, herself committed to the interaction of theory and practice [her sphere is education] patiently tolerates my compulsive addiction to a word processor. Our youngest son, now four, saw me preparing this page in the study and announced to the remainder of the family, gathered in the kitchen that "daddy was typing his church again"! For their forbearance and support I am grateful beyond measure. Without it the work could never have begun let alone be completed.

Each Monday evening for an hour a prayer group meets 'within the ministry of healing' [as we describe it] in St Andrew's Church, St Andrews. Time is given for silent petition and intercessory prayer, vocal intercession, prayers of thanksgiving, reflection and Bible study. All the Bible passages in this book, as well as the notes which accompany them, have been shared within this hour of prayer and reflection. I owe a great deal to everyone who prayed and shared with me on those Monday evenings. To them all I dedicate this book with blessing and appreciation.

R.A. Gillies
St Andrews, April 1998

PART I

Chapter 1
SOMETHING FOR EVERYONE

BACKGROUND READING

Upon the bookshelves of any Christian literature shop you can find a great volume of material on the Christian Ministry of Healing. Inevitably the quality will vary, though the standard texts which should be read remain the same. Morris Maddocks has produced a fundamental reference work *The Christian Healing Ministry*[1]. A lesser known work is by Stephen Pattison, *Alive and Kicking*.[2] Pattison's very readable book is well worth study. His critical approach and the keen analytical eye of a professional theologian and social scientist are brought to bear upon much of the Church's ministry of healing. Where questions are begged and definitions lacking Pattison spares no blushes in posing the relevant questions. Those of us who exercise a ministry of healing need regularly to delve into Maddocks for helpful resource and into Pattison for critical self-appraisal. As I prepared these pages, The Handsel Press was about to publish a major work by John Wilkinson, *The Bible and Healing: a Medical and Theological Commentary*. Wilkinson's concerns are close to my own and the congruence of much of our thinking is providential.

INTRODUCTION

In this chapter I will explore the biblical basis which might justify wide ranging involvement of churches and individuals in a Christian ministry of healing. As the chapter moves to its close I will offer some thoughts which link healing with God's purpose of salvation for all.

I tend to take it for granted that all churches should be involved in the ministry of healing. It is the case however that for many the jury is still out and, for others the possibility of a ministry of healing is not even entertained. My view, and I shall be encouraging it in the material which follows, is that all churches are involved in a ministry of healing and should make this explicit. Some might be reluctant to admit it, others might not recognise it. But, and I repeat, all are engaged in it. I will return to this in due course.

In the next few pages I shall be addressing some background issues. This will serve two purposes. First, it will locate everything I say within the context of the relatively recent renewal of a ministry of healing in the mainstream Christian tradition. Second it will serve to demonstrate both the Biblical foundation for this ministry as well as to point up one or two issues concerned with the interpretation of particular Biblical material.

Any study on the Ministry of Healing does well to begin with the Bible. Luke's Gospel in Chapter 9 [also found in Matthew 10] speaks of the twelve disciples being called together and given power "to overcome all demons and to cure diseases, and sent... out to proclaim the kingdom of God and to heal the sick." The closing verses of Mark's Gospel indicate the disciples continued this work: "...they went out to proclaim their message far and wide, and the Lord worked with them and confirmed their words by the miracles that followed." Perhaps most famous of all is the passage from the letter of James:

> Is one of you ill? Let him send for the elders of the church to pray over him and anoint him with oil in the name of the Lord; the prayer offered in faith will heal the sick man, the Lord will restore him to health, and if he has committed other sins they will be forgiven. Therefore confess your sins to one another, and pray for one another, that you may be healed. A good man's prayer is very powerful and effective.

The Church of Scotland minister J. Cameron Peddie, working deep in Glasgow's Gorbals, wrote of his own feelings as the call to begin a healing ministry impressed itself upon him:

> ... the first thing I did was seek guidance from the bible. My thoughts had flown to Our Lord's commission: 'Preach the Gospel, heal the sick.' We had been taught as Divinity Students that the second half of the commission was meant for the Disciples only and their immediate followers.[3]

Before he began a healing ministry in any public way Peddie had to test the call within the arena of his own conscience. He recalls walking Prestwick beach late at night during the August holidays of 1947, hearing nothing but the swish of the waters without and the sound of His voice within. Part of Peddie's anxiety was the credibility which would be attached to this call by his fellow ministers:

> If I were to tell my colleagues I was taking up this work, they might only laugh and think me insane. If I were to try to persuade them of the possibility of it, marshalling my arguments on the basis of Scripture, they very soon would argue me down. Yet my purpose was to get *all* ministers to take it up and the outlook seemed unpromising.[4]

With confidence gained from scriptural inspiration he was sure of his conclusion:

> ... if the second half of that commission does not apply to us, how do we know the first half does? The words make sense only if we believe Our Lord s commission is indivisible and act on that belief. Our responsibility is both to preach *and heal*.[5]

Peddie however, could have found support in words from the Church Fathers. In the *Apostolic Constitutions* [probably late fourth century] the writer says:

> These gifts were first bestowed upon us the apostles when we were about to preach the gospel to every creature, and afterwards were of necessity afforded to those who had by our means believed; not for the advantage of those who perform them, but for the conviction of the unbelievers, that those whom the word did not persuade, the power of signs might put to shame.[6]

Even in these early centuries it was therefore recognised that instructions and commands given to the earliest apostles applied also to believers in succeeding generations.

Before we move any further we should look briefly at the crucial last verses of Mark's Gospel. This will involve a short digression - to consider the extent to which we can take scriptural texts at face value or when more extremely put, as literally prescriptive. In these verses there is a commission from Jesus - to proclaim the gospel.

The original ending was at verse 8. The last twelve verses are an addition and come from a pen other than that of Mark. These later verses were however known in AD140, and quoted by Irenaeus in AD180. They seem to be an attempt to 'round off' the peremptory ending at verse 8, where the women "went out and ran away from the tomb". Mark records that they said nothing to anyone for they were afraid. The extra verses thus serve to unfold a proclamatory conclusion to the gospel whereby they went out to proclaim their message far and wide. We are told that God worked with them and miracles followed.

But the question can be posed, 'Are we at liberty to give these later constructions, namely the last twelve verses, the same credence we more readily give to the remainder of the gospel, that which was written earlier?'

What do we find in these later verses which form the longer ending of Mark's Gospel? In Mark 16:18 the idea that Christians are immune from poison is given. However such is unknown elsewhere in scripture. By contrast the injunction to spread the gospel, also from this later ending, is broadly spread across the New Testament in one form or

3

another. It is a command to 'go everywhere' and is crucial to the message of good news proclaimed by Jesus.

Could it be the case that in this longer ending of Mark's Gospel we have several levels of interpretation operating simultaneously? Perhaps by speaking of drinking poison, these later verses of Mark are providing a metaphor of Christians coming to no harm in an era of persecution; for those called to suffer and die in such an environment a more perfect life awaits. In other words they should not be read literally. Their richness lies in figurative, or metaphorical understanding. For this reason I would venture to suggest that even though they are of later provenance, these verses do in fact accord with the remainder of Mark s Gospel. The hope of eternal life after this one is a highly relevant New Testament theme. And in terms of difficult textual interpretation, where metaphorical interpretation is possible and yields understanding it may be put to use. Where literal application is the more appropriate reading it equally may be offered. Morna Hooker comments enigmatically, "Like Jesus, the disciples are to cast out demons and heal the sick; but, unlike him, they are to speak in tongues and be preserved from physical danger."[7] Quite clearly, Hooker's opinion is somewhat extreme. It was not so much the case that the believers were to be preserved from physical danger as given assurance of ultimate deliverance from its effects through faith in the risen Christ.

I have digressed long enough. Let us now return to the mainstream of my argument. Were the injunctions of Jesus meant for the first apostles alone? Like Peddie I answer 'clearly not'. For support I draw upon not only the *Apostolic Constitutions* as mentioned above, but also the lists of gifts given the church in Paul's Letters to the Corinthians, Romans and Ephesians[8] and the fact that these gifts encompass ordinary qualities of life for all Christians of all times as well as more specific gifts to enable particular aspects of ministry to be carried out for a particular feature of building up the body of Christ, the church.

It is my view that the ministry of healing is now a ministry which has both a general character for all Christians at all times as well as defining a specific focus of work for some Christians at particular moments. A reminder then; in the first part of this book I am aiming to give substance to the complementary nature of healing as both a general quality of all Christians and a specific gift to some. It will be seen that neither is more important than the other; both are necessary and equally so.

CALL AND RESPONSE

At the heart of the Christian faith two features present themselves as crucial for living the life of the Christian. One is the 'call' from God, the other is 'response'. British Christianity of the 1990s does not easily take either of these on board at a personal level. They tend to sound too 'churchy' or too 'religious' for ordinary people who simply want to get on with life and be 'good' Christians. And yet, they are vital aspects of the Christian life which once properly understood at a very basic level can be seen as relevant for every British Christian without exception.

The Call to Jesus and his Response

I shall for sake of ease not consider the eternal relationship of Jesus within God as Trinity. My concern is rather to focus upon the scriptural record of Jesus being called in specific terms to do his Father's work on earth. A passage I have in mind is Luke 3:21-22, Jesus' baptism by John the Baptist in the River Jordan. This is paralleled in Matthew and in the opening verses of Mark's Gospel. John's gospel also contains an account of Jesus' baptism. In Luke the passage is:

> During a general baptism of the people, when Jesus too had been baptized and was praying, heaven opened and the Holy Spirit descended on him in bodily form like a dove, and there came a voice from heaven, "You are my beloved Son; in you I take delight."

The passage is reminiscent of Psalm 2:7, "You are my son ... this day I become your father" and of Isaiah 42:1, "Here is my servant, whom I uphold, my chosen one, in whom I take delight! I have put my spirit upon him". In one sense this need not necessarily be read as God's call to Jesus for he was with God "at the beginning" [John 1:2]. But it was an occasion of great significance in the earthly life of Jesus; he was especially charged with authority by the explicit divine voice of God. Given this how did Jesus respond?

Clearly he did not take it as an item of individual spiritual blessing or benefit meant for him alone to the exclusion of others. Luke's account continues [as does Matthew's and more briefly, Mark's] with Jesus beginning his work and, "full of the Holy Spirit" he wandered in the wilderness experiencing every kind of temptation.

There is a lesson to each of us here. After an extremely uplifting spiritual experience we naturally want to remain within the experience. But reality is different. We have to come back to earth! It may even be the case that a wilderness experience is the natural follow-on from an event of great personal religious uplift. During such an experience we can well expect temptation of every kind to come our way [some would account for this by saying it points to the personal reality of demonic temptation]. This is a real testing of the call which came to us in the experience; have we been strengthened to withstand the temptation or not?

By way of anecdote, I once knew a woman who had lived with intense religious experience for about a year and had become obsessively extreme in her religious observance and devotion. Inevitably a period of testing came - and despite much quality counselling she failed to recognise it for what it was. Tragically she saw it as God's punishment for some imagined wrongdoing rather than the normal outcome of a genuine call from God. Perhaps inevitably she lost her faith and began almost to rejoice that she could be so 'bad'.

Returning now to Luke's Gospel. We read of Jesus coming from the wilderness, "armed with the power of the Spirit" returning to Galilee and teaching in their synagogues. It was evident that Jesus' words had authority - both to inspire and to enrage [Luke 4:21-30]. But his ministry was not only one of word, it was also one of work. An exorcism is recorded in verses 33 to 37 of chapter 4 and then the healing of Simon Peter's mother-in-law in 38 and 39 with further healings and exorcisms following in verses 40 to 41. From this high activity Jesus sought a lonely place [4:42-44] but once again crowds pressed in on him. His mind was set on further travel for as Jesus told them, "I must give the good news of the kingdom of God to the other towns also, for that is what I was sent to do."

It is in this last direction that we can see the response of Jesus to be focussed. He was sent to do what the previous verses have been telling us he was doing; to engage in a ministry of word and work arising directly out of his call from God.

The Call and Response of the Disciples

In his long prayer before dying as recorded by John, Jesus prays the following words concerning those who had responded to his teaching:

I have made your name known to the men whom you gave me out of the world. They were yours and you gave them to me, and they have obeyed your command. Now they know that all you gave me has come from you; for I have taught them what I learned from you, and they have received it: they know with certainty that I came from you, and they have believed that you sent me. [John 17:6-8]

Amongst others Jesus is here referring to those he had previously called to follow him. The stories of these calls are very famous. By the northern edge of the Sea of Galilee Jesus speaks to a group of fishermen:

Jesus was walking by the sea of Galilee when he saw Simon and his brother Andrew at work with casting nets in the lake; for they were fishermen. Jesus said to them, "Come, follow me, and I will make you fishers of men." At once they left their nets and followed him.

Going a little farther, he saw James, son of Zebedee and his brother John in a boat mending their nets. At once he called them; and they left their father Zebedee in the boat with the hired men and followed him. [Mark 1:16-20]

The same narrative is followed in Matthew 4:18-22. In Luke different situations are presented [see Luke 5:1-11 and 6:12-16, cf. Mark 3:13-19. A further variant is in John 1:40-51]. What is significant however is that in each Gospel the disciples followed Jesus as he set about his ministry of word and work. In Luke 9:1-6 the twelve are sent out with power and authority to overcome all demons, to cure diseases, to proclaim the kingdom of God and to heal the sick. A longer version of the same account is to be found in Matthew 10. In Mark 16 verses 8b and 20 we have, respectively:

Jesus himself sent out by them, from east to west, the sacred and imperishable message of eternal salvation.

...they went out to proclaim their message far and wide, and the Lord worked with them and confirmed their words by the miracles that followed.

The significance of what I am saying here must now be clear. If one is to believe in God and trust in Jesus as his Son and as Saviour then one has a call from him which leads to a response - namely to do as he did. But before I draw out the implications of this further I must also look at God's call to the church. In a later chapter my mind will focus on the implications of call when viewed from the standpoint of Jesus sending out his followers to share the good news.

The Call and Response of the Church

By this I am referring of course to no one specific Christian tradition, but rather to all equally as well as to individual Christians specifically. We may begin by quoting from the 'Catholic Epistles':

> You have not seen him, yet you love him; and trusting in him now without seeing him, you are filled with a glorious joy too great for words... [1 Peter 1: 8-9]

Some more verses from 1 Peter:

> So come to him, to the living stone which was rejected by men but chosen by God and of great worth to him. You also, as living stones, must be built up into a spiritual temple, and form a holy priesthood to offer spiritual sacrifices acceptable to God through Jesus Christ. [1 Peter 2:6-8]

> But you are a chosen race, a royal priesthood, a dedicated nation, a people claimed by God for his own, to proclaim the glorious deeds of him who has called you out of darkness into his marvellous light. [1 Peter 2:9]

How does all this relate back to the church responding to the call God has given it? Some words from 1 Thessalonians will help:

> With this in mind we pray for you always, that our God may count you worthy of your calling, and that his power may bring to fulfilment every good purpose and every act inspired by faith, so that the name of our Lord Jesus may be glorified in you, and you in him, according to the grace of our God and the Lord Jesus Christ.

Before I move on to another section it should not go without mention that the most significant example of someone hearing God's call and then responding is that of Paul. From Chapter Thirteen onwards almost everything in the Acts of the Apostles is concerned with Paul's missionary journeys. Having been dramatically called, Paul responded with untiring vigour.

GIFTS SUFFICIENT FOR THE TASK

Having called his followers God does not then leave them unequipped for the task. From Paul's First Letter to the Corinthians [12:28]:

> Within our community God has appointed in the first place apostles, in the second place prophets, thirdly teachers; then miracle workers, then those who have gifts of healing, or ability to help others or power to guide them...

In total Paul offers four lists of gifts given to the church:

1 Corinthians 12: 4-11	1 Corinthians 12:27-13:13	Ephesians 4: 11-13	Romans 12: 6-21
Wise Speech	Apostles	Apostles	Inspired Utterance
Deep knowledge into words	Prophets	Prophets	Administration
	Teachers	Evangelists	Teaching
Faith	Miracle Workers	Pastors	Counsel
Gifts of Healing	Healers	Teachers	Giving to charity
Miraculous powers	Helpers		Leadership
	Tongues		Helping Others
Prophecy	Love		Love
Distinguish true spirits from false	Giving		Hope
	Martyrdom		Hospitality
Tongues	Knowledge		
Interpretation			

Each of these could well merit a chapter on their own. Some of them are general qualities for all Christians all the time - faith, hope, love, hospitality and so on. Others, such as praying in tongues, martyrdom, administration, counselling could be gifts for all Christians but in reality are given only to some. Some have gifts which require development and formation. It could be that a gift is given so that it might be enlarged upon in practice. Wise speech and deep knowledge for example. In this respect, I remember hearing Richard Holloway in an ordination sermon charging the new deacon to "learn and develop the gift of oratory for preaching". In theory I suppose, everyone can and maybe should preach. But in most situations such a prospect is a practical nonsense. Therefore it is right and appropriate that those charged with that specific responsibility engage the task with a fitting admixture of confidence and humility.

This line of thought has repercussions upon our thinking about the ministry of healing. If this is a general gift for all Christians all the time then it could, no it *does*, mean that the meal taken personally to the house of a recent bereavement, the kind word to the student in examination difficulties, standing by and remembering the worried mother waiting for the results of medical tests are all part of a general ministry of healing. But amongst those who exercise a general ministry of healing in this sense are some who are called to develop and form the gift of healing in a more specific way. This will be through prayer, through counselling, through miraculous powers maybe, through leadership, inspired utterance. The context might be the 'healing service' set aside for such a purpose. It might be in a period of time towards the end of the morning service when people are available to listen to and pray with any who come forward to one of the side altars in the church.

For many the healing sought and offered will be unapologetically for physical intervention by God upon a definable physical condition. For others it may be for support through prolonged and unremitting pain and for others support through a time of personal crisis. For others it will be a healing of past hurt and damage. A friend recently wrote to me:

> ... one week I made a decision to go to church in a committed way again. A big decision and I was quite nervous. I sneaked into evensong and felt unsure of myself and of God. Then the organist played 'Nimrod' from Elgar's *Enigma Variations*. When I was a teenager at youth fellowship we had been asked to choose something which reminded us of God and bring it along one evening. I took 'Nimrod' to play because I associated it with the story of the prodigal son. The music builds up gradually and I imagine the son walking up to meet his father, and then the father going to meet him. I always think of how forgiving and loving God is when I hear the music. So when I heard it that evening I knew that I was being told it was OK, that God just wanted me back. I can't dismiss as coincidence the fact that on that particular evening, having made that particular decision, I should hear that particular piece of music.
>
> I felt that this new church was a safe place, though I didn't know much about it. My decision to speak to the priest was in part bound up with the sense of 'rightness' I felt about it. I am certain it can't just be coincidence because that church has now turned my life around. I am saying this because all the slow [and sometimes painful] healing of my past difficulties and hurt is all part of the journey up the path to meet God. It is about returning home. Whilst even now the thought of it scares me half to death the goal is one I can't wait to reach.

Perhaps that vignette was a digression. But it was one not without its significance because the issues it raises clearly had implications not only for my friend but also for those in the church with whom she came into contact. All of them in one way or another would in some way or another, whether consciously or intuitively, be engaging in the ministry of healing. For some it would be 'general' in the way I describe it and would involve various measures of reassurance, kindness, support, firmness, discipline and maybe even careful rebuke and caution. For others it would be specific involving the definite and quite explicit reassurance of God's healing variously through cleansing and renewal of life.

I can amplify what I mean here by looking at the meaning of some of the Greek words associated with healing in the New Testament. My remarks earlier indicate I am one singularly ungifted for such a task! The challenge of what follows is that in preparing it I have had to develop a hitherto unformed [and often suppressed] talent!

Within the words and work of Jesus two principal themes recur repeatedly. One is the concern he has for curing people of their illness. I use the word cure quite deliberately for many of the contexts in which Jesus cures people are therapeutic conditions. The word *therapeuo* can be found 38 times in the New Testament, most of these being in the first three gospels. An associated word *therapeia* [roughly meaning 'attendance in healing'] has two occurrences. Again, therapeutic activity is associated with other words too. One such is *iaomai*; it has 26 occurrences again the greater majority of these being in the gospels. The word *iama* has three instances, all associated with the gift of healing in 1 Corinthians 12 and *iasis* with its single location in Acts 4:22.

The second concern of Jesus is for salvation. This concern, like that of curing from illness progresses from him into the life and teaching of the early church. Prime words for this in the New Testament are *soteria* and *soterion*. Also used extensively is *sozo*. *Sozo* has a number of different applications mostly with the connotations of making sound, making whole, rescuing, bringing to safety and so on. But there are a few crucial passages where it is applied to healing, both in the sense of therapeutic curing as well as in a number of other senses meaning, more broadly, to make whole. With profit these can be listed:

Mark 3:4-5 [Luke 6:9-10] Then Jesus turned to them: "Is it permitted to do good or to do evil on the sabbath, or to *save* life or kill?"... he said to the man, "Stretch out your arm"; he stretched it out and his arm was restored.

Mark 5:23 [Jairus' daughter] "My little daughter is at death's door", he said. "I beg you to come and lay your hands on her so that her life may be *saved*."

Luke 7:3 *[diasozo]* [A centurion ...] sent some Jewish elders to ask [Jesus] to come and *save* his servant's life.

Luke 7:48-50 [The woman living an immoral life anoints Jesus' feet with myrrh] ... "He said to the woman, your faith has *saved* you; go in peace."

Luke 8:36 Eye witnesses told [Jesus and his followers] how the madman had been *cured*.

Luke 18:40-43 Jesus said to [the blind beggar on the Jericho road], "Have back your sight; your faith has *healed* you." He recovered his sight instantly...

Acts 2:46b-47 [With reference to the early believers' enthusiasm] ... and day by day the Lord added new *converts* to their number. [The *King James Bible* reads, the Lord added to the church such as should be *saved*]

Acts 4:9 [Peter is speaking] "...if it is about help given to a sick man that we are being questioned today, and the means by which he was *cured*... it was [by] the name of Jesus Christ of Nazareth."

Acts 14:9 Paul fixed his eyes on [the cripple from Lystra] and, seeing that he had the faith to be *cured*, said in a loud voice, "Stand up straight on your feet."

James 5:15 ...the prayer offered in faith will *heal* the sick man, the Lord will restore him to health, and if he has committed sins they will be forgiven... [and in 5:20] ... you may be sure of this: the one who brings a sinner back from his erring ways will be *rescuing* a soul from death and cancelling a multitude of sins.

These references are crucial in the church's healing ministry today. They encompass a range of situations portraying therapeutic healing, deliverance, forgiveness of sins, the name of the one in whom Christian healing is effected, conversion and setting free from a past life. All these are linked with the work of the ordinary Christian all the time who is directed to bring people to God's healing, his salvation.

The relevance of this excursion of mine into New Testament Greek interpretation will be becoming clear. Jesus and the early church focussed upon such matters as salvation and healing. If we question to the point of denying our own part in the outworking of these two facets of Christian life and faith we, and I put this with deliberate force, risk undermining much of the basis if not the actual content of what we believe and of that which we profess. My contention in all of this is that the Christian cannot avoid making real God's plan of salvation. Part and parcel of this is the ministry of healing.

Chapter 2
THIS GLORY HAS CHANGED
MY LIFE

This chapter aims to cover a wide compass of material. It will include prayer within the ministry of healing, 'bearing the burden' of others' sufferings, and connect each of these with Transfiguration. I also return to a theme of the first chapter namely the ministry of healing as a gift for every Christian in general as well as for some in particular. My purpose in doing so will be to introduce counselling into the agenda of this book.

At a recent Bible Study within the hour of prayer which we set aside every Monday evening, as part of the church's ministry of healing, a passage was offered by the leader which resonated in a way that perhaps I could not have predicted. The passage was well known. It was Matthew's account of Jesus praying in deep distress in the Garden of Gethsemane:

> Jesus then came with his disciples to a place called Gethsemane, and he said to them, "Sit here while I go over there to pray." He took with him Peter and the two sons of Zebedee. Distress and anguish overwhelmed him, and he said to them, "My heart is ready to break with grief. Stop here, and stay awake with me." Then he went on a little farther, threw himself down, and prayed, "My Father, if it is possible, let this cup pass me by. Yet not my will but yours."
>
> He came back to the disciples and found them asleep; and he said to Peter, "What! Could none of you stay awake with me for one hour?" [Matthew 26:36-40]

The study deliberately foreclosed at this point, though the narrative does continue the events of that first Maundy Thursday at the foot of the Mount of Olives. The focus for that study was the section beginning, "Could none of you stay awake with me for one hour?" I have to say I prefer those translations which use the phrase 'watch with me', rather than 'stay awake'. 'Watch with me' is evocative of a much richer sense of meaning. Jesus' agony in the Garden is plain for all to read; "Distress and anguish overwhelmed him..." He asks his disciples to remain awake with him. Though they are directed to pray that they will be spared the test which Jesus increasingly recognised was his destiny he wished them to pray with him in his personal hour of need.

How might this be applied to a ministry of healing? The answer is straightforward. The principal action within the ministry of healing is prayer. Without prayer the ministry of healing would be seriously depleted if not diluted to near non-existence. Touch, perhaps but not essentially in the form of laying on of hands would remain, so would compassion and understanding. Clinical action would continue to effect much healing. But without the action of praying there would be little to identify anything specific in the ministry of healing as the engagement of ordinary Christians with suffering.

As the Bible Study unfolded we began to realise in a very profound way that when someone asks us to pray for a particular situation we are like the disciples being asked by Jesus 'to watch and pray'. Very suddenly our roles were reversed. Previously it had been our unthought assumption that when people ask others to pray they did so because they expected something of Jesus from those involved in the prayer for healing. Our Bible study had taught us something new. We saw that the person in need is the one most like Jesus and those of us who are asked to pray most like the disciples being required to 'watch and pray' with that person in their hour of need.

Being with someone who is in need, being able to listen to them and hear what they have to say and sharing this time with them before God is a crucial part of the ministry of healing and, I believe, fundamental in the mystery of salvation.

I recently heard a story from someone who had had to go through an extremely serious operation. The effects of this operation have been staggeringly successful - mobility is restored when previously it was vanishing almost by the hour. That person said:

> After my operation I asked [the Rector] how I might give thanks to God to repay the wonderful new life I had been given. He quietly responded that I was now in a position to understand others' situations better and could offer them something by way of comfort and understanding. Before my experiences of being immobile I failed to watch and listen sufficiently to others. Now situations keep appearing from nowhere, and I immediately know I am in that place at that time for a purpose. Knowing that I shall never be frightened of anything again, I feel I can communicate this to the other person, and I think somehow this gives the other person a little more confidence as well.

This is a simple, but quite profound example of the way by which quite unexpectedly a person can enter into a ministry of healing without special training, without special knowledge. Put more straightforwardly a set of life experiences gave this person a capacity - a gift - to do something which before the operation seemed impossible. It is in this sense that every Christian believer can be part of the church's ministry of healing.

A picture image might help us consider this more completely. The person in need has a 'burden'. They wish, or need, to share that burden with another. As they do so the burden might either be removed completely or the load it imposes be eased by another taking up the task of carrying it along with the person whose burden it has to remain.

The person who has a permanent condition - such as diabetes, epilepsy or maybe constant pain, and who seeks regular and frequent prayers for healing is the person whose burden has to be shared given that its complete removal is only an outside possibility. For such a person knowledge that someone is prepared to 'watch and pray' with them in their hour of need is crucial. The burden does not have to be carried alone. Nor should it have to be. No one could remove Jesus' burden, yet he asked his disciples to share it with him in preparation for that fate which had become increasingly unavoidable. Bearing the burden of another - for them or with them - is vital in either a general or in a specific understanding of the ministry of healing.

Burden bearing is an important image. It helps us resolve the problem which confronts Christians when the question is asked, "What happens when there doesn't seem to be any healing?"

Many asked themselves this same question when, after much 'soaking in prayer' the great pastor in the Church of England, David Watson, died of cancer at an early age. "Why did God not answer our prayers?", said so many people. And yet such a question betrays a misunderstanding of the ministry of healing. Whilst a ministry of healing is in large part about the curing of illnesses - Jesus' own ministry and that of the disciples showed us this was so, it is also about bringing people into a wholeness whereby healing takes place in spite of the continuing presence of illness and suffering.

As I indicate elsewhere, I have no ready definition of what wholeness is, though I know what it means. The person who is made 'whole' is one who has come to terms with his or her situation in life. They are able to be open about their situation, and where they feel they have to be closed about something it does not dominate or gnaw away at them. If the person is dying then it involves an open awareness to that fact. Where sin has been a problem then the whole person is confident of God's forgiveness and they know of their acceptance by God in all they have been, all they are, as well as being in process of transformation towards that which they shall become. Wholeness has been found. It constitutes healing in a broader and deeper way then does curing, I suggest.

I once had the privilege of visiting a man with a terminal illness. He was a doctor and expressed in my early visits some disquiet with what I had been teaching about healing in my ministry. We conversed a little about the subject but not to any great depth. The visiting continued, spasmodically and irregularly and with varying degrees of frequency - all this was his wish. As the condition progressed he asked if when I called I would say Morning Prayer with [or rather, say it alongside] him. There needed to be no discussion about the translation to be used. In such circumstances almost always I would choose the *Book of Common Prayer.* As time and illness progressed the combined foundation of conversation and prayer gave way to a deep mutual trust and recognition. There were no explicit prayers for healing but there was a healing into wholeness for us both.

Morris Maddocks[1] has offered the Transfiguration narratives[2] as stories in which one might understand what is meant by being changed through 'personal communion with the living God'. He quotes the monk, Herbert Slade, "[transfiguration] is the self-expression of that God in whom we live and move and have our being; so that whatever finds expression there is true now..." Let me trace what Maddocks says. The relevance of this for those knowingly in a ministry of healing will emerge.

Preparation and mental adjustment are a prerequisite for a major 'happening' in our lives. It might be an operation, marriage or a birth in the family. The event will need some personal adjustment beforehand if its effects can be growth points for us. The disciples ascending the Mount of Transfiguration were at a crucial turning point in the life and work of Jesus. His messiahship would inevitably lead to his suffering.

One wonders what sort of preparation the human body needs in order to prepare it for the 'attack' culture of much of modern business and industry. It used to be the perception that clergy more than most others had stressful jobs. In many ways that is still the case for much parish turbulence and turmoil has to be carried within the soul of the cleric. To compensate for this however the clergy have a wonderful freedom to build meditation and quiet into their lives. A freedom about which many in business can only dream. Quiet is a powerful preparation of the mind and body for the stresses of daily life - in church, in work, in the family... wherever. Quietness in the form of meditation has a powerful effect of strengthening and building both physical and mental resources.

At another level Maddocks stresses physical fitness as important preparation for the body. The place of the physical body in all aspects of our lives is crucial. But let us not deceived into thinking the body has to be made fit at all costs. I say this for there is a danger in viewing physical fitness as a latter day deity to be worshipped and venerated in its own right. Very few male models in fashion and clothes magazines have a portly silhouette whereas muscles as part of an alert, assertive physique ripple across the pages. The Bible however [as if to challenge the twentieth century God of the toned-up thorax] speaks of giving up 'self'. Perhaps significantly just before the Transfiguration experience Jesus says to his disciples, "Anyone who wishes to be a follower of mine must renounce self; he must take up his cross and follow me..." [Matthew 16:24] and again where more explicitly we are told that the body can actually get in our way, "If your right eye causes your downfall, tear it out and fling it away; it is better for you to lose one part of your body than for the whole of it to be thrown into hell." [Matthew 5: 29].

Obviously a balance has to be struck. If physical fitness is a means of responding to God's call to live a healthier life then it is clearly good. If it is a deity to be venerated as an end in itself then ultimately a fit body will fail to satisfy as it ages and begins to tire and wear out. It is a deity which cannot be replaced.

In the transfiguration experience our human experience is contrasted with the glory of God - but not to our own undoing. Rather it is the case that our weakness is charged with God's strength. Our own finite world is penetrated, or filled, with his glory. Peter, James and John went with Jesus up the mountain and their experience was this. The law - the religion - of their forefathers [embodied in Moses and Elijah] encountered the person of Jesus. The past of Israel encountered its present in the person of Jesus. Central in the Christian faith is the perspective that in Jesus all things are reconciled. Peter attempted to capture and preserve the moment by offering to build three shelters. But time had to move on, Jesus was required to go his way of earthly suffering and thereby unite his present with the future [but already present] kingdom of God.

Maddocks makes the important point that along with Jesus, the physically fit and those whose lot is to suffer, can be sharers in the glory and healing of the cosmic Christ . The appearance of Moses and Elijah is significant too: there is no middle wall of partition between the living and the dead. All are one in the transfiguring power of Christ. Romans 14:8 can be quoted, "If we live, we live for the Lord; and if we die, we die for the Lord. So whether we live or die, we belong to the Lord."

As the foursome of Jesus, Peter, James and John went down the mountain they did so in silence. At the foot of the mountain they encountered an epileptic whom Jesus healed. Asking why [in Matthew's account] they could not do this the disciples learnt the hard truth that their time had yet to come. In due course they would be able to bridge the gap between the temporal and the eternal, the temporary and the permanent. They would - to employ Jesus' metaphor - be able to make the mountain move. To cure, heal and make whole.

Those who ask for prayer, and those charged with the task of praying within the ministry of healing can rightly expect much. Each is in a special relationship with God because of the particular fact of asking for, and offering prayer. This doesn't make one different or distinct from others in any way. The fact of asking prayer for healing, and being the person who is asked is not unlike receiving communion. This may sound complicated so let me explain what I mean. All may come forward to receive communion but the act of each individual receiving the bread and wine is quite special and everyone involved from the person receiving the bread and wine to the person 'administering' the elements of bread and wine as well as all those around can rightly expect God's full offering of himself to them in that situation.

Whether you are asking, or offering prayers for healing, you are in the presence of God in a most special way. Expect the moment to be a transfiguring one. It is being in the presence of God where healing into wholeness can take place. Where the past tensions and worries can be resolved and the future made plain. Where the torn individual can be made one in Christ and know it to be so.

Viewed against this background the ministry of healing has a dimension far richer than any simple situation such as might be covered by this caricature: "I've got a sore toe, please pray for it." In due response to this request you 'put up' a prayer with rather the same sort of dismissive abandon as might a doctor writing a hasty prescription. Whilst situations like this do inevitably present themselves, the ministry of healing is much broader and deeper.

A MINISTRY FOR EVERYONE

I want now to focus briefly but not without significance on the role of everyone who is a Christian and who, in my terms of reference, is thereby a part of the Christian ministry of healing. Once when discussing this thought with someone they commented to me that the ministry of healing in this general sense was identical with the gift of love.

The comment is insightful. It is true that the general character of love as a gift which must permeate all Christian life in general and each person's life in particular will overlap extensively with a ministry of healing. Perhaps one way to view the overlap of the two would be to see the gift of love, being the greatest gift, as something which is given one focused or explicit expression in a ministry of healing. Another aspect of this is the indissolubility of a ministry of healing within the wider Christian framework of evangelism and mission where love is given its fullest expression. More will be said upon this in the chapter 'Healing Moving Outward'.

A SPECIFIC MINISTRY

In this scenario particular people are given a charge to exercise a specific ministry of healing and have the church's authority to do so. This might be within the context of a ministry team, a group given authority by - for example - a presbytery or a bishop or whatever. Whatever the local circumstances, the situation of each will differ. The main feature for each however must be accountability. Whilst each person in the specific ministry of healing is given an authority by the church that person must never be authoritarian. Those in this ministry of healing must maintain confidentiality. They must be openly accountable to the structures of their church and they must be prepared to cease their specific role within the ministry of healing if required to do so. This may sound heavy-handed or officious. In practice it need not be so. All those who come forward, to seek prayer and guidance within a more formal ministry of healing situation [and many do so with much nervousness and after much painstaking soul-searching] must have utmost confidence in the people who are to receive them and minister with them. Equally the persons charged with a ministry of healing in this sense must understand the need for training and for correction if need be.

It is quite likely that by now the place of counselling within a ministry of healing will have occurred to you as something to consider.

A definition of counselling has been given, the language is dated and non-inclusive, but the meaning is clear:

> ... assisting an individual to develop insight and ability to adjust to successive events in his life through the appraisal of his capacities, aptitudes and interests; helping him to understand motivations, emotional reactions and compensatory behaviour; and helping him to attain a degree of personal integration whereby he can most effectively use his potentialities and make the greatest contribution to the society in which he lives.[3]

A senior colleague of mine in the Episcopal Church has spoken of the training he received for ministry many years ago, and has reflected upon the minimal guidance given for pastoral work. He summarises it as "writing promptly to thank anyone who has given you hospitality!" My own training, only twenty years after his, involved much time given to 'group dynamics', learning about and reflecting upon 'interpersonal skills' and being taught the basics of various issues within counselling. It involved training to discern when to be involved with people and when to 'let them go'. This input will be familiar to most clergy trained within the period from the late 1960 s onwards.

Counselling is now undertaken by a wide variety of people, mostly volunteers who work, for example with marriage problems [RELATE] and bereavement [CRUSE]. A network of self-help support groups have sprung up to enable the vulnerable, those with financial difficulties, learning difficulties and many, many more to share experiences and offer mutual support. For many of these people pastoral support would, in a former generation, have been provided within a stable community framework where the local church would have been the centre. Whilst it is the case that many of these specialised counselling and support systems have a strong Christian input [not least from participating personnel] their ethos is largely governed by secular theories from the human sciences, which whilst not non-Christian, are not explicitly Christian. In my own counselling much of the framework within which I work does not necessarily have a reference to specific Christian teaching. My motivation is however thoroughly Christian even if the content and format of the counselling does not obviously refer to texts in scripture, tenets of Christian doctrine or traditions of practice within the Christian church.

At a professional level counselling has been given increased and much needed credibility in recent years. The founding of umbrella organisations such as the British Association for Counselling [BAC], and the Convention of Scottish Counselling Associations [COSCA], has provided a discipline and a standard for work where very needy people could so easily suffer at the hands of the untrained and unskilled unaware of their limitations even if well-intentioned. Anyone entering counselling as a career, or saying they are a counsellor, ought to have some affiliation either personally or through their agency with a recognised authority such as the British Association for Counselling. This will indicate a recognised standard of quality is being followed and a Code of Ethics adhered to.

However this must not be interpreted to mean that counselling is only for the specialists. In exactly the same way that the ministry of healing has both a specific task for some charged with the exercise of that gift as well as a general role for all Christians, so counselling has also both a specific responsibility for professional and qualified counsellors as well as a role for everyone all the time. A recent definition offered by the BAC encapsulates this superbly:

> People become engaged in counselling when a person, occupying regularly or temporarily the role of counsellor, offers or agrees explicitly to offer time, attention and respect to another person or persons temporarily in the role of client.
>
> The task of counselling is to give the client an opportunity to explore, discover and clarify ways of living more resourcefully and toward greater well-being.[4]

Counselling has in a number of ways eclipsed the role of many clergy - who perhaps by their own tacit admission were ill equipped for the tasks required of them.

But this raises a question for us in the ministry of healing. What is the place of counselling in such a ministry? For many, if not most people counselling is required at times of crucial transition in their lives: bereavement, marriage crisis, perhaps an impending operation and so on. In most cases the benefits of the counselling are sufficient for it to take place over a relatively short period of time. For others where perhaps long-term trauma resulting from an incident or series of incidents in one's life is a lived reality then the counselling will variously need to be intensive as well as long term. One of the most significant and demanding periods of counselling I have had to do lasted 2-3 years and involved someone returning to 'life on the outside' after having served several years in prison for culpable homicide. For this person the scars of guilt and self-doubt will never be gone. The intended outcome of counselling in situations like this and others of long-term trauma will be to seek ways by which the past can best be accommodated into the present and future life. In such a scenario the past, though never forgotten, will cease to be parasitic upon the person in any destructively pathological way. The past can never be undone, it will always be remembered. Successful counselling will however seek to leave it behind as far as is possible and accommodate it within a coherent life-view. Perhaps even a transfigured life-view. More needs to be said on all these issues and in my next chapter I will dwell upon a number of these.

Chapter 3
GIVING FORGIVING

A MISCELLANY OF IMPORTANCE
WITH WHICH TO BEGIN

I have to admit this Chapter might seem to flit about! There is a lot of material which needs to be presented and which has no better place than here. All the material is essential in one way or another and in various ways is linked to so many other of the issues which have to be to outlined. Not least among these is abuse. I shall begin this miscellany of topics by starting from where I left off at the end of Chapter Two.

There I considered the place of counselling within the ministry of healing. Crucial for all counselling in a formal setting is the counsellor's supervision.

I understand supervision to refer to a formalised debriefing and guidance process that those engaged in a specific ministry of healing might undergo; maybe on a monthly or two monthly basis - more frequently if necessary. No situations should be discussed in relation to named people, though scenarios can be and might have to be rehearsed in non-specific terms. Crucially, confidentiality must be maintained. Anxieties about the ministry of healing, or hopes for it, or practical difficulties with it could be opened up for sharing. The purpose of supervision is at the very least twofold. On the one hand the supervisor eases or helps 'lift' the burden held by the person who is the counsellor. On the other hand the supervisor stresses the essential nature of supervision as contributing to the counsellor's guidance and growth as well as that of the client.

In all probability neither the altar rail at a healing service nor yet the prayer group are appropriate places for counselling [most especially where extensive and careful attention is necessary]. In each setting the environment is not present for quality counselling and the facility for in-depth work sustained perhaps over weeks or months is not available. The lack of privacy in these contexts is very much a constraining factor upon many who present for ministry. However, even with all this said, words of counsel and encouragement with prayer could well be appropriate. Appropriate also might be what is called 'first aid' counselling which might or might not entail the giving of advice. It could well be that counselling perhaps at an in-depth level might flow out of, and indeed be a part of a broader ministry of healing taking place at other times of the week when those circumstances so present themselves.

There are many dangers in the ministry of healing for those who are involved in it either in a general or a more specific sense. If a ministry such as this is successfully meeting a need in a congregation then one can expect it to be under attack in one way or another. I do not intend to dwell on this aspect but there is much that is dark in the world, and much that would wish to suppress the light of Christ shining in the midst of the darkness.

For those involved in the ministry of healing potentially there are personal dangers. The manipulation of people by others in a ministry setting, or by people exercising otherwise legitimate authority inappropriately is also a potential problem. One's ego can take over that which perhaps began as a genuine call from God. In such a situation one forgets that it is God who does the healing not the person exercising a gift of healing from God in the ministry of healing.

In his book Cameron Peddie speaks of hot and cold feelings, vibrations and electric needle sensations as he laid hands upon peoples' heads.[1] I do not question what Peddie, a deeply devout Church of Scotland minister says, but those who are open to intensity of feelings like these can so very easily consider that the power to heal belongs to them rather than to God. The converse of this is the sense of disillusion which many might feel when after much involvement in the ministry of healing no such feelings begin or one enters a desert. There is no 'feedback', no 'successes', seemingly no encouragement either. As a consequence one might find oneself giving up. The causes of this might be numerous - one could have been attempting too much, not sharing enough of the responsibility with other caring and restorative agencies, perhaps not maintaining an objective view of particular situations through over-indulgence in them.

In Cameron Peddie I spotted another danger. After having identified the need for a process of complete sanctification, cleansing and purifying to enable an absolute surrender of his personality, body, mind and spirit he says:

> I therefore set apart a room in our home as a personal Sanctuary reserved exclusively for prayer and meditation, and waiting upon the Lord. Each night I went there. And, so under God, my ministry of healing began.[2]

Later in the book however Peddie says this:
In 1952 I started an open clinic in my church prayer room in order to meet an overwhelming call for services...[3]
Cameron Peddie had begun his healing ministry in a room he described as a 'santuary'. In due course he began to describe the location, or his practice, as a 'clinic'. This alteration of terminology betrays a shift of some significance, I believe. Working in a clinic portrays the model of a doctor or politician attending to the needs of patients/constituents rather than a pastor at prayer with the sick. Peddie I am sure did not intend this, but with the advantage both of hindsight and overview I venture to suggest he had, perhaps unconsciously, adopted a less helpful model than the one with which he had started his ministry of healing.

In his early days at least, Peddie worked and ministered alone. For today's church I am convinced that the balance between a general ministry of healing with which all can engage and a specific ministry of healing in which only a relative few are chosen to minister is an appropriate balance. In my experience the wider ministry of healing is brought to a focus in the more specific activity of particular people. Either activity, the general and the specific, is part of the wider work of the church. Each gives the other a combination of support and explicit outworking.

The way in which this outworking flows is crucial. If the manner of the person charged with the task of ministering to others is busy with his or her personal agenda for the situation [rather than being attentive to what God's agenda might be] then the ministry of healing will fall short of that for which God intended it. A wrong word, perhaps one of hasty judgment, a failure to listen to what the person is saying, inappropriate forms of touch in the laying on of hands, nervousness in prayer all might in their own way compromise the ministry being undertaken. The thought that one might be careless, or negligent, or might miss the point in the ministry of healing places considerable burdens upon the person in the ministry of healing. In part this is because the situation is so pregnant with expectation [and rightly so] that one has to be totally attentive to all God wishes in the ministry of healing.

I am at fault so far in what I have been saying, for I have been dwelling upon the situation of the individual and of the individual congregation. Ought I not to address myself to bigger, broader perhaps even national and global issues of healing? The question is pertinent. But I have difficulties with it and to these I shall return shortly.

Stephen Pattison in *Alive and Kicking* considers various perspectives upon illness: the medical model, the psychological, the epidemiological and social administrative approaches, sociological and anthropological approaches.[4] His purpose in doing so is to enable the most effective response to illness. From an anthropological perspective one could ask how different cultures in different parts of the world describe and present illness. People in traditional African society will describe it differently and thereby respond to it in a manner likely to be quite different to that of almost any British teaching hospital I would suggest.

The sociologist might seek to make distinctions between 'disease', 'illness' and 'sickness'. The first is objective and observable. Illness is the presence of symptoms of disorder presented by the sufferer. 'Sickness' is a socially sanctioned role. An example of this might be a person I know who has habitually described himself for more years than most of us who know him can remember, "Ah'm no' a weel man". Knowledge of these three categories helps one to respond in the manner most appropriate to what is being said by the person.

From an epidemiological perspective one must ask why given diseases occur in particular populations at particular times and what significant factors come to bear upon these. When I was a curate there arose much anxiety in and around Bonnybridge [near Falkirk] because of an industrial plant which treated toxic waste. It involved much burning of poisonous and otherwise dangerous materials. What health risks were present to the locals, particularly children? Many of the same arguments continue around such industries as the reprocessing plant at Sellafield. In 1995 the owners of a former asbestos plant in Leeds were found at fault in a civil court action because children who had played in the asbestos fallout from that plant some forty years ago are now developing asbestos related cancers. If it is the case that specific clusters of conditions arise in locations such as these, ought not the most appropriate response to their conditions be to campaign against the removal or closure of those installations? I put this option in provocative form deliberately for that is the way such options are presented by their proponents. Perhaps it could be the case that prayer and an individual ministry of healing to those who are ill from industry-related conditions risks obscuring our vision of that which ought to be our most appropriate response to that condition - namely a political pressure campaign to have that industry closed down or made safe and pay due recompense.

Equally if it is found that certain groupings in society are more susceptible to illness than others ought not the most appropriate response within a ministry of healing to be the removal of this inequality? If mortality tends to rise inversely with falling occupational

26

rank or status, or if infant deaths are higher amongst manual and unskilled workers then does not this offer us the course of action a ministry of healing should take in order to ameliorate such situations? The conclusion that outgoing activism is required to remove the cause is hard to avoid.

One of the most taxing situations I have ever had to engage involved a young man who was paranoiacally obsessed with a need to see his [girlfriend's] new baby; he was the father. Little was well in the situation and relationships between them were severely strained. Those of us in the middle of it were at a loss as to how the situation could be managed let alone improved. There were faults on both sides, yet the threat and the worry for all of us arose from the behaviour of the man. Eventually his behaviour was so extreme that he was hospitalised for a month. No treatment was prescribed other than as much counselling and support as could be made available. I am truncating the serious problems which presented for they lasted many months and have had a lasting effect upon all who were involved. My purpose in reminding myself about this and sharing it with you is to remark that someone's behaviour characteristics affected not only his own but everyone else's response to the situation. What had begun as a compassionate and sympathetic response led to control, and this in turn led to restraint. This chain of reactions came about because of the way in which the young man expressed what was in many ways justifiable anger at the situation he was in. The problem was that the level of his anger and the obsessiveness of his demands were more than could be contained and directed within the support structures of the church within which I was working at the time.

I need not dwell on medical models of healing to the same extent. Gene control of cancer formation is an example of a medical response to disease quite independent of any situation beyond the molecules and microstructures involved.

Most of this I happily, and rather uncritically endorse. Though I can see problems with some aspects of Stephen Pattison's presentation he is broadly and quite substantially correct in what he says. But I have to confess a difficulty with the outcomes. This in part reflects my own personal make-up. Let me therefore be quite open about my shortcomings in the hope that further debate may be stimulated and hopefully my own mind opened up in a way that it currently is not.

Part of my problem is that I more easily fall into the role of someone given to prayer, rather than someone who is given to radical politics. My few excursions into community activism and social politics, into voluntary agencies [beyond the church] and awareness raising bodies have told me that I am not comfortable in such surroundings. Equally I do not revel in the cut and thrust of political debate, in fact I find myself disabled in many forms of conflict.

Now I do not think I am painting a false picture of myself in all this. I know only too well the counter arguments against what I am saying. For example there is a vast literature available upon the relationship of prayer and political activism. I know that the one who prays for social justice is falling short if he or she is then not part of that action movement which seeks to make social justice an ever greater reality in our day. I know that my concern for my community is muted because I feel I am unable to make genuine response to requests to work for and within movements dedicated to community betterment. Equally what do I say to myself when I pray for someone for healing from cancer if I do not in the same breath give a donation towards research which will eventually contribute to the alleviation of that cancer? These examples are very parochial in many ways. I could repeat many or all of them for more global issues.

And yet, to defend myself, I do not hide or bury my head in the sand. My understanding of national and international problems is very high for I attend quite consistently to several major news broadcasts and comment programmes on radio each day. My knowledge of local affairs, less comprehensive I have to admit, is also well informed and in each area I offer considerations both from the pulpit and, less frequently, on television.[5]

The problem with both of these media is that I am out of reach for criticism. Very few will challenge the preacher during a sermon - the number of people who have walked out of church when I ve been preaching number less than the fingers of one hand. It is also less than easy for a television audience to complain to a pre-recorded 'speaking head'.

So I offer criticism of myself and own up to my limitations [recognising that they are shared by many others] and in spite of some mitigating circumstances the limitations are quite substantial. But this notwithstanding I must also be honest with myself and others for it is only in this way that I can be of most use to the world.

I have friends who cannot join or undertake a ministry of healing [despite otherwise strong and unreserved support for it] because of the emotional demands it would of necessity draw. My position is the same with respect to political activism. It is necessary, I value it, I support others' action within it - but I invariably find myself having to eschew it. Do I have a sufficient *raison d être* which permits me, and

28

others like me, sufficient grounds for such limited responses to given dilemmas and problems?

Some would never ever be convinced that I have but nevertheless I offer a response which at the very least will not foreclose the discussion. In the formation of a 'healing community' and being part of that community I am part of a movement of people who each in their own ways respond to the needs of others as they impress upon oneself. I know that within this 'healing community' [I would like to offer the word 'church' as a synonym for 'healing community'] there are some more gifted than others in political activism. Some are more aware of social dilemmas requiring to be addressed, and many others capable of critique and evaluation to ensure no one is drawn too close to detail and so prevent the wood not being seen for the trees.

If this is so it means that the locus, the place, of the healing response is not so much the individual but the community. In this some will have gifts of prayer, others of administration, others of leadership, others of inspired utterance and so on. These gifts will find expression both in the local church as well as in the society and perhaps even the nation of which that church is a part.

One of the hallmarks of a 'healing community' will be its readiness to forgive. One of the sadder features of life in the town of St Andrews where I currently live and minister is the old habit of "no' speakin'". "No' speakin'" arises when some dispute in the past becomes a part of one's daily life and one will avoid any form of commerce and interaction with the person who is the perceived 'cause' of the offence. It has to be said that many will recognise the same phenomenon elsewhere. In my boyhood home village in north Lincolnshire my grandmother lived next to a person who had not spoken to his neighbour on the other side for over thirty years. The cause of their disagreement had long since vanished into the ether but the fact that they would not and did not speak had somehow etched itself into his way of living.

It has to be said that this represents a desperately poor state of affairs. It is no doubt the idealist in me rather than the human realist which is totally baffled by any attitude which sees a trivial conflict-situation more adequately dealt with by refusal to communicate than by some form of rapprochement however contrived it might need to be initially. A 'healing community' should have no part in such deification of non-communication. A 'healing community' will be a forgiving community.

An unknown Irishman was catapulted into the national and international headlines when he spoke on television after his daughter, Marie, was killed by a terrorist bomb at the Remembrance Day parade in Enniskillen, Northern Ireland in 1988 I think it was. Gordon Wilson, with no hint of false bravado, publicly forgave those who had planned and planted the bomb which murdered his daughter. His words were linked quite explicitly to the Christian faith which held him. His words and his gesture of forgiveness was a model for others to admire if not copy. His spoke from the heart of a forgiving mind, formed from within the faith of a believing community - perhaps also a 'healing community'. Such unconditional forgiveness, even when from a single individual, can have a ripple effect, can spread far and wide and be both broad and deep.

In the fifty or so years after the end of the Second World War many find themselves unable to forgive, especially it seems, the Japanese. The reasons are complex and in large part are due to Japanese inability [at least until recently] to accept culpability in the events and atrocities carried out by its wartime machine. But it is worthwhile to reflect in this chapter upon one way by which forgiveness can become real for those who find reconciliation hard to entertain.

AN APPROACH TO FORGIVENESS

I will approach this by unapologetically adapting a sermon I preached in Saint Andrew's Church, St Andrews on VJ ['Victory in Japan'] Day 1995. I offer it, because it is relevant in the context of this study but perhaps more pertinently in the hope that even though I find political involvement burdensomely difficult this may contribute in a small way to the healing of the nations as I ask people to extend forgiveness to one another. From this I will then offer some thoughts variously around themes of guilt, forgiveness and healing and relate these particularly to the situation of those who are victims especially of abuse, particularly sexual abuse. Firstly though my thoughts concerning the memory of war. I have read recently a definition of celebration: "A celebration is an occasion when a number of people gather to honour or commemorate." Human beings are in many ways defined by the celebrations we keep. Our birthdays, our anniversaries, our community, national and religious celebrations not only identify us, they are a part of our growth and development.

As Christians we 'gather in numbers' to celebrate the life, death and resurrection of Jesus Christ. We celebrate initiation into the body of Christ at baptism, we celebrate the creation of a new family in

Holy Matrimony. At other appropriate times - Lent, for example - our liturgical celebration takes on a tone of penitence as we gather in numbers to confess our sins and accept the gift of God's forgiveness.

As Christians we do not 'go to church' for we are the church. We go to liturgical celebrations as a crucial part of our identity and our maturation. There is much in the celebration of our liturgy, the holy communion, which performs a remembering function, and by this means enables us to identify who we are now. Much of this can be encapsulated in the words of the absolution of the Scottish Episcopal Church: it is the God who is power and love who

[1] forgives us and frees us for our sins,

[2] heals and strengthens us by his spirit, and

[3] raises us to new life in Christ our Lord.

We are identified as the people we are by the memory of where we have come from and by the future which God lays open for us. Writing, in very critical vein in his Diocesan Magazine Bill Burrill, the Bishop of Rochester in New York State USA, once said:

> The bombing of Hiroshima stirs up many memories and many strongly held opinions ... As a nation we have not worked through the feelings we have about August 6th 1945. All of our nation does not share the same feelings. It is important for us as a people to remember and then to make offerings. Our offerings will include repentance for the killing of many thousands of innocent people, thanksgiving for the end of World War II ... and for a world at peace.

It is not easy to be open in repentance and to say sorry. I am given to understand that in some of our own business practices it is bad form to say 'sorry' if one has made a mistake. It carries overtones of weakness.

And yet many veterans of the Far East Campaign do not seem willing to accept apologies when, even though guardedly the Japanese Premier offered his own apologies for his country's wartime atrocities during the build-up to the VJ commemorations of 1995. It is a big step to say sorry, whether for oneself or for one's country. Perhaps it is an even bigger step to accept the apology of an another.

Maybe from within our Christian memory we can recall aspects of Jesus' own forgiveness of others. There are two passages which are significant in this respect. One is of the paralysed man being brought to Jesus. In Matthew's account of the story Jesus commands the man to take heart and then says, "My son, your sins are forgiven."

By way of background there was in Jesus' time the common linkage of illness and sin. If you were ill some personal failing might be deemed to be the cause. Whilst God was seen as a forgiving God in the Judaism of Jesus' day it would be most unusual for an individual teacher to personalise this forgiveness, as Jesus did with the man with the paralysed legs.

If God forgives, has Jesus usurped the divine prerogative for forgiveness by offering this forgiveness himself? This was the cause of murmuring amongst scribe and pharisee onlookers. Was not Jesus blasphemous by offering the forgiveness which could only come from God?

It is in this sense that it is harder to offer forgiveness than it is to offer a healing for which a physical end-proof could be called. That we are told the paralysed man got up and walked away with his mat indicates at the very least God's power both to forgive and heal through Jesus. The onlookers see this, recognise its significance, and give thanks that God has given such power to people.

The other occasion came about when Jesus offers the forgiveness of God from the cross. He uttered the words, "Father forgive them for they know not what they do". I heard a recent BBC Radio 4 presenter argue that Jesus wasn't offering his own forgiveness to his persecutors whilst on the cross. Rather, the presenter said, Jesus was bypassing his own emotions and was offering a higher forgiveness, that of God.

I have to say I think the presenter was wrong. The indissoluble bond between Jesus and the Father is such that when Jesus offers forgiveness it is the forgiveness of the Father which he asks to become real. And when he calls upon the Father to forgive he is of one mind with the Father.

But at a human level when we find offering forgiveness difficult, there may be a pastoral benefit in adopting for ourselves what the Radio 4 presenter said. If you, or anyone else you know, has difficulty in forgiving personal wounding caused as a result of any injustice then I ask you to pray the words, "Father forgive them", and imagine Jesus by your side saying those words with you.

By doing this you will be entering the mind of God by following his will for forgiveness. As you continue to ask His forgiveness to be given, so over a period of time, if need be a long time then your mind will become closer to his and you will find yourself more readily able to own that forgiveness yourself. As forgiving is real for God, it will become increasingly real for you.

I will close by being personal. When the priest is in the confessional and offers the penitent God's forgiveness the priest asks the penitent to pray for him for the priest too is a sinner.

[When this address was preached the following two sentences ended the sermon. Although they are subject and time specific their wider applicability is clear]

Today we ask God's forgiveness for the Japanese. We ask him to make that forgiveness a reality in our own hearts. Let us never mask our own failings, and ask of the Japanese their prayers for we too have sinned.

HEALING AND GUILT

A good point at which to begin some thoughts about guilt, confession and forgiveness is the Adam and Eve story! From the story in Genesis 3 the only basis it seems to me God had for forbidding them eating the fruit of the tree in the middle of the garden is that they actually had the freedom to do so. If they hadn't had that freedom there would have been no reason for him to say they should neither eat nor yet touch it. Disobedience of God would result in death. The serpent was correct in saying that they would not die if they did eat it for they didn't. The sensual pleasure of the fruit to Eve's eye and the desirable outcome of knowledge, rivalling that of God, was sufficient to lure not only herself but Adam also to eat. Having eaten, their nakedness before God [clearly metaphorical, but also in a sense historical for they confronted their maker in their guilt without mask or protection] was clear to them. Hiding behind leaves was to no avail. God, their judge, sought them out and exposed their wrong doing to them. There could be no escape from the consequences of their disobedience.

John Calvin is the next resource to whom I shall turn. His treatise, *Penitence as explained in the sophistical jargon of the schoolmen, widely different from the purity required by the Gospel. Of confession and satisfaction*[6] is especially valuable as an insight into the depth of his feeling about the mediaeval church's corrupted emphasis upon confession for wrongdoing as the means of obtaining grace sufficient for forgiveness. It is additionally worthwhile for its reminder of the sole sufficiency of God's grace, without any necessary need for human mediation, as the means of finding forgiveness from him and of gaining righteousness with him. As one might expect Calvin castigates the mediaeval church for its many errors.

We do well to recognise that Calvin did not proscribe confession altogether. He writes:

We are to deposit our infirmities in the breasts of each other, with the view of receiving mutual counsel, sympathy, and comfort.[7]

This is of course coupled with prayer to the Lord:

If however it is the case that confession to another, a peer, is either not possible or for whatever reason not desirable then, it is not necessary to confess before witnesses; let the examination of your faults be made in your own thought: let the judgment be without a witness: let God alone see you confessing ... I do not force you to disclose your sins to men; review and lay open your conscience before God .[8]

And to this is added of course the general confession of the whole Church which "in a formal acknowledgment of its defects, supplicates pardon".[9] No priest has the power to withhold or give forgiveness. If any confession is defective the priest, at best, can only pronounce God's absolution. If the confession is defective or deficient, judgment rests with God alone. The words of the *Agnus Dei* come to mind.

Having considered the Fall narratives of the Old Testament and John Calvin's application of the New Testament in his criticism of the mediaeval church I turn now to a modern protestant scholar, Paul Ricoeur, to complete the backcloth against which I shall shortly present some thoughts upon guilt and [in particular sexual] abuse. Ricoeur's philosophical phenomenology of guilt, sin and evil is a very valuable resource.[10]

In his analysis he seeks to distinguish between ethical and religious discourse on the question of guilt. First however he offers what he calls a semantic analysis of guilt. His phenomenological treatment sees him bracketing off from consideration psychological, psychiatric and psychoanalytic usages of the term and focussing preferentially upon the "*texts* where its meaning has been constituted and fixed". These texts are the "penitential literature wherein the believing communities have expressed their avowal of evil; the language of these texts is a specific language which can be designated ... as 'confession of sins', although no particular confessional connotation is attached to this expression".[11] This opening sets the direction of Ricoeur's subsequent analysis for which he situates his point of departure to be within a '*phenomenology of confession*' or avowal .

Ricoeur points us to our deepest experiences and their origin within the most fundamental levels of human being. Behind confessions of evil and their rationalised latter day expressions, lie "myths, traditional narratives which tell of events which happened at the origin of time and which furnish the support of language to ritual actions".[12] What is the experience in the language of confession which brings to the light emotions of fear, anguish and so much more? In answer Ricoeur offers a consciousness of fault.

He directs our attention to the symbolism of evil "conceived as defilement or stain", something which contaminates from the outside. Within the modern day love of money we can see the way in which the symbol still operates. Likewise with racism. Each in their own way can defile the person. If these constitute a stain from outside then we can identify a pathway from the sense of being stained to the commission of a sin. The stain is external whereas the sin comes from personal action. The rich power of symbolism here is very obvious.

Guilt is an interiorisation of all this, It describes the consciousness of being overwhelmed by a burden which crushes ... "It indicates ... the bite of a remorse which gnaws from within, in the completely interior brooding on fault".[13] Ricoeur sees guilt as a way of situating oneself before a sort of invisible tribunal which measures the offence, pronounces the verdict and inflicts the punishment. The sentiment of guilt is "the consciousness of being inculpated and incriminated by this interior tribunal". It is a form of self-observation, self-accusation and self-condemnation by a consciousness doubled back on itself .

Ricoeur's writing endlessly fascinates me and my task at the moment is to resist the temptation to follow him further. But enough has been said to demonstrate that in this simple sweep of three diverse subjects there is little or nothing offering a message of hope to the victim of abuse, particularly sexual abuse. I stress sexual abuse because it is at the extreme of violence by one person to another. Whilst I am in no way minimising that cruelty inflicted upon people by emotional and physical abuse, victims of sexual abuse in my experience have these to contend with as well as a shocking litany of sexual violation, humiliation and degradation.

So very often it is the case that abusers are extremely clever people who satisfy a pernicious need to dominate another person and then behave in such a way as to ensure there is little or no trace of their activity. The psychology of this revolves around the twin linking themes of dominance and power. The abuser seeks to dominate his victim by the exercise of either or both mental or physical power over them. Gradually the victim has his or her facilities to resist stripped away. Ridicule, taunting, teasing and threat are among the most common means of shaming the victim into a submissive state. Paradoxically perhaps the victim is made to be dependent on the abuser - perhaps for livelihood if, let us say, she is the wife of the abuser and mother of children who in turn are dependent upon the abuser's income. Or the victim might be a child made to be too frightened to turn to anyone for help - such has been the level of threat heaped on him or her.

Another form of dependence occurs in terms of self-identity. The abuser's actions create a sense of defilement in the victim who then comes to understand this not as an external act but as an interior state of being. As the one who has stripped the individual [the victim] of positive self-identity, who has removed the capacity for accurate self-perception and self-judgement it is this person to whom the victim so often looks as the only one who can restore it. When later, perhaps in the context of therapy, perhaps in a friendship or deep relationship, others can provide alternative perceptions of the victim. Even then dependence upon the abuser's judgement is only overcome with much struggle. If my own words are unclear let me defer to a letter I received from a woman with whom I had spent much time in counselling conversation:

> Dad told me and showed me I was nothing - I was vile, disgusting... He wasn't [as I came to understand it] treating me wrongly; he was treating me as I ought or deserved to be treated. What did I do? I struggled for years to become a better daughter, a more successful person so that one day I'd hear him approve of me. I had teachers who praised and encouraged but only dad's opinion counted because [in a way which I still find hard to articulate] he dominated my mind in such a way that it was putty in his hands - he could manipulate it in whatever way he chose. Result: I was dependent upon the person who abused me for approval and positive regard, in other words for those things which which help a human being to flourish and to grow.

Another very tragic scenario told to me over a very long period of guided counselling involved a young child whose facility to weep had been removed by the abusers. If tears appeared a leather belt would be firstly produced as a threat and then used unsparingly. Further threats involved the likelihood of death. Accordingly as an adult the person was so severely emotionally emasculated that when unwanted and threatening sexual advances were made by others of the same age the power to resist had been removed by the earlier abusers in childhood.

In discussing this issue with Naomi Higham, one of the text readers of this book, she showed me one of her undergraduate essays. This was a quite brilliant critique of Simone Weil in which Higham used the issue of abuse to highlight what I want to say next about guilt:

The crucial element [in abuse] is the offender's unilateral position of power... rendering [the victim] helpless to withstand the violation of his/her person. This leads to feelings of complicity and responsibility. The child, let us say, is unable to resist and eventually develops the 'accommodation syndrome' which is typified by passivity, fatalism and submission. By such a means one can so easily see how and why guilt - which is actually the abuser's - is transferred to the abused.[14]

By the progressive humiliation and degradation of the victim, coupled sometimes with sweetening treats blurring the distinction between right and wrong, by the process of forcing the victim into a state of passivity and submission the victim is thereby made to feel complicity in the event. Even though intellectually he or she may recognise the nonsense of this view, emotionally it is the more dominant and is more than amply able to negate the otherwise more sensible voice of reason. Thus the victim of abuse grows up feeling they were responsible for what had happened. Accordingly they feel guilt and culpability for those sins which belong to the perpetrator and of which they were the victim.

Now we must ask how this measures up against the three situations we mentioned earlier. Adam and Eve felt guilt because they had done wrong. Calvin argued for mutual confession, or private confession to God, in respect of sins committed and with this the acknowledgment of God's absolution. Then thirdly Ricoeur's phenomenology of guilt points back to individual wrongdoing and the realisation of a need to externalise by ritual and action, by word and promise, the confession of that wrongdoing.

Each of these three clearly recognises guilt as present. And yet each refers these back to some wrongdoing whereby one is the guilty agent. No substantive or sensitive thinker of whom I am aware addresses that pathology or psychology whereby the person who feels guilt is the victim of someone else's sinful and evil action.[15] The greatest part of the Christian heritage has focussed upon the sense of guilt as the sign which generates the need to be put right with God. And yet for so many, so very many, victims of abuse their sense of guilt is the outcome of progressive brainwashing by those who sought to dominate their lives in pursuit of their own perverted power-urge to control another and from them to gain personal gratification.

Christian theology has yet to address this issue in any substantive way, though I know of one author who intends to consider it by way of a treatise on 'shame'. More crucially the Christian Church has no means of offering to victims of abuse a ritual or verbal form of sacramental cleansing whereby the stain or contagion which underlies this sense of guilt might be washed away. Counselling over a long and sustained period is the most effective and healing process currently available. Sadly even counselling does not have within it the means of enabling victims of abuse, deep from within themselves, freely and confidently to admit to themselves and others that what was done to them was fundamentally wrong and evil. Recognition and admission of that state of affairs is however part and parcel of the healing process. Only once one has recognised that fault and blame do not reside with oneself [as the victim] and can admit this is so may healing take place. Otherwise any healing which comes through counselling, or indeed any other means, will remain only superficial at best.[16]

Chapter 4
HEALING MOVING OUTWARD

THE COMMISSIONS OF JESUS:
TO THE TWELVE AND TO THE SEVENTY TWO

In this Chapter I develop in greater substance some of the implications which arise from biblical injunctions for healing. This I shall do by reference to what are known variously as the commissions of Jesus. This will move us towards a consideration of what is meant by healing in our own day.

In Chapter One I considered the commission given at the close of Mark's Gospel with its injunction to heal in Christ's name. For the purposes of this chapter I will begin by examining the commission to the twelve in Matthew 10:1, 5-14 [parallels Mark 6:7-11, Luke 9:1-5] and then to the seventy two in Luke 10:1-11. The other gospels have no parallel accounts of this.

The setting described in Matthew 9:35-38 where Jesus sees the crowds "like sheep without a shepherd" gives the context for the sending out of the twelve as well as its occasion in the compassion of Jesus. The authority the twelve are given is denoted by the term *exousia*, namely the same as used of Jesus in Matthew 7:29 when his teaching authority is contrasted with that of the scribes. It is an understanding of authority which is derived neither from the Law nor yet from the interpretative tradition surrounding it. It is rather an authority which resides in, and is given by, Jesus in his person as the Word of God. In other words it is authority which must be understood from the perspective of his messianic mission. It is a mission we now see him sharing with the twelve. The issue or problem of the authority of Jesus occurs in its most acute form in Mark 11:27-33 [parallels in Matthew 21:23-27 and Luke 20:1-8].

It would seem that Jesus put the same restriction upon the twelve as he did upon himself in that their ministry was to "lost sheep of the house of Israel". The sparse attire allowed the twelve for their work indicates they were not to travel far. Wherever they would appear to people they would be as barely shod as they would be before their maker. Equally they would be as dependent upon those whom they met for their sustenance as they would be to the God in whose name they had been sent.

By way of aside it is worth noting that the earliest ministry in the church to be accorded stipendiary support is that of apostles who functioned as travelling missionaries. Paul in 1 Corinthians 9 is strongly arguing the case for stipendiary support for those who preach from the communities to whom they preach although he is unlikely to extend this to the locally based ministry of preaching and teaching. Those engaged in such work earned their living and ministered in their spare time. And although he does not explicitly restrict stipendiary support to preaching and teaching ministries alone, we do well to remember his words and compare his situation to our heavily sacerdotal and sacramental stipendiary priesthood today.

I would take issue with Krister Stendahl in *Peake's Commentary* when he says that the commission to the twelve is to those "lost Jews who do not follow Pharisaic appropriation of the Law, those known as the *am haaretz*." Why should Jesus' commission be limited in this way? My own view, along with other current scholarship, is that the commission was only restricted geographically. The setting I describe above, where Jesus moved around the towns and villages of Galilee, gives both content and location for quick response on the part of unencumbered disciples to extend Jesus' teaching in his name.[1] Stendahl is not entirely clear on this point; for example, in his commentary on Matthew 15:24 ["Jesus replied, 'I was sent to the lost sheep of the house of Israel, and to them alone...'"] Stendahl interprets Jesus' call to the 'children of Israel' to mean a call to the whole house of Israel.

Much can and has been made of the particularist nature of ministry to be only for the Jews [let alone any one group of Jews] from these verses. Other passages however [5:13, 10:18, 21:43, 24:14] place any such interpretation within a broader sphere. Jesus was moved with compassion and pity for those he was currently encountering. Consequently a 'quick reaction' task force of disciples was sent among these people who, because they were lightly equipped, could move fast and therefore encounter more people with the message of good news in word and work as entrusted to them by Jesus. Accordingly they were not to go in the direction of Gentile lands in the Decapolis [ten towns] beyond Jordan, nor yet to the Samaritan towns to the south, nor to Phoenicia [modern day Lebanon] in the north. Galilee it would seem was their sphere of operation.

Like Jesus himself [4:17], John the Baptist before him [3:2] and the Christians of the first churches [cf. 1 Cor 9], the twelve were to to proclaim here and now the presence of the kingdom of God. This was Jesus' messianic message - to be given in word, and demonstrated in action, by healing the sick, raising the dead, cleansing lepers and driving out demons.

Matthew's verb for 'heal' is *therapeuo,* whereas Luke has what seems his preferred term *iaomai* [Luke 9:2]. Mark's narrative of the same commissioning omits the injunction to heal though it is clear from Mark 6:13 that they did so in response to what Jesus had said through both exorcisms and anointings with oil.

It is only in Mark 6:13 that we are given any indication of the way in which the disciples healed. Mark it seems was not quite so austere in his restrictions upon accoutrements for the disciples journeying. I do not intend any detective work as to why the gospels vary in their accounts of the travelling wear of the disciples. Morna Hooker follows T.W. Manson's interesting note from Mishnah teaching [M. Berakoth 9.5] that entry into the Temple Mount in Jerusalem is forbidden to anyone with staff, sandal, wallet or with dust on one's feet. Perhaps there is an echo here that the journey being instructed by Jesus has similarly sacred overtones. More than this cannot be said however. Both Morna Hooker and David Hill seem to concur that Mark's narrative is likely to be closer in detail to the original events.[2]

Elsewhere in this book I have cause to consider the revivification of corpses as part and parcel of the healing ministry. If it was a given in the ministry of Jesus then so be it. But, there is no evidence nowadays which compels me to consider that revivification of the dead is an aspect of his work which either has been continued since the time of Jesus or should be continued by us today. Where I have read examples of latter day raising the dead they invariably come from the developing world and lack any facility for proof that would in any acceptable way compel us to believe. Perhaps the so-called 'near death' experiences recorded by an increasing number who have been brought back from the brink of death through prompt and accurate clinical intervention are the nearest episodes we have in the western world where perhaps death has been postponed.

Against that however I have the account of a friend of mine who is a surgeon. He was in hospital for a hip replacement [a consequence of older-age marathon running!]. Quite soon after his operation he took a massive epileptic fit and was unconscious for some five days and gravely ill. Upon recovery his anaesthetist from the operation said, with a measure of amicable tactlessness only possible between medical colleagues, that my friend was "the closest to a 'box job' as he's ever seen who managed to recover". My friend recounts none of the 'tunnel of light' experiences of so many other near death experiences. He has no recollection either of the experience nor yet of even going to the hospital for his operation. Near death narratives are alluringly compelling but they offer at best little more than an account of some people's subconscious workings *in extremis*.

In the expository notes which form the bulk of the later part of this book I note that Jesus commanded lepers to present themselves to the [Levitical] priest. It is not so much that Jesus was obeying the law, but rather enjoining lepers to do so in order that their cure might be certified, and they thereby be permitted to resume a place in the community. Jesus himself observed this Mosaic regulation [see Matthew 8:4 and Mark 1:44, Luke 17:14.]. The word for 'cleanse' refers both to the cure of the leprosy and the priest's ritual pronouncement of the cure. It seems likely here that Jesus would similarly be requiring the twelve to remain within the same Mosaic regulation.

My treatment of the driving out of evil spirits has also been sufficiently considered below to require no further mention here. Perhaps I ought however to offer some justification for my use of the word 'exorcism' when referring to the deliverance ministry. Some commentators object to the words exorcism, exorcise etc on the grounds that they derive etymologically from the casting out of demons by various spells, incantations and the like rather than by the name of Jesus. Similarly the word does not appear as such in the New Testament. My response lies in the current use of exorcism / exorcise where it regularly describes the deliverance ministry of Jesus and those who do so in his name.

In Luke 10 there is a commission to seventy two who, being sent in pairs to those places where Jesus was himself shortly to visit, were given the injunction to go, exchange greetings on the road, offer the word of 'Peace' to houses that are visited, enjoy hospitality and heal *[therapeuo]* the sick and proclaim the kingdom of God. As in the other passages those charged with this task were to travel light and I am led to think that the commission was given for a specific time, place and purpose. Arguably the passage is a doublet of the commission to the twelve. Although no reference is given to the casting out of demons when the seventy two returned, jubilant with the success of their work, they reported that demons had submitted to them. From this it seems clear that the work of the proclamation of the kingdom could be effected in ways other than those directly mentioned by Jesus. It is clear also that the inclusion of this seventy two by Jesus in his mission indicates at the very least he was not restricting his commission to preach and to heal only to the twelve disciples.

The message the seventy two were to preach was very much in terms of the teaching of John the Baptist; the kingdom of God [10:9-11] and repentance [10:12ff.]. For obvious reasons they could not offer the post-resurrection kerygma of the early church. This in itself is a further feature indicating the limited nature of these first commissions by Jesus to his followers. There is no record of any reviving of corpses by the disciples until those recorded in the Acts of the Apostles and my earlier references to its dubiety as a part of the healing ministry today are relevant also. If then we are to look for more specific injunctions for the spread of the healing ministry as the church's natural outworking of the ministry of Jesus today we need broader and deeper evidence from material beyond the first and limited commissions of Jesus to the twelve and to the seventy two.

THE GREAT COMMISSION AND THE EARLY CHURCH

References to the 'Great Commission' most often point to Matthew 28:18-20 though there are four other versions of this. The one contained in the longer ending of Mark has already attracted our attention. Luke 24:45-49 contains a third with Acts 1:8 and John 20:21-23 being others. Along with these there are other locations where indications of the work required by Jesus are presented. A summary listing will be sufficient for my purposes: Acts 10:42 [proclaim and witness], John 14:12 [the believer will do even greater works], John 14:13 [whatever you ask in the name of Jesus will be granted], Acts 4:30 [in a prayer to God that healing may be effected through the name of Jesus], gifts of healing are given to the church [see my lists from the Pauline Epistles in Chapter One above] and then James 5:13-18 where the practice of the visitation of the sick is presented as the normal work of the church. There is no indication in these verses that James thought the ministry of healing was anything other than the normal work of the Christian community. The framework of the ministry was to be set in prayer. The facility for confessing sin was presented as a given and the prayer of the righteous man, like that of Elijah, was given as efficacious. The consequences of the ministry are the salvation of the sick person, his raising up - literally a return to standing upright again - and along with this the forgiveness of sin.

Further testimony of an active ministry of healing moving outward in the life of the early church may be found in the Acts of the Apostles. A quick count of locations in my expository notes below tells me that over twenty such instances may be found. It seems the case then that even though definite specification of a precise nature was not given by

Jesus that his followers should heal they saw it as a natural outflowing of his life into their lives as both individuals and as church. Thus it seems that the ministry of healing began then and clearly continues today.

In the Epistles many of today's problems and dilemmas concerned with the ministry of healing were present. It could be thought [at a superficial level only] that everyone with whom either Jesus or his early followers came into contact were healed of all sickness. This is patently not the case. Mark 6:5 demonstrates this. In the Epistles we find a very familiar wrestling with the seeming inevitability of ill-health and permanent pain. Paul's famous 'thorn in the flesh' more obviously relates to the problem of pain and to it I will return in the next chapter. But other references, three in all, tell of those whose sickness persisted with accommodation having to be made for each. In many ways the lack of specific references to healing accounts in the Epistles may be thought a problem for those who, like myself, strongly advocate a continuing ministry of Jesus for healing in and through his name today. My view remains however that the references to the gifts of healing by Paul, echoed in part in 1 Peter 4:10, the clear evidence of active healing work in Acts and James are sufficient to offset silence in the remainder of the Epistles. The Epistles do serve to remind us of the frailty of the body and that it will in natural course wither and decay. Illness is unavoidable within this. Our advocacy of healing is framed within this context.

Arguments based on silence are always problematic. Why then are the Epistles intriguingly silent about a ministry of healing? One scenario could be that it caused no real concern within the life of the early church. Amongst Paul's concerns were the improper use of the more dramatic gifts such as tongues and prophecy, the correct place of women in, say, the church at Corinth, and teaching on the resurrection. Within other letters we find issues of church order being addressed as well as other situations where the local church needed counsel on, for example, its concern for widows and so on. If the ministry of healing was giving no cause for concern its relative absence from the Epistles may be explained on these grounds [though Romans 15:19, 2 Corinthians 12:12 and Hebrews 2:4 most conceivably refer to healing and in all likelihood, exorcism]. A not insignificant comparison may be put with respect to the eucharist. There are no references to it in the Epistles except in 1 Corinthians 11 where its disarray was giving Paul real cause for worry.

A counter-case can be put however. There is no mention either of exorcisms [in an explicit sense] or of raising the dead in the sense of revivifying corpses. On my logic does this mean that both practices were active and maybe even flourishing and thereby causing no concern? In this case I think not. It seems to me, on an intuitive level, that revivifying the dead was not being practised and that exorcisms whilst practised were in the process of being transferred to baptismal rituals. The whole picture is more complicated than is possible to describe here. My purpose in raising the issue in this way is simply to raise a question mark against any position which seeks to justify itself on the basis of, as I put it, an argument from silence.

Within the Epistles we come very close to an understanding of the inevitability of illness in a manner not unlike that known today, notwithstanding our keenly modern eagerness to strive officiously to keep it at bay and wherever possible to remove its hindrances from our life. From this the question will arise as to why illness should persist when the Christian church actively pronounces healing for those who suffer. The question faced the believers in the early church, and after some exegetical notes, will be one to which I shall shortly return.

Epaphroditus [cf Philippians 2:25-30] had been sent by the church in Philippi to minister to Paul in his prison cell. In the course of his visit Epaphroditus fell gravely ill and it would seem became depressed that his illness had been heard of in Philippi. Whether Epaphroditus risked extra hazard or simply travelled on when he should have taken rest in an infirmary [cf. v.30], as is indicated by the reference to "risked his life", we cannot be sure. But we can be certain that he received no ministry of healing such as might have required especial mention in the letter. The emissary was doing on its behalf that which the church at Philippi could not do. Because of that, and because of all the suffering he went through, he should be held in honour, the readers of the letter are told. Can we say then that the illness of Epaphroditus was given, or was the occasion perhaps, of further glory and that it was required for the purposes of that glory? This argument has its problems clearly. But we must not easily overlook its force. Vicarious suffering, particularly when freely accepted, is ennobling and sets a generous example.

The writer of 1 Timothy 5:23 seems impatient with the prudent carefulness of only drinking water and counsels in favour of some alcohol consumption to help stomach upsets. Kelly[3] relates the moderate drinking of draughts of wine for a patient for whose stomach, water alone is dangerous [citing, Hippocrates, *De med. antiq. xiii*] and Plutarch *[De sanit. praec. xix]* for whom wine is the "most useful of drinks and the pleasantest of medicines". Not least, though perhaps more puzzlingly, we are also referred to Proverbs 31:6 [and following]: "Give strong drink to the despairing and wine to the embittered of heart; let them drink and forget their poverty and remember their trouble no more". By way of aside it seems in this last respect that Kelly does not notice that alcohol is being cited here as a means of avoiding recognition of trouble in the manner of a 'drown your sorrows' attitude. This hardly constitutes sufficient evidence for healing.

Returning now to the Biblical text, the purpose of caution to Timothy seems to be given in the context of relaxing the personally austere manner of this young disciple. Whilst Timothy's self-discipline is good and holy, in certain of its respects it is over fastidious. Therefore it seems that for the good of his health his diet and drinking should have broader latitude. As with Epaphroditus there is no reference to a specific ministry of healing though once more the context is of someone undergoing privation in one way or another for the sake of the gospel.

Trophimus is mentioned a number of times in the Acts of the Apostles [20:4, 21:27-34] and in 2 Timothy [4:20]. In this last location Trophimus had to be left behind at Miletus for he was ill. There is no mention of prayers or actions consonant with a ministry of healing. For his health it seems best that he journey no further with Paul. In this third instance it seems that Paul and the Epistle writers were content to allow illness to be attended to by conventional medical means. There seems no conflict between this and the specific outworkings of "gifts of healings" [both nouns are given in the plural in Paul's lists in Corinthians].

Paul and the others are here showing genuine concern for their fellow believers. In the case of Epaphroditus and Timothy they are situating their conditions in a wider frame of reference. For the former his illness is seen as a cause for glory and with the second it adds little to his already exemplary discipleship. Indeed it needlessly detracts from it, since its ill effects are capable of mitigation.

Within the early church, following James and the narratives in Acts, we can identify a ministry that is specifically interventionist with prayer and actions. In many other situations it would seem that believers offered a "natural gift of sympathy or empathy combined with a capacity of knowing the right thing to do in any individual situation and with any individual patient. This intuitive knowledge was sharpened and made more sensitive by the operation of the Holy Spirit on the mind of the healer, and had no necessary connection with medical knowledge or surgical training."[4]

46

This conveniently coincides with much of what I said in my opening chapter about healing having both a specific understanding and application as well as being the property of all Christians insofar as it is a gift given to each severally and to the church collectively.

ILLNESS AND HEALING

I must now return to the issue I raised earlier and consider the disturbing fact that even though the church proudly and legitimately proclaims a ministry of healing in Christ's name many people [most in fact] remain ill and all eventually die. A ministry of healing is no guarantee against premature dying and death, nor is it simply a means of escaping the harsh reality of so much undeserved suffering. I write these words with much unease for though I have seen many whose lives are ennobled through suffering, I know many are not. In my doctoral thesis I followed Edgar Sheffield Brightman's own trenchant arguments against those Christians who failed to recognise the fact of suffering and of so many who sought to resituate suffering within a tamed apologetic in which it was gently seen as 'God s will'. Brightman would have none of this. He had nursed his first wife to an early grave as she died of a hideous facial cancer not long after the birth of their first child.

I must not however give the reader the impression that my interest in this subject is one born of academic pursuit. As I write these words in early February the sky is icy blue and the sun of immense brilliance. Two days previously our childminder's sister had been diagnosed with Hodgkin's Lymphoma. She is aged twenty eight and her child is barely twelve months old. Chemotherapy is scheduled for the week I am writing these words with radiotherapy to follow. One can but only imagine the difficult days ahead for both her and her husband as he seeks to manage his shift work to the best advantage of all the family. Our next door neighbour is now chairbound with a terminal bone cancer. In church this morning at a needleworkers' coffee morning one woman with a terminal leukemia arrived with cheery greetings to everyone and a joy at being out on such a lovely day. Some people place the mystery of suffering into a broader and deeper context for us. They portray a mystery of tragedy, pain and confusion set against the potential of the brilliant and the beautiful.

In the remainder of this chapter I will reflect upon matters of meaning and definition and in my next chapter return more explicitly to the additional problems of understanding which unremitting pain cause a ministry of healing.

HEALING AND MEANING

In 2 Corinthians 12:8ff, as we shall shortly see, Paul spoke of the thorn in his flesh and of his view that in his weakness God's strength is most accurately shown. In my early years of ministry at Saint Andrew's, St Andrews I was put under some considerable [and quite justifiable] pressure to organise a congregational group to go to the large Christian gatherings known as Spring Harvest, held in English holiday camps each springtime. Having read the material, seen the costing involved, and having prepared a draft budget I came to the view that the scale of what would be involved was beyond my personal capability to organise. Totally frustrated by my inaction two members of the congregation set to and organised in the first year for fifty to go to Spring Harvest and in the second year for seventy. From that start youth work in the church took off in a spectacular way.

The purpose in recounting this narrative is that the two women who were the prime movers in this were both chronically ill and in so very many ways quite weak. And yet their weakness proved to be their greatest strength. Through it God shined in a way totally impossible through my comparative 'strength'. In many ways their work demonstrated the power of faith at work. There may not have been a healing in conventionally understood ways but there was a full trusting in the power of God to demonstrate his power in the seeming weakness of his followers. In the case of these two women chronic illness was overcome by the intensity of trust in a God who could effect mighty works through them.

Some writers have offered a criticism against my earlier book *A Way for Healing* in that I neither offer definition of health nor yet of healing. In that this is true I would also point out that neither did Paul when he identified the gift of healing in his lists of charismata. Presumably he could take it that no definition was required by his audience. Even the reformer John Calvin wrote, "everyone knows what is meant by the gift of healings [sic] with seeming little need for further comment."[5] However if I am to be honest it is stories such as the one I have just offered which lead me to feel that definition is at worst impossible and at best arguably misleading. In clinical terms I was the one who was healthy and yet it was the chronically ill and weaker women who were able more effectively to draw into practice the strength of Christ.

The English theologian Alan Richardson wrote[6], "The healing ministry of Jesus introduced into the world a new compassion for the sick and it is impossible to over stress the significance of [Jesus'] healing work in the ... expansion of Christianity". Richardson goes on to say:

The bringing together of scientific medicine and humane compassion is undoubtedly one of the supreme achievements of [Christian] civilisation. It was brought about by a refusal to recognise a distinction between men's spiritual and physical afflictions: both must be healed by medical and 'spiritual' treatment, working together. Whether charismatic or purely spiritual [non-medical, non-psychological] healing is something which Christians today ought to attempt to revive or encourage in our scientific age is a question which will be answered variously by different theologians; but there is evidence to point to 'gifts of healing' in the church which cannot be ignored.

Richardson's words, put together in the 1960s, seem prophetic. It is possible for us to know what healing and health are without the requirement to frame either into definition.

I may well be criticised for not being prepared to offer such definitions but by way of rejoinder I would have to argue that definitions do not settle any issues. My preference is to work with problems in a descriptive format and leave definition to arise in the mind of the reader or critic. Let me outline one approach which I believe fulfils that remit.

The Belgian theologian Edward Schillebeeckx has offered valuable insights into the nature and purpose of Jesus' healing ministry through his examination of the New Testament miracles. Although his book *Jesus*[7] is an enormous volume, and again even though very few pages are devoted to the miracles of Jesus, what Schillebeeckx has to say is very relevant. He begins by asking what significance the miracles of Jesus have for us today. If Jesus fed five thousand people, what is the significance of that to the starving millions since who have died through lack of food in every generation? He asks whether Jesus' contemporaries understood by 'miracle' something different to that by which we know the term. Schillebeeckx considers that being confronted by a miracle caused the people of Jesus' day little problem. The real problem for them was being confronted by a miracle done by Jesus. They knew his origins, knew his parentage, his teaching, his forgiving of sins, his habit of table-fellowship with those with whom one would not normally wish to associate, and all this caused offence. How could *he* be one who could suspend, or transcend, the law of Moses and work miracles as signs of God's kingdom becoming real in their presence? Was this man 'of God' or 'of the devil'? This was the stark alternative facing those who might choose to believe in him or to reject him.

In the Gospels the description of the effect of Jesus' words and actions upon people is given by the word, *thaumadzein* [the sense of surprise and amazement]. His actions are denoted by the terms *semeia* [signs] and *dunameis* [mighty acts] or the more self-effacing description *ta erga tou Christou* [works of Christ]. Nowhere Schillebeeckx tells us does the profane Greek *thauma* [meaning 'miracle'] appear. For those of faith in him such signs could be interpreted as God continuing to work his marvellous way with his chosen people. For his opponents everything said or done by Jesus was perceived as threat. The one reaction led people to Jesus' exaltation as recorded in the later parts of the Gospels, in Acts and in the Epistles and Revelation. The outcome of the other was his crucifixion.

In Mark 7:37 there is a summary of Jesus' reaction to his combat with forces opposing the will of God: "All that he does, he does well." This is a comment about Jesus' opposing the force of evil with the force of good. Questions as to whether he is seeking to usurp the understood laws of science do not enter the heads of those around him. Schillebeeckx argues with force that the miracle narratives are recorded in the gospels not only as historical reminiscence of something that happened but also as something which has a 'post-Easter interpretation' for faith. In all the words and works of Jesus there arises in those who confront him the question 'who is this man?' The question at the one remove is a historical question which people ask of someone who lived at a specific point in history. But because it is a question which cannot be separated from the will of God for his people it becomes also a Christological question. Schillebeeckx concludes:

> Who is this Jesus who is able to extend to people the help of God? Who is this man who can arouse people's faith? In his earthly life Jesus shows himself to be the one who, through his very ministry, summons men to faith in God. That is the point and purpose of Jesus mighty acts.[8]

This perhaps should be the focus in our evaluation of the healing work of Jesus. It is not so much that we should seek to offer a definition either of health or of healing but that rather we should offer to place before people the option of that faith towards which Christ's healing is continued through his church today. It is not only the case that Jesus could feed five thousand people from a few scraps of food in his day but rather that he could still do so today were it not for the obstructive politics of late twentieth century greed. The hungry people of the world are right to have faith that God can do the impossible and feed them. There is upon us the injunction to submit to his authority and enable his will to work through us, however incapable, weak and chronically sick we might otherwise seem to be.

Chapter 5
THE PROBLEM OF PAIN

Attending to those who suffer unending pain has been one of the most taxing pastoral tasks in my ministry. This chapter offers insights from that pastoral practice with reflections upon it not least upon what is referred to in the Bible as Paul's 'thorn in the flesh' as well as more recent writings.

There are many writers whose work is read by lots of people who then in turn refer others to these same inspirational books. Not least among the many often quoted authors from the middle of the twentieth century is C.S. Lewis. When so many people quote him with such fervour one has to take seriously the fact that Lewis is one of the most significant Christian visionaries of our day. And yet one must not read him uncritically. In preparing this chapter I have read a number of his books. I shall refer to his later material briefly and favourably at the end of this chapter. But as we begin I shall indicate my disatisfaction with his early reflections particularly as focussed in *The Problem of Pain*[1]. Doing this will helpfully serve as a foil for the perspective I wish to outline.

Let me begin by saying that his analysis of pain and its derivation from human freewill with the need of a loving God to make us ever more lovable [pain being one of the means for this] is compelling and provocative. There is much in Lewis with which I concur but pain is a more complex phenomenon than he discerned in his early writing. Let me illustrate what I mean.

In the previous chapter I spoke of Edgar Brightman's first wife dying of facial cancer. It is worth emphasising that Brightman's consideration of this and of suffering in general led him to the view that so much suffering in the universe is pointless. He applied searing logic to his argument; namely that if God is all loving and all powerful he both could and should remove suffering. Since he either does not or cannot then God is not both all loving and all powerful. From the perspective that personal existence is the action of a God who wishes people to share in his [loving] work of creation God cannot therefore be all powerful. Brightman's view was that there is much evil in the world which is ultimately meaningless and which God has no power to remove except through the eternally ongoing and painful drawing of creation to its eventual fulfilment.

But I must not allow myself to be drawn into solely academic discourse on the subject of pain. The issue is much closer to real life for everyone. For several years I have been counselling, and laying on hands with prayer, a woman in her forties who has had unremitting pain for twenty six years located in the nerves of her neck / jaw below her right ear. There was pain previously but an attempt at surgical correction went wrong and made matters far worse. From time to time she has written of her situation for me. The following is self-evidently poignant:

> I have pain but nothing visible to show for it; no spot, no mark, no missing leg or arm, no cancer. Just pain - something you can't see but something that is hell to live with. God, you had pain when you sent your Son down to earth to die for our sins to be forgiven. You were able to see your pain. I'm not. Why?

Does unremitting and seemingly purposeless pain have any meaning in God's plan? C.S. Lewis speaks of it being part of God's way of training us to become more lovable. He gives an example of owning a puppy. The little puppy which we love is trained and disciplined so that it might become an even more lovable dog. Pain, Lewis argues, serves much the same function for us. He also speaks of our submission to pain within the wider context of our submission to God. In fairness to Lewis he also raises the paradox that on the one hand whilst submission to pain is right and proper, seeking means to alleviate pain is equally correct. Nonetheless Lewis' view, when I am sitting opposite my pained parishioner gives me no words to offer as comfort. Somehow his approach seems too remote, even detached.

That is enough introduction. I have set down the parameters of this chapter. By and large my focus will be upon pain which comes to us through no deliberate fault of our own. By this I mean the sort of pain which is with us either by accident or perforce by the context of our place within creation. To begin this some background information is necessary and to that extent let me offer a layman's narrative on the physiology of pain.[2]

Imagine a silhouette of the human person lying face upwards on the floor. There are three 'boxes' comprising head, shoulders and hips. Each is joined to the other by the cantilevers of spine and neck. All twists applied to the body will rotate around spine and neck. This is straightforwardly explained by the various evolutionary processes which have come to play as the human body ceased to move on four limbs and adapted to movement on the rear two limbs with the skeletal frame standing vertically. It is very easy to subject the modern person to stresses which the body cannot accommodate. For example, the soft tissues stretch and with them the nerve fibres which they channel. The various connective tissues will recover given time and rest but the nerves never will. The outcome will be damage resulting in paralysis, at worst, ranging along to loss of feeling or conditions of pain any of which might well be accompanied by a range of mobility losses.

An example of such a situation involved a buildings officer on a construction site. He was carrying a clipboard in his right hand as he opened the door of a portacabin with his left. He slipped on ice and involuntarily used the left hand to grasp the handle tighter. The brachial plexus nerves from the neck to the arms were pulled, indeed stretched, with the result that the man is now unable to move his hand, he has a lot of pain, his sleep is spoiled and he can no longer drive. Clearly also he is unable to work.

Another situation is that of a care assistant who was grasped tightly by a demented patient. This caused internal damage to the radial nerve for it was squeezed between the patient's finger and the assistant's own bone. As a consequence the extensor muscles are now dysfunctional. Because there is no external sign of anything amiss, the local authority, neighbours and even relatives refused to believe something was wrong.

For the person who has to suffer the outcome of these traumas the problem of the pain is made worse by the misery of non-belief on the part of others who might well involve crucial figures such as employers, lawyers, doctors, friends, relatives and so on. The pain may not be removed, but it will be relieved by others listening attentively and sympathetically to the person's account of their situation. This may well be a repeated phenomenon. It is crucial that the person listening be prepared to say they believe the person. When, for example, unbelieving former employers have to be taken to litigation the outcome may well be financially very satisfactory for the former employee though the fact of the litigation means that the trauma has been spread rather than eased.

Other scenarios come about for other reasons. Osteoporosis - Dowager's Hump - is a function of increasing longevity. Its presence is perhaps also the outcome of an early oophorectomy giving rise to an accelerated gradual decline in bone strength and density. Pain arises by bone crumbling down and impressing upon nerve trunks. Health will be increased by exercise along with non-smoking and healthy eating. All of these can accompany pharmaceutical prescription. In other situations surgery may help. A prolapsed intervertebral disc for example, where the soft inner tissue of fibrous material presses outward onto the nerve, may be excised in theatre.

Migraine offers a different set of issues. Put very simply and rather hamfistedly, a biochemical mediator causes the meningeal blood vessels around the brain to constrict. Drugs are designed to inhibit the adrenaline-like hormone mediators which cause this contraction. Well known foods and drink such as chocolate, cheese and rich clarets are factors which also trigger migraines. It seems that once a person has been revealed to be susceptible to migraine attacks they are more likely to have repeating migraines.

In all of these a range of treatments are possible. Surgery has been mentioned. Anaesthesia, such as the 'block' freezing as it is called of the lower body with an epidural injection, is a radical procedure which though short-lived may give some respite to a chronic sufferer. Pharmaceuticals and holistic remedies may also offer relief of variously short and / or long periods. But what seems crucial for all chronic sufferers is the attentive ear of others who are prepared to believe what they say and prepared to give time and attention to them in times of especial need. The attentive ear and understanding counsel will help relieve tension and stress and thereby help reduce the burdensome nature of the pain. What was clear in the case of the parishioner I mentioned above was that if tension increased then the intensity of the pain also rose. This is not the case with everyone though it seems to me that simple common sense procedures and facilities [including I suggest, prayer] which seek to alleviate anxiety are bound to be of benefit to those with chronic and maybe intractable pain.[3]

The situation of my parishioner is a good illustration of this. She attended the pain clinic on a regular and frequent basis at Ninewells Hospital in Dundee. There was a 'round the clock' facility for her. Additionally I saw her on a frequent basis for counselling and conversation in connection with the pain. And further to that she received laying on of hands with prayer for healing and relief at the altar rail Sunday by Sunday. Significantly impressive in all of this was the acceptance by the hospital staff of her participation within the church's ministry of healing. Although surgery was eventually attempted as a 'last resort' stratagem it was not before the woman had been to the lowest and most anxious depths and returned. She periodically recorded her feelings on paper. Of her most anxiety ridden fears and intentions I can repeat nothing but in the midst of deepest despair the following appeared:

I ask myself where do I go from here? I feel I must trust in God, he is my only hope. I have seen doctors, specialists ... I have had acupuncture[4], I have had everything possible. I must go on although to be completely honest I don't want to with this pain.

About eight months later she also wrote in the form of a prayer to God:

Today and for the last four months you have been with me. I know because my Faith in you, my knowledge of you, has grown. Maybe that is what I have learned out of my suffering. I put my little crucifix back on - a sign to me that wearing it is like putting a wedding ring on to C. It means "Yes God, you are there, although I don't totally understand why I had to have doubts. Whatever it was I think you have certainly strengthened my Faith to feel your presence... To know your healing would be above us. To do your will is to put down in writing the shame I feel in not wanting to carry on..."

There is much here that C.S. Lewis would applaud. But we must not be lulled into the false sense of security which would result from offering this as the happy outcome of a long and pained struggle. My parishioner, even in these more lucidly real moments of deep spiritual awareness could never accept that pain was part of the processes of God to make us ever more lovable. Writing in a more medical context Patrick Wall characterises the sad lot of many with peripheral or central nerve damage who do not have such support facilities as did my parishioner:

Talking to such chronic cases tells one a lot about their disease and about their doctors. They move on like draught horses, uncomplaining, heads down in continuous driving snow. Not only have their multiple treatments failed but they have suffered the indignity of being told that their pain will go away and / or that it is all in their head. They have learnt that to continue to complain is to alienate and to isolate. These stoical characters plod on, often counted as cured because they no longer go to the doctors or take their ineffective medicine.[5]

Perhaps this is a convenient point at which to offer a passing conclusion. My unease with C.S. Lewis writing his *The Problem of Pain* in 1940 and my own experience of those suffering pain prompts me to direct this chapter away from any attempt to find purpose designed by God within the experience of pain. It seems to me that many facets of creation have no purpose within God's economy. It would be blasphemous to say that the massacre of little children and their teacher in Dunblane in March 1996 has a purpose in God's ultimate ordering of creation. Rather I tentatively venture first the proposition that meaning may be found in the reality of pain and, second, I intend to set us investigating whether anything can be redeemed from it. I hope the sense of these words will be clear. By 'purpose' I am referring to the view which sees God as visiting pain upon his creation specifically to bring forward a disciplining or refining aspect within it. By 'meaning' and 'redemption' I indicate the perspective that pain is an inevitable given within creation with which God has to contend and out of which he seeks to bring meaning as well as bring to redemption.

Let me continue this chapter by enlarging upon pastoral and physiological aspects of pain with a consideration of Biblical material. Paul's "thorn in the flesh" will prove fertile ground for examination.

Paul's apostleship was grounded in a blinding revelation of the risen Lord. To avoid him being led to boasting of it and thereby claiming some sort of spiritual superiority he was given, as he puts it, a "thorn in the flesh":

> To keep me from being unduly elated by the magnificence of such revelations, I was given a thorn in my flesh, a messenger of Satan sent to buffet me; this was to save me from being unduly elated. Three times I begged the Lord to rid me of it, but his answer was: "My grace is all you need; power is most fully seen in weakness." I am therefore happy to boast of my weaknesses, because then the power of Christ will rest upon me.[6]

In 2 Corinthians 12:2 and 7 Paul tells us that the onset of the "thorn in the flesh" accompanied an ineffable vision. Whether this is the same experience as that of his Damascus road conversion is unlikely for the dating of Second Corinthians may be about AD56 giving AD42 as a plausible dating for this particular vision and the 'thorn' which came as its sequel. The time of its appearance is given quite precisely, some fourteen years before the writing of this letter. Curiously perhaps there is no mention of pain resulting from the thorn, though the imputation of its painful discomfiture is reasonably inferred. It weakened him and it humiliated him in the sense of stopping his inherent tendency to over elation.

The significance [the meaning] of the thorn for Paul was very definite. Though commentators have to resort to conjecture in their efforts to try to identify the nature of the thorn its effect upon Paul was very clear. It was not there by chance. It served to keep him from spiritual pride. Although a parallel may be drawn with Job 2:1-7 where God seemingly gives authority to Satan [the 'Adversary'] for the fate of Job, I cannot conclude from the text that the same delegation of authority befalls Paul. He is quite clear that the affliction is from God because the intention "to keep me from being unduly elated" can't come from Satan. Whether its meaning is general [the painful nature of all mortality], or literal [eye trouble, disfigurement, recurrent pain] or metaphorical [the weakness of his preaching word compared with the greatness of the grace of God] we can be sure its effect upon him was that of pain, however interpreted.

From the text it is quite clear that Paul considered it perfectly appropriate to pray for his own release from the thorn. Again some of those whom I have counselled who suffer pain feel such self-directed prayer is wrong as there are others far more worthy of God's attention with their sufferings being greater. Equally strong are the feelings of guilt from the many who find their pain relieved whilst others, who shared the pain clinic waiting room, benefit no such release of their affliction. This may be paralleled with the prayer of Jesus in Gethsemane that the cup of suffering might also be taken from him [Matthew 26:39-44]. Like Jesus Paul came to recognise the way he unavoidably had to go. For some there will be release, and improvements in medicine make this ever more likely, but for others the pain will have to continue. For Jesus the way of pain was ultimate salvation for all. For Paul it was an antidote to pride. In each and for each the meaning became clear; in weakness is God's power most forcefully presented. Paul continued [2 Corinthians 12:10], "So I am content with a life of weakness, insult, hardship, persecution, and distress, all for Christ's sake; for when I am weak, then I am strong."

Herein lies Paul's sense of the purpose of his suffering. It is in the time of weakness that Paul most relies upon and it would seem is granted God's grace. Rather than ask a fourth time for the thorn to be removed Paul now sees his affliction as a source, or channelling, of God's correspondingly abundant grace. In falling victim to this condition, this thorn, Paul was no different to any other person. In seeing God's work of grace overcoming the effect of his condition he was truly apostolic. Perhaps in passing it is worth noting that Paul's thorn did not arise as a consequence of sin. Many in his day would argue that illness [and thereby 'pain'] was derivative from wrong doing. For Paul it would seem the case that his thorn arose out of mystical experience. It seems that it did so with the purpose of protecting him from spiritual pride. Thus although we are told the thorn was given by Satan, and for this reason we might assume his intention was malevolent, Paul was able to see, through grace given him, its redemption from evil intent to the greater work of controlling pride. Crudely put it served as a preventive measure.

Throughout the development of my thesis within this chapter will be seen the contrast between what might variously be called traditional perspectives on the problem of pain with others which might challenge these. Often the latter arise within pastoral situations. One such is the pain which arises from the power of emotion, not least when associated with tragic memories. My experience of survivors of childhood abuse is that much repressed memory of trauma struggles to emerge and give rise to a coherent sense of self during adolescence and early adulthood. If such meaning and purpose is not allowed to form during this crucial period then the likelihood of a lifetime of damage is very real.

I have encountered one situation where indescribable sexual and other physically violent brutality inflicted upon a young girl generated an emotional response during adulthood which in turn triggered chest and stomach pains which were to last several years. No analgesic could assist these. As their cause was in the deep trauma of a fractured childhood release from the pain could only begin as the effects of this past were gradually [and with immense difficulty] overcome. Hearing and listening to the story of those in such situations is as important as is the close attention given to others with a more physiological cause for their pain. In her writings[7] the woman has written the following as a means of both documenting as well as sharing the intensity of her pain:

> ... the hurt is so physical that I don't know how else to contain it / bear it. And I say 'Oh God' over and over again, as though that's going to make him take it all away ... Every few seconds it comes and it's like being gripped suddenly. My stomach muscles tense - in the same way that they would if I was being sick ... I could barely speak because the muscles in my stomach kept squeezing up ... it stops me breathing.

The tragic situation being so graphically offered in this vignette indicates how similar is the experience, in survivors of abuse, with others bearing the loneliness of an equally invisible, but no less real, pain.

In all of this it will be obvious I hope where my sympathy resides. Nonetheless, I cannot but admit a sense of admiration for those who firmly believe as does John Wilkinson that, "In the hour of pain and suffering the Christian can know that his experience is not an accident outside the purpose of God resulting from a suspension of his providence, but a situation in which God is active for the Christian's good with everything under control."[8] And again, I know a young woman who is severely disabled with cerebral palsy. She skis, holds a

PhD, drives a car, goes on cycling holidays with her tricycle and is eloquent testimony that in weakness there is indeed strength. She adds, controversially to my mind, that God does not make mistakes. Both these exemplify the Lewis position I was questioning at the outset of this chapter. Even though I have my own contrary views to Lewis and to Wilkinson I nonetheless remain deeply impressed by those who do submit to the ennobling outcomes of suffering and can see within it the purpose of God unfolding. My illustration from the previous chapter where the two women, one largely wheelchair bound and the other weakened by significant illness and deafness demonstrates again how God's grace abounds in power in the presence of weakness.

It has to be admitted that however powerful such testimony as this might be ultimately it can never prove a point. Its purpose is declaratory. By this I mean that if through theological terms we can assert that in weakness and suffering [and by extension pain] there is strength then for this to have 'cash value' we must look for actual examples whereby the teaching is seen to be a lived reality. The efficacy of testimony therefore is that it gives empirical instantiation to the propounded truth.

In our examination of the New Testament it is also important to note the seeming paradox of taking up the cross of suffering and pain ["God forbid that I should boast of anything but the cross of our Lord Jesus Christ, through which the world is crucified to me and I to the world!"[9]] as the actual means of following the way of Christ. Perhaps this is in part what C.S. Lewis meant by submission to pain. And yet submission to unnecessary pain should be avoided by the removal of the pain. The taunting which seems to have befallen Paul [2 Corinthians 4:8] was not something he clearly enjoyed and yet he was able to see in what he bore something of the death of Jesus being carried about in, or on, his own person. That is the ambiguity; on the one hand bearing pain as a reminder of the pain borne by Jesus and yet [with both Jesus and Paul] praying that the cup of suffering be taken away.

There is a long and strong tradition of pain-bearing within the Christian heritage. At worst it has led to various and regrettable disciplines of a sadomasochistic form. At best it has significantly advanced the life and witness of the church. In our own day the lives of Dorothy Kerin and Cameron Peddie offer testimony of this. Respectively they were the prime movers in the recovery of the mainstream Christian ministry of healing in the Church of England and in the Church of Scotland.

I have referred earlier to J. Cameron Peddie's epochal little book *The Forgotten Talent* as a Scottish classic upon the reopening of the mind of the Church towards the Ministry of Healing. It is also a wonderful window to the mystical tradition within the Church of Scotland. In a national church so heavily dominated by the ministry of the word [and with it all too often many unthought words] there has been a rich and much neglected mystical tradition that has fed the heart and minds of many Scots Divines whose preaching and teaching have been gold mines of spiritual erudition. Donald Baillie in his Gifford Lectures *The Sense of the Presence of God*[10] documents the epistemology of this. Cameron Peddie meanwhile gives us the insight of a disciplined pastor.

Chapter Three of Peddie's book [entitled 'The Nail in my Palm'] traces the course of Peddie's devotional commitment. In content this involves his submission to the scrutiny of God, his self-opening and self-examination within a context of regular and strict meditation, and his searching of the scriptures as he sought his own command to begin a ministry of healing. At the culmination of this he was looking for a second sign which would trigger the start of his ministry of healing [the first had been a direction to Luke 21:15]. As Peddie was praying for a sign he saw the imprint of a stigma in his right hand. Peddie's account runs thus:

> I saw something very strange. My hand grew smaller, and became all bruised, as if it had been hammered. Then down from the roots of the first two fingers and between them, a large nail appeared driven in to the very head; from it blood trickled down the lines on the palm and round the wrist. I cannot say how long the vision lasted for time did not exist for me.[11]

Peddie presents this as a vision, the content of a mystical experience. His previous searches of the scriptures had taught him of the veracity of such experiences as overtook Paul in 2 Corinthians 12:2-4. Peddie had come to realise that the same could come to him. And it had. It seems the case that this was a vision only rather than an actual impress of the stigmata in a physical sense upon his hand. What is crucial is that the vision of the nail in the palm led Peddie into his public healing ministry. A complementary contrast may helpfully be made with Dorothy Kerin.

Being a lay woman with an emerging vocation to the Christian ministry of healing would present its own problems for a member of the Church of England. Whereas for Peddie his concerns were persuading his ministerial colleagues and academic mentors of his ministry, for Kerin her problems resided initially in finding clergy who might take her vocation seriously. Providentially there were within the emerging Anglo-Catholicism of the first quarter of the twentieth century sufficient priests of calibre and depth who could recognise the clear and profound mystical greatness of this woman.[12]

Morris Maddocks locates Kerin within the tradition of the greatest of the mystics. In a fascinating comparison with Julian of Norwich, she asked for the mind or memory of Christ's Passion, so that she could experience the Passion in the same way His mother and closest friends did at the foot of the cross. And she goes on to quote Mother Julian, "I wanted His pain to be my pain... I was not wanting a physical revelation of God, but such compassion as a soul would naturally have for the Lord Jesus... Therefore I desired to suffer with Him".[13] Kerin was called into the healing ministry by a similar pathway into and through suffering. Maddocks cites one of her prayers:

By the bruising of my whole life,
Strengthen me with sympathy for every wounded soul;
And let my prayers be a balm for the wounds of thy children
That they may be healed.[14]

Maddocks begins his next chapter of Kerin's biography, "Suffering seems to have been the normal accompaniment of sanctity throughout Christian history". Her experience of suffering and pain was intense. Maddocks offers the following narrative which may be allowed to speak for itself:

While her [spiritual] director gave her the laying on of hands, she experienced what he described as the most terrible attack of pain he had ever witnessed. With his intuitive awareness he perceived it was no ordinary pain. It was especially acute in her left hand which seemed to be the focus of her agitation. He then saw a red mark gradually appearing on the back of her hand. Later on, she became more distressed and showed him the palm of her left hand where a wound could be clearly discerned... he also prayed that if it were God s will, the stigmata might be given also in the right hand to convince her and reassure her that this was a visitation from her crucified Saviour and Lord... The following day, 9th December [1915], Dorothy received the wound in her side and in her right hand.[15]

For the sceptical reader I defer to Maddocks' book for he quotes at length eye witness testimony with graphic description of the stigmata of Dorothy Kerin. Though clearly different in form from the experience of Peddie the outcome was the same for each. After deep preparation and searching experience of the stigmata for both Peddie and Kerin was to be the watershed which opened for each the movement into the ministry of healing.

In writing these words I can see that so much of what I am saying flies in the face of my opening pages. Having levelled so much criticism against such notable figures as C.S. Lewis for example I now find myself using the life and witness of those whose own experience of pain and suffering [St Paul and Dorothy Kerin most especially] has been the way into the healing ministry. Their acceptance of it [even yearning for it] because of the grace it correspondingly released has proved a blessing for countless of other sufferers. So what is the case I am seeking to prove when my own presentation teems with such contradiction?

My argument has to be I believe, that pain and suffering for their own sake are an unacceptable part of Christian life and practice. Equally abhorrent and contrary to the gospel are any form of ascetic practices which seek to make the deliberate inflicting of pain a virtue. Furthermore I cannot accept the pastoral practice of saying to a person who suffers pain that they are sharing in the suffering of Jesus. Nonetheless when I examine my own ministry and recall those occasions when I have said something similar to the person of whom I mentioned earlier her legitimate reply to me was that Jesus only had to suffer his pain for a few hours at least and for three days at most. She had had her pain for twenty six years. Now suppose you counter this and say that Jesus is eternally suffering at the heart of the universe: while this may be a correct perspective, it is regrettably a spiritualisation of pain which offers little solace to a woman whose pain prevents her sleeping in readiness for work the next day. It is especially problematic for someone such as me to offer such counsel. I suffer little or no ill health.

So the resolution of the dilemma is to recognise that certain people can and do accommodate their pain within the vocation to which God calls them. Even though they may wish for the pain to be taken from them [as did Jesus and Paul] if it is to be inevitable then they are ready to accept it as such and to go with it where it leads. Others seek deliberately to share in the pain of Jesus so that their understanding of and compassion for others who suffer may deepen. The purpose, or redemption, of their suffering pain in this way is to exercise a ministry of healing aimed towards the relief of pain and suffering in others for whom it clearly serves no such divine purpose. It seems to me therefore that only in the sense that pain and suffering bring some willingly and freely into the redemptive work of Christ may we count each as worthy Christian virtues. In this and only in this way may pain and suffering have meaning and be understood to have some purpose in God's work of redeeming his creation "heaving in travail".

I began this chapter with reference to C.S. Lewis. It would seem that his mind moved, most especially so after the death of his wife. By the time of writing *A Grief Observed* he was fully immersed in all the personal dilemmas of the pain of grief. In *Shadowlands* Brian Sibley wrote about this period:

> What happened to Joy [Lewis' wife] was that she had been set free: free from the endless battle against an insidious disease; free from the pain and the agony; and free from the torment of waiting for death. For Jack [i.e. Lewis] the pain went on.[16]

Lewis was experiencing from within something of the human side of pain. The post-1960 C.S. Lewis is a more human, less dispassionate man that was the C.S. Lewis of *The Problem of Pain*. In this respect I at least find his writing in these latter years much more approachable and helpful.

PART II

Chapter 6
HEALING WORDS

Let me summarise my aim for this chapter. I want to help the non-Greek speaker who is interested in the Christian ministry of healing come to appreciate the importance of the 'healing words' of the New Testament. I feel this task is at the very least justified because fewer and fewer pastors, priests and ministers are as competent in the biblical languages as has been the case hitherto, even though there are more theology graduates across the length and breadth of the land!

Accordingly I am offering this essay to help others who like myself lack a formal training in New Testament languages to come to a broader and deeper understanding of what I call, for purposes of simplicity, 'healing words'. In the pages which follow this essay I am offering a sweep of the New Testament healing narratives with the relevant 'healing words' italicised in English along with their Greek root in its Anglicised form. It is especially important when consulting the expository notes for one passage that others are followed up where perhaps the same sort of miracle [eg healing of leprosy] is being considered. I have aimed in these notes to offer cumulative information across a range of passages rather than to cram everything about each narrative into each and every location. This is especially true where there are parallels. Many of the expository notes in one parallel will be relevant to the parallel texts and should always be studied along with the particular passage which has drawn the eye of the reader. Let me begin my task with a sentence or two about Fred:

> Fred went to the hospital *to see about* the itchy skin trouble on his arms to see if it could be *dealt with* and properly *fixed* in time for his summer holidays.

I have italicised the 'healing words' in this sentence. They are 'see about', 'dealt with' and 'fixed'. Each of these of these has a non-specific meaning in normal use. Meaning is given when they are applied in a particular situation. Let me explain what I mean. Following popular trends one could go into a garden centre to *see about* a new climbing rose which has just been developed. One could go along to the local tax office to see if one's tax claim had been *dealt with* and one could ask the plumber if a leaking tap could be *fixed*. Each of these terms has we can see a multiple range of potential applications. It is the application which gives meaning to the term. In my illustration concerning Fred it has a healing application. Now let's reword this illustration:

Fred went to the hospital *for an appointment with a dermatologist* concerning the itchy skin trouble on his arms to see if it could be *treated* and properly *healed* in time for his summer holidays.

Here the words have a more specific application. An *appointment with a dermatologist* can only have meaning within the framework of clinical treatment. Its meaning is specific to that setting. Fred's itchy condition will likely be *treated* within that same setting and so the word *treated* has a healing connotation. It has to be said however that the word *treated* is not exclusively a clinical term as clothing, for example, can be *treated* to render it more waterproof. But the third word, *healed*, does have a more thoroughgoing even if not exclusive relation to the relief of ailments, illness and other such conditions. However it may also be used in relation to the resolution of difficulties between two previously warring parties in a marriage dispute. Let me reword Fred's situation once more:

Fred went to the hospital *for an appointment with a dermatologist* concerning the itchy skin trouble on his arms to see if medication might encourage normal *epithelial tissue to form* in time for his summer holidays.

In this third extension of my illustration each of the 'healing words' [more accurately phrases] I have italicised has a highly distinctive, if not exclusive reference to a clinical or scientific setting. These words have little use outside this setting. Even though their use still speaks of Fred's skin condition their reference and meaning is quite different to the more general terms of my first and, to a degree, my second illustration. Consider now this narrative drawn from Matthew 8:

As Jesus entered Capernaum a centurion came up to ask his help. "Sir," he said, "my servant is lying at home paralysed and racked with pain." Jesus said, "I will come and *cure* him." But the centurion replied, "Sir, I am not worthy to have you under my roof. You need only say the word and my servant will be *cured.*"

Here the 'healing word' is *cure*. We can ask whether the word 'cure' is being in a general or specific sense. Scrutiny of the Greek reveals that two words are used, *therapeuo* and *iaomai* . We can further ask whether this means that the single English word 'cure' should be interpreted in different ways in the context of this passage.

In the healing miracle narratives a relatively close circle of words appear and reappear. Principal among these are the two I have just mentioned *iaomai* and *therapeuo*. Furthermore they have widespread usage. Other healing words seem to have specific reference more to certain conditions. *Ekballo* is especially used in those texts where there is a demon to be driven out. *Katharizo* is a term used for the cleansing of skin conditions, these normally being referred to in a general sense as leprosy in English translations of the New Testament. *Apokathistemi* is a further word with the meaning of something being 'made sound' such as the man's withered arm in Matthew 12:13.

The time has come for me to investigate these words in greater detail before embarking on those expository notes in which we will see the words put to use. There are two volumes which are crucial resources. The first, *The New International Dictionary of New Testament Theology*[1] is a massive four volume work unequalled as a reference source for the theologically competent reader lacking language skills. Both this Chapter and the Expository Notes which follow have drawn upon the encyclopaedic wealth which Brown has brought together. For those with language competence, and even myself as a beginner in this regard, the ten volume *Theological Dictionary of the New Testament*[2] edited by Gerhard Kittel has little to equal it. I am singularly privileged to have very ready access to the Divinity library of St Andrews University. Access to these great works presents therefore no serious problem. Either volume is unlikely to be found in the average public library, or the majority of pastor's studies, and given the size and reference nature of each is not the sort of work available on the usual run-of-the-mill inter-library loan. If these words of mine succeed in any way I hope they will help at least to bridge the gap between parish and academy.

Therapeuo and *iaomai* form the two principal word groups around which revolve many, indeed the majority of healing narratives in the New Testament. A start can be made with that which is most frequently found, *therapeuo*.

In its New Testament usage *therapeuo* diverges from its secular Greek origins where it means 'to serve', 'to be of use to someone' in the sense of 'being willing and ready to attend upon someone'. In these contexts expression is also being given to the interpersonal dynamics between the person who serves and the one being served. As I understand this the relationship being implied within the term is that of mutual benefit between the parties concerned. Connotations of 'slave labour' or of forced and unwilling 'serfdom' are not implied. In this same popular context through religious observance one would also be reckoned to 'serve the gods' by due veneration and acts of appropriate obeisance. Only once in the New Testament is this meaning given to *therapeuo*. Paul in the thoroughly Hellenistic Council of Areopagus, and no doubt wanting to apply his oratorical skills says in Acts 17:25, "It is not because [God] lacks anything that he accepts *service* at our hands, for he is himself the universal giver of life and breath - indeed of everything."[3]

Within the secular understanding of *therapeuo* it is not too far to see linguistic evolution gradually including application to situations of illness wherein one might 'attend the sick' in the sense of caring for them, or waiting upon their needs. *Therapeuo* came increasingly to have its place secured within clinical contexts. In the New Testament a straightforward or direct clinical understanding of *therapeuo* is present only in few exceptions of its forty three appearances [of which forty are in the synoptic gospels and Acts]. In Luke 4:23 ["Physician, heal yourself"] and in Luke 8:23 where the woman with the issue of blood could not be healed by anyone the reference is to clinical processes. In all the remaining locations [excepting its cultic imaging in Acts 17:25, just mentioned] *therapeuo* refers to the miraculous healings recorded as performed principally by Jesus as well as by his followers. There is no secular understanding of *therapeuo* in the sense of 'serving others' in the New Testament.

The scholar, H.W. Beyer, writing in Kittel[4] gives evidence that Jesus' healing ministry had few parallels amongst the rabbis of his day. He cites Fiebig, and refers us also to Bultmann, "In Palestinian Judaism of the time there were no workers of miracles, nor were there any who were honoured as such". It would seem that only isolated accounts of healings by rabbis are to be found. In this context however we should note Jesus' comment in Matthew 12:27, "If it is by Beelzebul that I drive out devils, by whom do your own people drive them out?" Leaving aside the birth and passion narratives of Jesus the two most dominant motifs of Jesus' ministry are his healing work and his teaching. Both are intertwined and both led him into controversy. Two verses in Matthew 4:23 and 9:35 [respectively, "He travelled throughout Galilee, teaching in the synagogues, proclaiming the good news of the kingdom, and healing every kind of illness and infirmity among the people" and "... Jesus went round all the towns and villages proclaiming the good news of the kingdom, and curing every kind of illness and infirmity"] top and tail a major section of teaching discourse [chapters 5-7] and healing narrative [chapters 8-9], act as a prelude to the commissioning of the twelve and herald the context of increasing opposition to what Jesus both said and did.

The use of the word *therapeuo* as descriptive of Jesus' healing work is such as to distinguish it from normal clinical processes which might not succeed. In the healings of Jesus there is never any question of his healings not succeeding though from Mark 6:1-6 it appears that lack of faith is a barrier to carrying out a ministry of healing. In his healing work Jesus did not seek to identify himself with those others who might claim divine healing prowess but explicitly placed himself in the tradition of Old Testament prophecy and carried out his ministry of healing in the framework of a messiah who in his own person and work embodied and inaugurated the new kingdom of God. Jesus does not draw upon these Old Testament texts to prove he is Messiah but rather places his work in that framework of obedient activity which is messianic and is part and parcel of the fulfilment of the hope of the prophets. Jesus' claim therefore that his work is compatible with the law of Moses, particularly in relation to the thorny dispute of healing on the sabbath, rests upon his obedience to his Messianic thrust. Matthew 8:17 is applicable, "...to fulfil the prophecy of Isaiah: 'He took our illnesses from us and carried away our diseases'."

Clearly Jesus was drawing upon his intimacy with God as Word of God to exercise a power *[dynamis]* in his healing work. Modern day understandings of healing as a 'power activity' risk misunderstanding the Greek *dynamis* here. *Dynamis* refers more to God's energy, or capacity, or drive to heal people. Whilst this also does mean power, power as we tend to understand it in popular terms has regrettable implications of hierarchical authoritarianism and despotic gratuity.

The word *therapeuo* is used both in contexts where its reference is general [Luke 4:40] and where the situation is presented in some detail [Matthew 8:6ff and 17:16ff]. It also appears in a variety of differing scenes and settings. Ought we to be bothered about the historicity, or historical facticity of the miracle narratives? In one sense the question is pointless because no definitive answer is possible. The relative simplicity of the healing miracles in comparison to others claimed elsewhere at the time indicates that the focus of attention should not so much be upon the process of the miracle but rather upon what lies behind it. Furthermore we can say that the texts clearly and consistently speak of the activity of this rabbi Jesus who in his teaching and ministering differed so markedly from other rabbis of his day that we are well advised to take the scriptural narratives as they stand with earnest seriousness. Although textual differences may alter nuances between one gospel and another, the overall direction of the content is quite clear; Jesus taught in a particular way and healed in a manner that was thoroughgoing and extensive.

From both these we learn the lesson that foremost in the person and work of Jesus is the in-coming of the kingdom of God demonstrating that both in word and work Jesus is victor over all forces [including ill health] which would conflict with God's reign in the universe.

Two derivatives of *therapeuo* are to be found in the New Testament. *Therapeia* refers to the medical healing people need in Luke 9:11 [and therefore also in need of Jesus' healing] as well as with eschatological application at Revelation 22:2 where leaves on a tree represent the 'healing' of the nations. A further derivative is *therapon*, where we find in Hebrews 3:5-6 a contrast is made with Moses the servant and Christ the son.[5]

By way of summary I would want to say that *therapeuo* finds in the New Testament a religious application in the messianic work of Jesus with precedents only in prophetic longing and the few healing miracles of the Old Testament and no contemporary parallel of any substance. I chose not to refer to the use of *therapeuo* in the exorcism narratives simply to avoid repetition with material still to emerge. It is sufficient to note as I move on in my investigation that Jesus conflict with powers which seek to submerge or negate his will extends no less to opposing demonic authorities every bit as much as it does to more conventional illness. We can turn now to *iaomai*.

The application of *iaomai* in the New Testament mirrors almost exactly that of *therapeuo* and much of what was said about *therapeuo* applies also to *iaomai*. *Iaomai* occurs some twenty six times, twenty of these being in the synoptic gospels and Acts. A derivative, *iasis*, has three appearances in Luke and *iatros* five times in the synoptics and one in Colossians 4:14. Another derivative *iama* is to be found in 1 Corinthians 12 where, in three instances, it is specifically related to the gifts of the Spirit given to those in the early church. In Matthew 10:18, Mark 6:13 and Luke 9:1 *therapeuo* is used in the extension of Jesus' ministry to others; in Luke 9:2 *iaomai* is used.

In the primitive world-view we need not be surprised at the perspective of illness being likened to a wound inflicted by an exterior force. Whether from an animal lunge or from the spear of an opponent the primitive man could understand the subsequent pain, bleeding, inflammation or whatever. By analogy, illnesses and other conditions would similarly be regarded as 'attacks'. The origin of these attacks might be seen to be various evil powers with wide ranging identity [gods, for example, or demons or whatever]. Healing would be sought by various vegetable and animal remedies as well as by magical processes deemed to be beneficial in their reversal of the malignant effects of the attack.

Whilst scientific medicine arose firstly amongst the ancient Egyptian civilisations it was the Greeks who developed it to a fine art and skilled practice with its own accompanying ethical code.[6] A range of remedies are offered in Greek culture for various conditions. Some of these conjoin the processes of the gods with the processes of humankind.[7]

In ancient Judaism illness carried with it both a human dimension as well as religious significance. The latter arose through widespread belief that illness was a result of the causal activity of malign forces. However as belief progressed God came to be understood as the sender or withholder of illness. It could be viewed as a sign of God's anger for someone otherwise enjoying prosperity [cf the account of Hezekiah's illness in Isaiah 38].

In other locations maladies of all sorts were viewed as the angered activity of a God seeking retribution for misdemeanours. Oepke[8] gives examples where ulcers and dropsy are deemed to have arisen from immorality and licentiousness, quinsy on account of neglecting tithes, epilepsy and crippling on account of marital infidelity. We are given that even foetuses could sin in the womb. Conversely illness, if borne with 'humility and resignation', would lead to increasing grace with freedom from the effects of sin recognised by their complete remission. Such, it would seem, was widespread Old Testament teaching.

Medicine was practised in ancient Israel. Jeremiah 8:22 reads, "Is there no balm in Gilead, no physician there? Why has no new skin grown over their wound?" The effects of venereal infection are recognised as the result of promiscuous behaviour [Ecclesiasticus 30:2b-3] and the benefits of good health and vigour given high prominence [Ecclesiasticus 30:14-17] and preference over any amount of earthbound riches.

There is witness to belief in the healing influences of religious practices. In Numbers 21:9 Moses erects a bronze serpent "in order that anyone bitten by a snake could look at the bronze serpent and recover". Moses did this as a direct result of instruction during his intercession with God on behalf of the people. They had been punished by God with a plague of snakes as a consequence of their lack of faithful trust [Numbers 21:5-9]. Whether the bronze serpent was effective we are not told, though it may well have served as a reminder to the people of their dependence upon God during their desert wanderings. The healing of Naaman in 2 Kings 5, the raising of the dead boy in 1 Kings 17 by Elijah and the similar story of Elisha raising a dead boy in 2 Kings 4 are each accompanied by prayer and ritual actions.

In ancient Judaism, with echoes to be found in the ministry of Jesus, healing was associated with the remission of sins - this last being accompanied by intention towards a new life of faith and the recognition of forgiveness flowing from God. Crucial for seeking God's healing is the recognition of relationship with him as well as explicit dependence upon his ability to heal and to save. In Isaiah 61:1 *iasasthai* relates to the binding up of a wound [a figurative reference to the healing of broken relationship with God], *iasis* in Ecclesiasticus 28:3 can mean forgiveness as well as help. This interpretation is also to be found in Deuteronomy 30:3 where once again *iaomai* is the operative 'healing word'. The healer in Old Testament prophecy is also the wounded saviour. Increasingly the wounded saviour becomes seen as God's specific agent. And then in verses pregnant with later significance when seen against the backcloth of the vicarious work of Jesus, Isaiah 53 looks forward to ultimate healing from God coming in one who can take our suffering into himself and by suffering vicariously cancels out the effect of sin.

Within the New Testament many of the Old Testament understandings of illness reappear though here the context in which they do so is as part of the battle which Jesus ranges against all that conflicts with God's creative plan. Jesus himself both healed and in his parabolic teaching extolled the virtues of ordinary [what we might call 'common sense'] caring and remedial practices [cf. the story of the Good Samaritan]. Paul clearly values Luke the physician [Colossians 4:14] and 1 Timothy 5:23 is I recognise often quoted with amusement and normally out of context.

The application of *iaomai* in the healing ministry of Jesus is quite literal. Figurative use occurs only when there is quotation; an example being Matthew citing Isaiah 6:10 at 13:15. The same quotation appears in John 12:40-41. In Mark 2:17 [and its parallels] Jesus speaks with both serious criticism and pointed irony when he speaks of himself as the saviour of sinners in the framework of the doctor who heals illnesses.

The New Testament Gospels contain the fullest, indeed the only, historical record of Jesus' healing work. That this is so should not in any way devalue their use or reference as source material. It is because they were deemed by the early church to be normative in their testimony to the life and work of the historical Jesus that they were included in the New Testament. Had their authenticity been in doubt then, like the Infancy Gospel of Thomas for example, they would not have been presented in the canon of scripture. Far from weakening their authority as evidence of the work of Jesus the presence of the four gospels within the New Testament actually strengthens the case for taking them more seriously than liberal critical scholarship might otherwise wish to indicate. A. Oepke in Kittel notes that after the first century the gospel narratives would not have received significant redaction, and that up to this date the written forms had already had their structure and content well constructed within the Christian communities which arose after Jesus died. These would have been based upon oral narratives initially but since well formed written texts existed within some forty five years after the death of Jesus it seems reasonable to propose that the gospels as we now have them are indeed a faithful record of the words and work of Jesus. If nothing of significance happened at the hands of Jesus how could such a corpus of writings have so easily and quickly arisen convincing so many as it did? If what happened at Jesus' hands has been corrupted by the New Testament writers how could they have done this without significant protest by those who could testify otherwise? Our conclusions lead inexorably to the authenticity of the New Testament accounts.

We may add to this by referring to the fantastical imagery of the miracle narratives in the Infancy Gospel of Thomas and the apocryphal Acts and by comparing them to the simplicity of the Gospel accounts [even though not entirely unfree of embellishment and arguable exaggeration] as we have them in the New Testament. These last do not so much point to the magical potency of Jesus but of his surrender to the will of God and the establishment of his kingdom. The healing miracles recorded in the New Testament freed people from sin, gave recovery of sight to the blind, enabled the restoration of leprous limbs, and offered God's gracious love to the humble person of faith. Healing is never refused though equally Jesus does not deliberately go out of his way to heal at every touch and turn; there being occasions when the teaching word takes precedence. There is no cash reward for Jesus for any healing; the requirement however to surrender in like manner to God is implicit throughout.

Dramatic actions in the healing work of Jesus are largely absent. Perhaps the use of saliva in Mark 7:33, 8:23 and John 9:6 are exceptions but only marginally so for the increased use of touch for persons deprived of either or both the senses of hearing and sight is highly relevant to their situation. Elsewhere Jesus also uses touch though never to displace the 'word' which pronounces healing. The word of healing is effective even at a distance [cf Matthew 8:5ff]. Anointing, though practised by the disciples and early church [Mark 6:13 and James 5:14], was not a method recorded as used by Jesus. Jesus' use of the 'word' for healing further distinguishes his work from that of contemporary accounts of healing. It is his word of authority which is required for healing though it does seem [Mark 6:3-6] that lack of faith on the part of people was a constraining effect upon the ministry of Jesus. By extension of this reasoning the inference might be drawn that for there to be healing the person should have faith in Jesus' power to heal.

In everything we have said the application of *iaomai* seems to mirror that of *therapeuo*. I began this chapter by asking whether the different healing words have different meanings one from the other. So far they do not. But we are finding that they are being given a distinctive application by Jesus in his life and work, or rather at the very least by the writers of the New Testament in their record of the word and works of Jesus. Let me move on to consider the usage of *hygies* (or *hugies*). This will help us consider more thoroughly what is meant in the New Testament by health.

Broadly speaking *hygies* means healthy with its derivatives respectively meaning to be healthy or to have health. More specific usage refers to mental health and the facility of rational and coherent thinking and in this sense *hygies* can mean 'intelligent' and 'rational'. By extension its ancient usage also extended to processes of rational or clear thinking, 'an intelligent or rational word'[9] and became also a greeting to begin and finish letters. Luck also indicates that *hygies* means 'farewell' on ancient gravestones.

Underlying these widespread ancient meanings is the view that that which is healthy expresses some kind of harmony or order in its being. In that which is healthy there is neither excess nor yet imbalance of any kind. It would seem that it refers to all circumstances being properly ordered in appropriate and given proportions. In ancient usage this refers both to the individual and to society where health was reckoned to be the valued norm with ill-health being the occasion for religious and medical concern. Health is the goal and the intended outcome of methods which seek to remedy the ill effects of sickness.

This view of the ordered state of well-being as an indication of the healthy person extends also into Old Testament Judaism. It is found in Joshua 10:21 in reference to the safe return of the Israelite army after their decimating bloodbath of the Amorite forces. In the healing of Hezekiah in Isaiah 38 his return to health is also represented as the normal state in which to be before God. In the passage from Ecclesiasticus 30 to which I referred earlier health is also given high worth and the doctor, the physician, accorded recognition in 38:1-15. Here it should also be remembered that the doctor's skill is derived from God from whom comes all healing and who seemingly delights in the presence of health.

Müller in Brown reminds us of the parable of the prodigal son who, having gone astray, is welcomed home and fully restored by the father who met him at his returning. The same applies to Luke 5:31, "It is not the healthy *[hygiainontes]* that need a doctor, but the sick; I have not come to call the virtuous but sinners to repentance".

Luck, in Kittel, makes the curious assertion that "health is not especially valued in the NT".[10] To me this seems an odd reading not even supported by his citation of Mark 2:17 and cross references to other volumes in Kittel. It seems to me [unless I am being unduly superficial in my reading of the New Testament] that Jesus' restoration of health to so many indicates health to be a preferred situation to that of ill-health, or non-health. Quite apart from that since so many in the gospel records apparently sought Jesus' healing this also highlights peoples' recognition of it. Luck continues, perhaps more appropriately, "The power to heal, to make whole, is also transmitted to the apostles according to Acts 4:10".

In the pastoral epistles correct, whole, orderly teaching of the faith is presented in terms of *hygies* and its derived forms. This has echoes of its early Greek usage when it related to the rational ordering of thought. Here in the pastorals it means Christian teaching coherent with the message and proclamation of Jesus in whom is the capacity to make people whole.[11]

Let us move into a discussion of, *apokathistemi*, 'restore'.

Oepke gives the simple meaning of *apokathistemi* as "to restore to an earlier condition".[12] In Israelite religion this developed its own messianic interpretation as well as its own ethical message. In the former the messianic interpretation is linked to the prophetic understanding of a saviour who would come and restore the chosen people of God. Linked to it is the latter understanding whereby inner recovery and restoration is the specific restitution of individual people paralleling God's action writ large with his people. Neither come automatically, they have to be worked for. Amos 5:15 reads, "Hate evil, and love good; establish justice in the courts; it may be that the Lord, the God of Hosts, will show favour to the survivors of Joseph". The words [like those of v.14] are addressed to the people of Israel but as is so often the case in the Old Testament have both a national and individual reference.

H.G. Link[13] gives a range of classical meanings which include restorative reference in terms of property, of borrowed goods, as well as of the restoration of a sick person. *Apokathistemi* and its derivatives have their origins it would seem in secular usage; religious application follows later. There is also astronomical reference to the restoration of 'cosmic cycles' though this has little relevance in our current discussion. In the Old Testament non-religious reference to *apokathistemi* has a wide range of application.[14] With more religious orientation we find focus upon the proclamation of eschatological deliverance to the people in exile. And we find a comparison made between the eschatological restoration of Israel and the nation's own earliest beginnings.

The messianic reference of *apokathistemi* to Jesus is voiced by the disciples in Acts 1:6, "Lord, is this the time at which you are to restore sovereignty to Israel?". Jesus' answer removes political connotations from their question but adds to it his recognition that the new age has already come in him and that the disciples will share in it as the Holy Spirit imparts his power upon them. In Jesus however, this restoration was to be achieved through the vicarious suffering of the cross.

The derived form *apokatastasis* which has only one New Testament location [Acts 3:19,21] draws much of its meaning from Old Testament eschatological hope; namely the restoration of humanity in line with God's purposive urge for his creation.

Although there is an implication in all this that conversion to a former life is part of God's will, *apokathistemi* does not refer to this in the New Testament. Rather its reference is the reconstitution or reestablishment of neutral things such as the man's arm 'restored' from its leprous condition in Mark 3:5 and parallels. The arm was restored to the state in which God had intended it to be. This represents its non-religious use in application to Jesus' healing ministry. It echoes the words of Hebrews 13:19, "...that I may be restored to you the sooner".

A universalist reading from such passages as Romans 5:18 ["acquittal and life for all"] seems in my view improbable at best. Whilst those of faith will be restored, those who refuse to acknowledge God without any semblance of faith elect their own non-restoration, indeed this constitutes their punishment.

If these considerations of *apokathistemi* tell us anything, they direct us towards a more universal vision of healing, when even though the gospels record specific instances of restoring withered arms. With *apokathistemi*, such occasions are types of God's wider restoration.

An interim or passing observation is in order concerning New Testament use of 'healing words'. It would seem, quite unsurprisingly, that the New Testament drew the meaning of 'healing words' from two sources. One was typical etymological evolution, in this case their formation within the language, thought forms and history of the people of Israel. Secondly, with the coming of Jesus and his own consciousness of his mission, these words gained greater poignancy. They no longer only looked forward to an eventual restoration of Israel [say], or towards a healing of that which was in contradiction to the will of God, but in the words and work of Jesus found their fulfilment. It is this latter which gives the 'healing words' their prime significance in the New Testament. It is this which gives them an understanding not found before, and by the extension of the ministry of Jesus' healing to us, gives them similar if not the same meaning today.

Some of the words refer to the individual healings of particular people. Some have a range of application both from the individual person to the wider people of God. That their meaning is both particular and widespread need cause us no surprise. That a variety of 'healings' should be encompassed within the meaning of one word such as *therapeuo* or *iaomai* again need cause no eyebrow to rise. It will come with no sense of wonder either that some conditions have words more specifically associated with the healing of very particular conditions. All this represents the very fluid and diverse way in which languages operate. Nonetheless we must not forget that, although given very special force by Jesus, the meaning of 'healing words' in the New Testament was not only conditioned by his use of these words but also by the history out of which he arose and in which he lived. Let us press on.

Ekballo is the word given for expelling, throwing out or propelling away. The root *ballo* is used of the fishermen in Matthew 4:18 'casting' their net. It is also used in the sense of 'placing' or 'depositing' in the context of new wine in old wineskins in Mark 2:22. *Ballein* is also used of the finger in the ears [Mark 7:33], the finger in the nail marks [John 20:25] and of Judas' malintent [John 13:2]. H. Bietenhard in Colin Brown cites eighty one New Testament locations representing the full range of meanings of both the root and its derivative forms.[16]

Within Jesus' healing ministry *ekballo* has particular reference to exorcism, the expelling of demons. These may have settled in property [as at Matthew 12:44] or persons [as at Mark 1:34 and elsewhere]. There was, however, by the time of Jesus a well structured framework for expelling demons by means and measures involving their binding by superior powers [see in this respect Matthew 12:29] and by the straightforward word of command.[17] Jesus it seems never questions the theological understanding of demons but refuses to operate within what we can take to be the normally given means of exorcism current in his day. This perhaps explains his dispute with the authorities recounted in Matthew 12:22-28. Jesus' own ministry of exorcism is given as the direct action of God upon the demons. It was an integral part of his preaching and proclamation of which his full range of healings were its real life outworking. The expulsion of the demon is a sign of the presence of the kingdom of God already here with the people [Luke 11:20]. It would seem also to be the case that other exorcists recognised Jesus as a superior force to the demons and began expelling demons in his name [Mark 9:38-40]. Jesus gave authority to expel demons to his followers.

It would appear that some cases of possession recorded in the New Testament are potentially at least reducible to modern-day understood clinical conditions. My inclination is to remain agnostic on this issue. It seems to me however that there is sufficient evidence for us to be very wary about discounting the possibility of demonic presence in a person or a place.

A pastoral footnote is appropriate at this point. Exorcism, the 'deliverance ministry', is the most controversial aspect of the ministry of healing today. I need not repeat myself at any length but I am one of those who hold to the view that this ministry must be exercised with the greatest level of caution and circumspection. I refer readers to Unit Seven of my workbook *A Way for Healing*.

In Hellenistic use the noun *aphesis* never occurs in a religious framework though it has widespread application in the sense of forensic release [from, say, marriage, an obligation, or maybe a position as well as from due debts or punishment]. Within the Septuagint its presence is also replete with wide ranging definition. Unlike its Hellenistic application however, in the Septuagint a religious understanding unfolds. God is one who also can forgive and release. Increasingly this becomes seen as release from sin. Isaiah 58:6 explicitly links this to a general pardon, an eschatological release, for the whole people.

With little surprise we find much the same spread of meaning in the New Testament. *Aphesis* almost always refers to forgiveness proceeding from God and offered in his name [Mark 1:4, Matthew 26:28] for people to accept. Of seventeen examples in the New Testament fifteen concern release from sin and the remaining two release from captivity. John 1:29 is significantly moving in the testimony of the Baptist. In the earliest New Testament texts, Paul's letters, *aphesis* and its other forms are largely absent, though at Romans 4:7 Paul quotes *aphiemi* from Psalm 32:1. Brown speaks of Paul's understanding of sin as a systematized doctrine of grace offered unconditionally as a result of the sacrifice of Jesus given once for all to redeem all cost of sin.

The forgiveness offered in this way as releasing from sin is however not cheap. Matthew 6:12 and the longer parabolic teaching in 18:23-35 enjoins the forgiveness of others as concomitant to one's own reception of forgiveness from God. In his healing miracles Jesus develops a dispute with the religious authorities of the day by uttering the forgiveness of God, an otherwise blasphemous act for a person to carry out. Seen from this perspective the coming in of the kingdom of God is made real because God's own forgiveness can be proclaimed from the mouths of his followers and in the act of making the proclamation the effect becomes real, alive and active in the forgiven person. The sin is wiped out by the proclaimed word and the sinner made welcome. [Luke 23:43] [Readers with a philosophical interest will recognise cousin-like kinship between this and notions like 'performative utterance'.]

Elsewhere I have told the story of the old man whom I once met on the Isle of Lewis. The day was a Wednesday and communion Sunday was approaching. The man, a deeply devout Christian contemplated his unworthiness before God and therefore his incapacity to receive the bread and the wine. My view was that this man, through this self-recognition of personal guilt was thereby more readily in a state of mind actually to receive the sacraments. However he could not take what for him was the ultimate momentous step and acknowledge that God's forgiveness could overcome and give release from his professed deep, deep sin [the actual depth of which I would seriously question]. The old man could only see into his past and bemoan it. He had no equal vision into the future and see the freedom from sin already won, ready and waiting for him. He recognised the condemnation upon him but he failed to see with it God's righteousness being showered upon him in superabundant measure. The situation is not only true of the Western Hebrides of Scotland. As I edit these pages before publication I have an identical scenario in my pastoral work - this time from mainland Scotland. In the New Testament a parallel situation exists with notions of uncleanness and impurity. God's healing cleanses not only the leprous condition but the ritual, cultic and moral impurity which goes with it. We shall look at this now as we turn to consider *katharizo*.

With *katharizo* and its various forms we are faced with some of the most primitive and yet perpetually reawakened processes of human life. Lady Macbeth tried in vain to wash from her hands the stain of murder. To rid hands of blood she had originally and naively considered that, "A little water clears us of this deed." Macbeth's own previous thoughts were to be the more pertinent, "Will all great Neptune's ocean wash this blood clean from my hand? No; this my hand will rather the multitudinous seas incarnadine, Making the green one red." [*Macbeth*, Act 2:2] Lady Macbeth's subsequent sleepwalking ablutions after the death of Banquo turned out to be the more real reflection that hands, having spilt blood, could never be cleansed [Act 5:1]. This is an ancient perspective. There is a primordial link between purity of deed and cleanliness of heart; between a foul deed and the sense of defilement which accompanies subsequent recognition of guilt. There is something very physical in all of this. The sense of defilement clings to the person. At a fundamental level the person seeks to wash away the dirt. Cleanliness and moral purity are linked and have been so since ancient times.

There are many echoes in Christian practice of this. Self-examination and confession before receiving the sacraments; the priest's symbolic washing of hands before the *anaphora* of the mass; various self-negations such as abstinence from sexual intercourse, food, work in different cultures and communities are all differently viewed ways of ensuring the participant does as little as possible to allow him or herself to be defiled in approach to that which is held sacred.

In the Septuagint, indeed in Old Testament thinking generally, uncleanness or defilement, is given dimensions which relate uncleanness to various categories of animals [Leviticus 11] , the baking of bread [Ezekiel 4:12-15], medical condition [Leviticus 15:1ff - this likely refers to gonorrhoea], ejaculation and sexual intercourse, menstruation [Leviticus 15:16-30] as well as childbirth, leprosy and corpses. That which is unclean may also transmit itself by contagion. Impurity is thought of as quasi-physical not unlike the way we might view a virus. In Hebrew, leprosy literally indicates being hit and often appears in conjunction with the words 'mark' or 'stroke' with God being the agent of the action.

It is important to remember that in most cases impurity is contracted inevitably and innocently. There is no guilt attached to it. Burying the dead is a good thing to do - a religious duty - but it gives impurity. Likewise childbirth and sex are good things, but make one impure in Old Testament terms. Richard Bauckham offers students the illustration of digging the garden and then washing off the dirt before joining the family for dinner. The soil gives impurity which has to be washed off by fairly simple processes normally. The same would apply to Hebrew people needing a form of cleansing before entering God's holy presence in the Temple. One is not usually *guilty* of impurity and one can't keep oneself free of it. Like garden soil on one's hands it needs removal by straightforward washing.

Continuing this we read that the God of the Hebrew people is a holy God, anything which in these and other ways detracts from this supreme holiness defiles in a manner understood as unclean [Leviticus 15:31]. Various forms of offering and cleansing rituals are prescribed to negate the effects of uncleanness. These included washing, sprinkling, bathing, offerings - namely sin offerings.

It was the prophets who later developed notions of ethical purity as opposed to merely cultic purity. Isaiah 1:4 is relevant in this respect, "You sinful nation, a people weighed down with iniquity, a race of evildoers, children whose lives are depraved, who have deserted the Lord, spurned the Holy One of Israel ...". Jeremiah 33:6,8 also, "...I shall bring healing and care for her; I shall cure Judah and Israel, and let them see lasting peace and security ... I shall cleanse them of all the wickedness and sin that they have committed, and forgive all the evil deeds they have done in rebellion against me." We can see that older ritual requirements of purity were not forgotten but that purity came increasingly to be seen as a purity of the heart, of the moral conscience and of sound intention all achieved through the upright life.

The use of *katharizo* and *katharos* in the New Testament reflects Jesus' opposition to the inherited cultic view of uncleanness. Jesus' criticism of those who held to the older views was uninhibited, "Alas for you, scribes and Pharisees, hypocrites! You clean the outside of a cup or a dish, and leave the inside full of greed and self-indulgence" [Matthew 23:25] though this needn't mean they should not observe purity rules, only that ethical concerns are more important. Jesus however, at least in the early part of his ministry recognised the priests' historic and legislative authority for pronouncing a cure had taken place [and therefore pronouncing clean] in cases of leprosy [Matthew 8:3-4]. Perhaps however we should not make too much of this for such would be a practical necessity - the leper needs to be certified, cleansed in order to be allowed back into society. Peter's fasting converse with God over unclean food in Acts 10:9-16 exemplified that God can pronounce cleanliness and this in spite of Torah food laws which held to the contrary. Mark 7:8-9 is worthy of scrutiny in this respect. Uncleanness in the teachings of Jesus seems to be linked more to what unfolds from the mind of the person through words and actions rather than in meats which might nourish and in vessels which require a simple scrubbing. A pertinent text is "...nothing that goes into a

81

person from outside can defile him; no, it is the things that come out of a person that defile him." [Mark 7:15]

In Jesus' teaching this inner purity is lived by obedience to God, and in Paul it is lived, or experienced, by God's grace flowing into the person. Individual moral acts, however worthy, do not amount to the same thing. The former lead to the obedient and blessed life and therefore to the moral life. If one starts with the moral life one puts the cart before the horse.

In the context of healing *katharizo* has its relevance most especially for the leper. Jesus not only heals the condition but more fundamentally pronounces the leper clean and therefore fit for all forms of social interaction and religious observance. It seems then that Jesus sought more than simple medicinal benefit for people as he healed them. He wanted to free them from constraints of religious legalism by releasing them from the additional burdens imposed by association of their condition with uncleanness. This is expanded further by its link with service of, and obedience to, God. In the requirement for purity of heart he did not require observance of a list of commands or prescriptions but something that is best and variously described as obedience, discipleship and a life lived in response to the grace poured into it.

Of all the words in the New Testament which take us to the richness of Jesus' understanding of healing there is none so powerful as *sozo*. To it we must now address ourselves albeit briefly.

Kittel documents extensively the wide ranging application of what it means to save, or be saved.[17] In the world into which Jesus was born *sozo* had come to mean the notion of preserving or restoring the integrity of a person or situation of some form or other. In the Old Testament this may be by the relief offered seemingly by human hands with little or no reference back to a deity [cf. 1 Samuel 11:3 and 23:5]. But human hands are limited, and where these fail - as suggested in Jeremiah 14:9 and Hosea 13:10 - God is there. Various leaders would have had as their responsibility the deliverance of the people of Israel, cf. Judges 8:22 and 2 Kings 6:26f. where the appeal for salvation is individual. Whilst in all senses deliverance is ultimately by God its circumstances vary according to empirical setting. It may even appear earthly through and through, from Exodus 14:13-14 "...Have no fear; stand firm and see the deliverance that the Lord will bring you this day; for as sure as you see the Egyptians now, you will never see them again. The Lord will fight for you; so say no more."

In the New Testament non-religious usage of the term *sozo* is restricted to a relatively few situations involving acute danger to life. Examples are the shipwrecked crew in Acts 27:20 and of the disciples in the storm tossed boat of Matthew 8:25. It appears also in the mocking taunts directed at Jesus upon the cross [Mark 15:30]. In all there are 106 New Testament appearances of *sozo*, and eight of *diasozo*. The related noun *soteria* occurs forty five times. Throughout reference is to soteriological outworking in the human situation.

In the early church *sozo* was applied to the work and word of Jesus as the central action of the gospel he lived. In Acts 4:12 there is no other source of salvation given anywhere either in person or in name except in Jesus [cf also Acts 10:43, 13:38 and 15:11]. Salvation as an opportunity for all to take up appears in an apocalyptic context in Acts 2:20-21, verses which refer to Joel 3:31-32.

As applied to the healing miracles *sozo* and *diasozo* have in total eighteen appearances [two of which belong to *diasozo*]. Its usage as a 'healing word' leaves open the interpretation that the healing which came through and from Jesus extends beyond the physical wellbeing of the individual. It is noteworthy to remark that in the healing narratives when the Gospel writers in their Greek texts use terms like *sozo* they never do so in connection with the healing of a part of the body, or condition, which had been malfunctioning. Reference is always to the whole person. A cautionary word must however be noted.

We cannot conclude that simply because the same word is used for 'salvation for the whole person' and 'heal' that New Testament writers meant the same when *sozo* was used in either concept. Neither can we say that 'healing' is therefore 'a particular form of salvation'. What we can say is that healing and salvation both fit into Jesus' overall teaching on the kingdom. With regard both to healing and salvation we need to ask the more fundamental question namely, 'Why is the same word used for each?' It seems to me that if Jesus had simply concerned himself with [that is, seen his mission in terms of solely] clinical cure he would have had no need to use the word *sozo* with its derivatives and cognates. *Iaomai* and *therapeuo* would have sufficed quite adequately on their own. But even with these terms, and also with the less frequent *hygies*, *apokathistemi*, *aphesis*, *katharizo* and so on we are finding that each word is being taken by Jesus and his New Testament recorders beyond the context solely of clinical treatment. There is a wider referential application, namely to the whole person, his or her general well-being in this life, and the person's relationship to God both in the present and beyond.

It is in this last area where something of the crucial reference of *sozo* and its cognates is to be found. Salvation as the ultimate victory has become a present fact through the actions and through the healing words and work of Jesus. This salvation is accompanied by signs including the forgiveness of sins, the cleansing of that previously deemed unclean, the restoration of that which is thought irredeemable, the generation of health where previously illness prevailed.

EXPOSITORY NOTES ON BIBLICAL PASSAGES CONTAINING HEALING TERMS

Chapter 7 MATTHEW

sozo

1:21 She will bear a son; and you shall give him the name Jesus, for he will *save* the people from their sins.

The verse is brief but of great significance for our understanding of the healing work of Jesus, as we shall come to see in due course. The language of Genesis 16:11 is brought forward, "The Angel of the Lord [said to Hagar], 'You are with child and will bear a son. You are to name him Ishmael'..." The same format appears when God spoke to Abraham, "...your wife Sarah will bear you a son, and you are to call him Isaac. With him I shall maintain my covenant as an everlasting covenant...". Jesus would have been given his name eight days after birth at his circumcision - our church recognises 1st January as the 'Naming of Jesus'. 'Jesus' is the Greek version of *Y'hosua* which when translated from its Hebrew reads 'Yahweh is salvation'. Two issues are worthy of note.

First the name 'Yahweh'; it is the written form of the divine name of God. This name in its ancient form, *YHWH*, was deemed too sacred to utter. The name *adonai* ['Lord'] was given by the Hebrew people as a substitute when speaking or when reading texts. The English 'Jehovah' is a compilation of the Hebrew consonants for YHWH and the vowels for adonai. George Anderson describes this transliteration as 'mistaken' and the resultant word, Jehovah, as 'absurd'![1]

Second there are important echoes from Psalm 130:7-8, "Let Israel look for the Lord ... He alone will set Israel free from all their sins". The Hebrew for 'set free' is *padah*, meaning redeem, and has clear eschatological significance.

From Matthew 1:21 and these Old Testament antecedents arises very significant Christian understanding concerning the person and work of Jesus. Matthew and his readers would have been well acquainted with the Hebrew scriptures. Imprinted within their heritage was faith in God. In his name and through his work is salvation made real. The New Testament writers recognised the person and work of Jesus as he in whom this salvation had come among them.

The use of the word *sozo* meaning 'save' will attract our attention below as it did above in 'Something for Everyone' and in 'Healing Words'.

<table>
<tr><td></td><td>4:23-24 [Jesus] travelled throughout Galilee, teaching in the synagogues, proclaiming the good news of the</td></tr>
<tr><td>*therapeuo*</td><td>kingdom, and *healing* every kind of illness and infirmity among the people. His fame spread throughout Syria; and they brought to him sufferers from various diseases, those racked with pain or possessed by demons, those who were</td></tr>
<tr><td>*therapeuo*</td><td>epileptic or paralysed and he *healed* them all.</td></tr>
</table>

It would be expected, or at least not surprising, that a visiting Jew should be asked to teach in the synagogue for the purpose of interpreting the scriptures. Matthew's gospel speaks of proclaiming the good news of the kingdom. Jesus' healing ministry is a sign to people of God's kingdom. Since the coming of God's kingdom is as real now as it was in Jesus' day the healing ministry continues in the Christian church as a sign of its proclamation.

David Hill[2] whom I am following at the moment, reminds us that Matthew and his first readership would connect sin with the conditions referred to in this passage. This connection would recognise such illnesses atoning for sin as well as being its due punishment. Prayer, amendment of life and medical attention were understood remedies. The importance of the doctor in finding and effecting a cure for illness is amply testified in Ecclesiasticus 38:1-15 as is also the 'arrogance' of the person who courts the risk of illness by continued sinning.

As this passage stands there is no indication that Jesus' healing of all these conditions might have the implicit connotation of forgiveness of sin. But this issue will arise and we shall in due course see Jesus and the authorities locked in significant dispute because of it.

<table>
<tr><td></td><td>7:22 When the day comes, many will say to me, Lord, Lord,</td></tr>
<tr><td>*ekballo*</td><td>did we not *drive out* demons in your name, and in your name</td></tr>
<tr><td>*poieo*</td><td>*perform* many miracles?</td></tr>
</table>

This verse, and those around it, pertain to Jesus' teaching on the last judgment. He is identifying himself as the one who also will be the judge [cf. Mark 8:38]. An interesting comparison can be made between the direct self-reference of Jesus in Matthew 7:22 and a parabolic counterpart to be found in Luke 13:22-30.

Matthew 7:22, like much of the gospel narrative, is situated in the context of late Jewish teaching. With reference to this verse Malachi 3:16-18 can be cited:

... those who feared the Lord talked together, and the Lord paid heed and listened. A record was written before him of those who feared him and had respect for his name. They will be mine, says the Lord of Hosts, my own possession against the day that I appoint, and I shall spare them as a man spares the son who serves him. Once more you will tell the good from the wicked, the servant of God from the person who does not serve him.

Verifying the credence of charismatic leaders who claimed to work 'in the name of the Lord' was clearly a problem for the early church as it is today. Acts 19:13ff. records such a situation. The *Didache* reflects upon it as well: "But not every one that speaketh in the spirit is a prophet, but if he have the ways of the Lord, by their ways then shall the false prophet and the prophet be known."[3] Distinguishing between true and false practitioners by reference to their actions is a crucial part of Jesus' teaching [Matthew 7:15-20] out of which this verse is drawn.

> 7:28-29 When Jesus had finished this discourse the people were amazed at his teaching; unlike their scribes he taught with a note of authority.

This narrative should be read as the conclusion of a long missionary and teaching section which begins at 4:13. The formula, "When Jesus had finished..." ends the five great teaching passages in Matthew; see also 11:1, 13:53, 19:1, 26:1. This verse, along with others, gives Joachim Jeremias the foundation for concluding that Jesus was a prophet - a charismatic leader and teacher, rather than a professional theologian.[4] Nothing further need detain us here except to recognise that the parallels for this verse are placed alongside healing narratives.

Parallels in Mark 1:21-28 and Luke 4:31-37

	8:2-3 And now a leper approached him, bowed before him,
katharizo	and said, "Sir, if only you will you can make me *clean.*" Jesus
katharizo	stretched out his hand and touched him, saying, "I will; *be clean.*"
katharizo	And his leprosy *was cured* immediately. Then Jesus said to him,

"See that you tell nobody; but go and show yourself to the priest, and make the offering laid down by Moses to certify the cure."

Beware of the too easy assumption that the leper in this passage has modern clinically diagnosable leprosy in one or other of its forms. In ancient middle eastern usage leprosy referred to a wide range of skin conditions including leprosy as we understand it as well as impetigo, psoriasis, eczema, acne and so on.[5] Colin Brown also cites classical writers employing *lepros* as describing "anything rough, scabby or scaly". Whether the condition is a full clinical leprosy is impossible to determine though from the passage in Luke it was clearly well advanced whatever it was.

In Luke 5:12f. below I will consider the term *katharizo*, though in humorous footnote we can add our recognition that the word was the one employed in classical times for the gardener clearing the ground of weeds!

Parallels in Mark 1:39-45 and Luke 5:12-14[-16]

8:5-10 As Jesus entered Capernaum a centurion came up to ask his help. "Sir," he said, "my servant is lying at home paralysed and racked with pain." Jesus said, "I will come and *cure* him." But the centurion replied, "Sir I am not worthy to have you under my roof. You need only say the word and my servant will be *cured*. I know, for I am myself under orders, with soldiers under me. I say to one, 'Go,' and he goes; to another, 'Come here,' and he comes; and to my servant, 'Do this,' and he does it." Jesus heard him with astonishment, and said to the people who were following him, "Truly I tell you: nowhere in Israel have I found such faith."

therapeuo

iaomai

8:13 Then Jesus said to the centurion, "Go home; as you have believed, so let it be." At that very moment the boy *recovered*.

iaomai

Capernaum was a significant Roman military base on the north western coast of the Sea of Galilee. The title 'centurion' represents a company commander within a legion of the Roman army and this gives the context for his militaristic understanding of Jesus' authority [verse 9] which Jesus goes on to recognise as an expression of genuine faith in contrast to that which he has found elsewhere in Israel. In part this seemingly strange interpretation on the part of Jesus can be explained by the centurion's manner of address 'Sir', often translated 'Lord'. Whilst at a secular level this would be a title of respect, for Matthew it would have additional reference to Jesus as the Christ. The framework for Matthew seeing Jesus in this way would be in his fulfilment of Old Testament prophecy [cf. 8:16-17] and by his standing for the cause of the weak and helpless [cf Isaiah 53:4]. This interpretation can be further reinforced by the centurion's trust in the power of Jesus' word to heal, though in this respect perhaps we must guard against too easy a reading into the text of perspectives from later belief, not least our own.

The word for servant, *pais*, can also mean child, young man, son - in this location we can take it to mean a servant [the Lucan parallel speaks of a servant as *doulos* at 7:2 and as *pais* at 7:7. John refers to a son, *paidion* in 4:49, *hyios* in 4.50 and *pais* in 4:50.] The condition was

88

clearly a major worry, the word *basanos* has the context of one who is tormented, racked by pain.

Brown[6] draws an interesting comparison between the accounts of miracles as performed by Jesus and those in other contemporary locations both from the non-biblical world and from apocryphal testamental material such as the Infancy Gospel of Thomas. Whilst there are later accretions in a number of the biblical passages they stand in marked contrast with these other narratives by their simplicity and by their stark refusal to draw glory either to the miracle or to the dramatic power of the miracle-worker. The power to heal in this passage is a function of Jesus' word in response to the explicit faith of the centurion [cf also 8:16]. Jesus' authority to heal comes from God and is a physical sign of Jesus proclamation of the kingdom of God.

Parallels in Luke 7:1-10, John 4:46-53

8:14-15 Jesus then went to Peter's house and found Peter's mother-in-law in bed with fever. So he took her by the hand; the fever left her, and she got up and attended to his needs.

It is perhaps curious to note the significance of Jesus extending his healing not only to men but also to women.[7] In the time of Jesus this exceptional compassion might have caused some surprise. Both Matthew and Mark omit the 'rebuke' of Jesus to the fever included by Luke.

Parallels in Mark 1:29-31 and Luke 4:38-39

ekballo
therapeuo

8:16-17 That evening they brought to [Jesus] many who were possessed by demons and he *drove* the spirits *out* with a word and *healed* all who were sick, to fulfil the prophecy of Isaiah: "He took our illnesses from us and carried away our diseases."

Matthew, unlike Mark and Luke, does not explicitly locate this event upon the Sabbath. Sabbath law would permit bringing sick people on the streets only after sunset. However, leaving aside for the moment reference to the parallels, one might more naturally think that people would wait till the end of the working day before they had time to bring the sick to Jesus.

The use of a 'word' to effect the exorcism mirrors the pattern of 8:8. In spite of what the text says we need not think that the exorcism referred necessarily to an actual driving out of an evil spirit as such. As verse 16 is very general in content it is perfectly admissible to have in mind the world view of the time that evil spirits everywhere dominated human life. These same evil spirits could well have been cited as the cause of illnesses and conditions which, with different clinical information today, we might understand differently. I will say more about this in due course.

Matthew's reference of Jesus' healing ministry to its foretelling in the Old Testament is characteristic both of Jesus' own self-awareness as well as the belief of the church subsequently.

Parallels in Mark 1:32-34 and Luke 4:40-41

sozo 8:25-26 So they came and woke him saying, *Save* us, Lord; for we are sinking! "Why are you such cowards?" he said. "How little faith you have!" With that he got up and rebuked the wind and the sea, and there was a dead calm.

I have debated with myself the reasons for including this 'nature' miracle in a series of expository notes upon New Testament healing narratives. In the Lucan parallel I offer my reasons for doing so. In the notes for the passage below I consider this passage as one of a trilogy which testifies to the authority of Jesus over the various elemental forces in the world. Having said that, however, I have decided, for purposes of brevity that only two verses need be included here. And this for two reasons. Firstly because of our interest in the use of *sozo* and secondly because of Jesus' word of command to the storm.

The Matthean narrative differs from the parallels in that the address to Jesus is 'Save us Lord', and then the response to the disciples criticising their seeming lack of faith comes before the calming of the storm.[8]

The use of the term *epitimao* for 'rebuke' points to the subduing of the elements in a manner similar to the quelling of evil under the authority of the establishment of God's kingdom.

Parallels in Mark 4:35-41 and Luke 8:22-24

ekballo
apostello 8:28-9:1 When [Jesus] reached the country of the Gadarenes on the other side, two men came to meet him from among the tombs; they were possessed by demons, and so violent that no one dared pass that way. "Son of God," they shouted, "what do you want with us? Have you come here to torment us before our time?" In the distance a large herd of pigs was feeding and the demons begged him: "If you *drive* us *out, send* us into that herd of pigs." "Go!" he said. Then they came out and went into the pigs, and the whole herd rushed over the edge into the lake, and perished in the water. The men in charge of them took to their heels, and made for the town, where they told the whole story, and what had happened to the madmen. Then the whole town came out to meet Jesus; and when they saw him they begged him to leave the district. So he got into the boat and crossed over, and came to his own town.

The location for this story is in gentile or mixed gentile/Jewish territory; the keeping of pigs would not be permitted in Jewish communities. Matthew, unlike the parallels, doubles the number of the possessed, neither does he mention the name of either man, nor yet indicate any wish they might have to follow Jesus. The story resonates with echoes of Isaiah 65:1-5.

In context the passage is the second part of a trilogy which tells progressively of Jesus' control over the natural elements, a storm on the Sea of Galilee is stilled in 8:23-27, and a paralysed man is healed in 9:2-8.

Clearly the townspeople were angered by the loss of the pigs and no doubt some local livelihood. Josephus[9] refers to exorcised spirits adopting very demonstrable behaviour patterns at the time of their expulsion. The purpose of Josephus recording such behaviour in his narrative seems to be his way of offering proof of the reality of the expulsion. In the course of his exposition of King Solomon, Josephus offers the following charming anecdote:

> I have seen a certain Eleazar, a countryman of mine, in the presence of Vespasian, his sons, tribunes and a number of other soldiers, free men possessed by demons, and this was the manner of the cure: he put to the nose of the possessed man a ring which had under its seal one of the roots prescribed by Solomon, and then, as the man smelled it, drew out the demon through his nostrils, and, when the man at once fell down, adjured the demon never to come back into him... Then, wishing to convince the bystanders and prove to them that he had this power, Eleazar placed a cup or foot basin full of water a little way off and commanded the demon, as it went out of the man, to overturn it and make known to the spectators that he had left the man... this was done...

Quite where demons go after their expulsion is itself a significant question. Matthew 12:43-45 has the unclean spirits wandering until a suitable habitation is found. Tobit 8:3 sees the demon expelled to Upper Egypt where it was bound and made fast by the angel Raphael!

David Hill offers a tantalising comment upon the 'factual basis' for the story of the Gadarene swine. He writes, "...some of the statements reflect notions current in popular folk-tales. But behind the embroidered version and the theological superstructure there may be a kernel of truth about the cure of a deranged person whose final paroxysm frightened a herd of swine and provoked a stampede."[10] Morna Hooker disagrees with this interpretation![11] However interesting we may find Hill's speculation, Hooker offers the timely reminder that we have no evidence for it.

Parallels in Mark 5:1-20 and Luke 8:26-40

9:2-8 Some men appeared, bringing to Jesus a paralysed man on a bed. When he saw their faith Jesus said to the man, "Take heart, my son; your sins are forgiven." At this some of the scribes said to themselves, "This man is blaspheming!" Jesus realised what they were thinking, and said, "Why do you harbour evil thoughts? Is it easier to say, `Your sins are forgiven', or to say, `Stand up and walk'? But to convince you that the Son of Man has authority on earth to forgive sins" - he turned to the paralysed man - "stand up, take your bed, and go home." And he got up and went off home. The people were filled with awe at the sight, and praised God for granting such authority to men.

The narrative differs from its parallels in a number of respects, not least in that there is no mention of an opening through which the paralysed man is lowered.

This is one of a number of locations where Jesus asserts his authority; over demons and illness, over 'would-be' followers, over creation and in this passage over sin. Furthermore, by claiming the capacity to forgive sin, Jesus is pressing his authority over against that of the Law of Moses and its interpreters.

What arose when Jesus gave the man God's word of absolution was the immediate accusation of blasphemy. The charge arose because Jesus was usurping the divine prerogative to forgive sin. His punishment would have been stoning even without the mention of the divine name. Since forgiveness of sin is an act of God Jesus' question to the scribes was rhetorical. Which was it easier for him to do, heal the paralysis of the legs or perform that action which was God's? Jesus, as Word of God, both offered the assurance ['take heart'] of God's forgiveness and effected God's healing.[12]

The onlookers, 'filled with awe', arguably reflect the situation of the early church vis à vis first century Judaism. The authority of God to forgive sin is given to the church to be exercised in God's name and is a clear departure from teaching arising out of the Torah. This passage therefore reflects a likely amalgam - of probably original oral tradition with later ecclesial polemic.

Parallels in Mark 2:1-12 and Luke 5:17-26

9:18-19 Even as [Jesus] spoke, an official came up, who bowed before him and said, "My daughter has just died; but come and lay your hand on her, and she will *live*." Jesus rose and went with him, and so did his disciples.

zao

9:20-22 Just then a woman who had suffered from haemorrhages for twelve years came up from behind, and touched the edge of his cloak; for she said to herself, "If I can only touch his cloak, I shall

<table>
<tr><td>*sozo*</td><td>be *healed.*" But Jesus turned and saw her, and said, "Take heart, my</td></tr>
<tr><td>*sozo*</td><td>daughter; your faith has *healed* you." And from that moment she</td></tr>
<tr><td>*sozo*</td><td>*recovered.*</td></tr>
</table>

9:23-26 When Jesus arrived at the official's house and saw the flute-players and the general commotion, he said, "Go away! The girl is not dead: she is asleep"; and they laughed at him. After turning them all out, he went into the room and took the girl by the hand, *egeiro* and she *got up.* The story became the talk of the whole district.

Verses 20-22 form an interlude in the otherwise continuous narrative 18-19, 23-25. Although there are only two references [I think] where explicit mention is made of Jesus laying his hands upon someone for healing in the Gospels the official's clear expectation was that Jesus would do this in order to bring life [*zao*] to his dead daughter.

In Daniel 12:2 'sleep' is used figuratively for death but in both Matthew and his parallels the inevitable conclusion we cannot avoid is that they all believed this girl was actually dead. At one level the story has a resurrection motif within it, namely that even death cannot usurp the lordship of Jesus. The same reference to Daniel also has echoes of this. 1 Corinthians 15 is majestic in its teaching about the dead being raised to life incorruptible. Death is therefore not the end but is rather a condition for eternal life. At times of significant doubt in the Christian message as well as in millenarian times credibility is sought for the possible resuscitation of corpses as a sign of the incoming establishment of the kingdom of God. Such credibility is gained by reference to the stories of Jesus raising individuals from the dead [interpreted as revivifying corpses]. I reflect in *A Way For Healing* that "serious questions must arise in our own minds... if we consider such ministry is repeatable or even appropriate today".[13]

The Matthean account of the woman with the haemorrhage is much shorter in length and omits much which is included in the two parallels. Matthew, it would seem, always abbreviates Mark. The woman's actions indicate her reliance upon magical practices. She seemed to view Jesus' cloak as a healing talisman though it is equally plausible that the crowd prevented her gaining any closer access. One might initially be tempted to think that Jesus, through the use of *sozo*, indicated that she was not only healed of the haemorrhage but was also completely made whole as a consequence of her faith in him. Such a supposition cannot be made without qualification. The woman herself used the same word when quietly, and without obvious wish to be noticed, she made her approach to Jesus. The narrative does not tell us that in her secret wish to be cured she intended anything more than the cure of her haemorrhage. I must therefore question commentators who might easily draw together physical cure and a healing of the whole person within the term *sozo*. It could be the case that Jesus did intend such a double reference, but with *sozo* enjoying the comprehensive range of meaning and application which it does, a conclusive understanding cannot be claimed.

Having thus flown my sceptical and critical colours let me also quote from John Wilkinson's most recent, and magisterial, work, *The Bible and Healing*, where he writes:

> ...it is not always easy to define its *[sozo]* meaning in any particular context. However it is clear that its wide application in the gospels indicates that the Christian concept of healing and the Christian concept of salvation overlap to a degree which varies in different situations, but are never completely separable. Healing of the body is never purely physical, and the salvation of the soul is never purely spiritual for both are combined in the total deliverance of the whole human being, a deliverance which is foreshadowed and illustrated in the healing miracles of Jesus in the gospels. [Wilkinson, p.82]

Parallels in Mark 5:21-43 and Luke 8:40-56

anoigo

9:27-31 As he went on from there Jesus was followed by two blind men, shouting, "Have pity on us, Son of David!" When he had gone indoors they came to him and Jesus asked, "Do you believe that I have the power to do what you want?" "We do," they said. Then he touched their eyes, and said, "As you have believed, so let it be"; and their sight was *restored*. Jesus said to them sternly, "See that no one hears about this." But as soon as they had gone out they talked about him all over the region.

This miracle narrative is like all others in the New Testament. Jesus does not seek to suspend the natural laws of the world in order to 'prove' the mastery and authority of God. Rather, the task of Jesus is to make real the conflict between and victory of good over evil, life over death, salvation over destruction.

Blindness, because it prevented study of the Torah, meant that those afflicted could not become priests though the inhibition in Leviticus 21:18 also includes the lame, dwarfs and the 'overgrown' [indeed virtually any physical 'defect'] within the same clan of cultic blemish. The priest, like the sacrifice, has to be unblemished. Blindness, we find, is also described metaphorically, Exodus 23:8, Deuteronomy 16:19 [one is blind to injustice] and Isaiah 6:10, 29:9f [one is blind to issues of truth and right]. Colin Brown[14] notes that in late Old Testament Judaism blindness was regarded as a consequence of sin again because it prevented study of the Law. It is this perhaps, which gives the context for the blind men pleading out of fear and need to Jesus [using his messianic title 'Son of David'] for pity.[15] Blindness had the significant consequence that the blind could not earn a living and were perforce required to beg. In Jesus' teaching the blind should have full fellowship with everyone else and, as will be seen in John 9:1ff, Jesus explicitly distances himself from any connection between human sin and blindness. The eschatological reference of this is made real in Jesus' own ministry by his acceptance of the blind and by his recommendation of table fellowship with them. The force of this is strengthened by Jesus' clear willingness to touch their eyes.

A partial doublet is in Matthew 20:29-34, with its parallels Mark 10:46-52 and Luke 18:35-43

	9:32-35 They were on their way out when a man was brought to him, who was dumb and possessed by a demon; the demon
ekballo	was *driven out* and the dumb man spoke. The crowd was astonished and said, "Nothing like this has ever been seen in Israel." So Jesus went round all the towns and villages teaching in the synagogues, proclaiming the good news of the
therapeuo	kingdom, and *curing* every kind of illness and infirmity.
ekballo	[After 'Israel' some texts add: But the Pharisees said, "He *drives out* devils by the prince of devils."]

In the synoptic gospels the capacity of Jesus to heal the deaf, the dumb and the blind is a messianic fulfilment of prophetic teaching, cf. Isaiah 35:5-6, 43:8 and of course 61:1-2. The effect of Jesus driving out the demon was the man's immediate recovery [or discovery?] of speech. The sense of 'seen' in verse 33 is that of 'made visible' or 'brought to light'.

There is a doublet in Matthew 12:22-24. Verse 34, missing from some MSS, is probably an insertion from 12:24.

	10:1 Then [Jesus] called his twelve disciples to him and
ekballo	gave them authority to *drive out* unclean spirits and to
therapeuo	*cure* every kind of illness and infirmity.

The same authority which Jesus has [cf.7:29] is here given to the disciples [*exousia*] though with one caveat upon which I comment in 10:7-8. They have been with him until now, will have witnessed Jesus' own exercise of his messianic authority and now are charged with it themselves. They are then listed [10:2-5], their travel arrangements given [10:5-6] and their share in his work specified [10:7-8]. More detailed instructions then follow.

	10:7-8 "As you go proclaim the message:
therapeuo,	'The kingdom of Heaven is upon you.' *Heal*
egeiro, katharizo	the sick, *raise* the dead, *cleanse* lepers,
ekballo	*drive out* demons. You received without
	cost; give without charge."
	['raise the dead' is omitted in some MSS]

Colin Brown[16] poetically summarises the ministry of Jesus as given by Matthew, "*didaskon... kai kerysson... kai therapeuon*: teaching... and preaching... and healing", citing Matthew 4:23; 9:35. The disciples' share in this ministry is given in the same way but without *didaskon*. Brown notes that "for Matthew significantly, Jesus alone is the teacher", there being no release in his gospel of teaching authority until the great commission of 28:20. All this is linked unmistakably with the kingdom of God 'coming near'; it is 'here now' through the person and work of Jesus in whose name the disciples are sent out for "those who receive the disciples will also receive Jesus, and those who receive Jesus receive also the One who sent Him" [Matthew 10:40, my paraphrase].

Though the phrase 'raise the dead' is omitted in some MSS the overcoming of death by Jesus, here extended to his disciples, is given high [even if metaphorical] relevance by Matthew in some of his teaching narratives. In this respect consider Matthew 3:9, "God can make children for Abraham out of these stones". In each the 'raising motif' is very prominent.

| | 10:22 Everyone will hate you for your allegiance to me, but |
| sozo | whoever endures to the end will be *saved*. |

Faithfulness to Jesus will not so much result in security and easy living but will lead to salvation through suffering. Thus those who share the work of Jesus also share his ultimate burden.

	11:2-6 John who was in prison, heard what
	Christ was doing, and sent his own disciples
	to put this question to him: "Are you the one
	who is to come, or are we to expect someone
	else?" Jesus answered, "Go and report to John
anablepo	what you hear and see: the blind *recover* their
peripateo, katharizo	sight, the lame *walk*, lepers are *made clean*, the
akouo, egeiro	deaf *hear*, the dead are *raised* to life, the poor
euangeleo	are *brought good news* - and blessed are those
	who do not find me an obstacle to faith."

The clause, "the dead are raised to life" is omitted in some MSS though its inclusion is consistent with a great deal of Jesus' and other New Testament teaching.

John the Baptist was, with the whole Hebrew nation, heir to the expectation that the Messiah would come. He would come in the tradition of Hebrew prophecy and in fulfilment of the peoples' longings. His validity [if that is not too simplistic a description] would be vouched by his standing in that tradition of Hebrew expectation. In this sense Jesus [and with him Christianity] is historically and irretrievably united with Judaism, the Jewish people and the religion of the Hebrew Bible. When John therefore asks if Jesus is the "one who is to come" Jesus replies in a twofold manner. First, his answer is in terms of Hebrew prophetic writing.[17] Second, he is pointing to the work he has already done for which the teaching and healing narratives so far presented in Matthew are both evidence and testimony. Colin Brown writes, concerning the miracles of Jesus:

> Jesus' ... miracles are a foreshadowing and a promise of the coming universal redemption. Ultimately, it is in this eschatological context that the accounts of Jesus' miracles are to be read. Thus, the casting out of demons signals God's invasion into the realm of Satan and its final annihilation... the raising of the dead announces that death will be forever done away with... the healing of the sick bears witness to the cessation of all suffering... the miraculous provision of food are fore-tokens of the end of all physical need... the stilling of the storm points forward to complete victory over the powers of chaos which threaten the earth.[18]

Brown then goes on to quote Karl Barth:

> When the biblical miracle stories excite serious and relevant wonderment, they intend to do this as signals of something fundamentally new, not as a violation of the natural order which is generally known and acknowledged.[19]

Parallel in Luke 7:18-23

	12:9-14 Jesus went on to another place, and entered their synagogue. A man was there with a withered arm, and
therapeuo	they asked Jesus, "Is it permitted to *heal* on the sabbath?" [They wanted to bring a charge against him]. But he said to them, "Suppose you had one sheep, and it fell into a ditch on the sabbath; is there a single one of you who would not catch hold of it and lift it out? Surely a man is worth far more than a sheep! It is therefore permitted to
apokathistemi *hygies*	do good on the sabbath." Then he said to the man, "*Stretch out* your arm." He stretched it out, and it was *made sound* again like the other. But the Pharisees, on leaving the synagogue, plotted to bring about Jesus' death.

The main issue in this narrative is Jesus' challenge to the Pharisees' understanding of the sabbath laws. The preceding narrative [12:1-8] concerns the disciples plucking grains of corn on the sabbath. In verses 9-14 although there is a healing, the healing as such is subordinate to the debate about the sabbath. Jesus' commission as Word of God in his own very being would perhaps inevitably bring him into conflict with literalist, or more likely formalised, interpretations of the letter of the Mosaic law. Nor did he teach like the scribes who themselves operated within their own *modus operandi*.

Matthew records a parable here and draws a deliberate conclusion omitted in both Mark and Luke. The reference to lost sheep is frequent and familiar in both Old and New Testaments. There was much humanitarian concern for animals in the Old Testament, from the Ten Commandments we read, "... the seventh day is a sabbath of the Lord your God; that day you must not do any work, neither you, nor your son or your daughter, your slave or your slave-girl, your cattle, or the alien residing among you." [Exodus 20:10, cf also Exodus 23:12 and Deuteronomy 5:14; Exodus 23:4f, Deuteronomy 22:1 and Deuteronomy 22:4] Whilst it was clear from the Law that animals required sound husbandry on the sabbath it nevertheless seems to have been controversial when Jesus sought to raise people to the same level.

The word *krateo* refers quite generally to 'take hold of securely'. In the context of healing stories it is the dead child's hand [Matthew 9:25 and parallels], the sick woman [Mark 1:31]. In 12:11 here, it refers to taking hold of the sheep and in Matthew 28:9, "Suddenly Jesus was there in their path, greeting them. They came up and clasped his feet..."

Although *sozo* does not appear in this passage it is quite clear from the use of *hygies* in verse 13 that the healing which results is a wholeness of the person through encounter with the Word of God in Jesus' person and in his individual word of healing.

Parallels in Mark 3:1-5 and Luke 6:6-11

therapeuo

12:15-16 Jesus was aware of it and withdrew, and many followed him. He *healed* all who were ill, gave strict instructions that they were not to make him known.

Those who have previously engaged with New Testament studies will consider as somewhat idiosyncratic my introduction at this point of what is familiarly called the 'messianic secret'. Normally discussion of this would take place in the context of an examination of Mark's Gospel. These two short verses in Matthew, however, very simply and very quickly take us into the subject so therefore I will consider it here. Whilst Mark has the greatest number of Jesus' commands to silence Matthew retains several, of which this is one.

The scholar, William Wrede, writing at the turn of the century[20] argued that Jesus was unconscious of his messianic mission. On these terms Wrede considered that the Gospel of Mark read back into the life of Jesus actions and teaching whereby he secretly gave his followers and others glimpses of who he was and then enjoined them to silence. His followers' appreciation of him could in any event only be partial up to the resurrection. Thereafter, when the full significance of Jesus' life and work were known they could proclaim him to the four corners of the world.

A number of key passages take us into the problem of the 'messianic secret', Mark 9:9 and 8:30 for example. Demons are made to be silent, Mark 1:25 and 34, 3:12. In addition Jesus wished some concealment Mark 7:24 and 9:30 and elsewhere we read of the restricted audience he saw as appropriate for his teaching, Mark 4:11f.

Colin Brown[21] helpfully summarises the main criticisms of Wrede's thesis by tracing the threefold critique offered by J.D.G. Dunn.[22] First, Dunn argues that nowhere in Mark did any recipient of Jesus' healing conclude he was the messiah. References are to the healing of the paralysed man in Mark 2, his home people saw Jesus as the carpenter's son [Mark 6] and others mistook his identity [Mark 6:14f and 3:22]. Clearly the exceptions to Dunn's account are found in the exorcism narratives [Mark 1:24]. Dunn's view was that Jesus' injunctions to silence are in part a procedure for deflecting misleading ideas as well as for ensuring that people did not anticipate nor yet accelerate a process which ultimately was to remain in God's hands.

Dunn avers that rather than secrecy there is more to the 'secrecy motif' than Wrede allowed. From a second angle a 'publicity motif' was at work in the ministry of Jesus. Mark 1:28 indicates this. Mark 1:45 also, along with 3:20, 5:19f, 6:2f, 14ff and others. Dunn concludes that this publicity motif running through Mark indicates that the requirements for secrecy failed. Quite apart from that it seems also that Mark was at pains to identify ways by which Jesus' identity could be made known [Mark 12:10, 8:31, 9:31].

From a third perspective Dunn offers [amongst other examples] the triumphal entry of Jesus into Jerusalem as the obverse of Jesus' injunctions to messianic silence. And to add to this the trial of Jesus revolved in large part around Jesus' alleged blasphemy [cf Mark 14:61-62]. Central to Dunn's thesis is the historical nature of his counter-examples to Wrede. It seems to the present author that evidence to consider them otherwise is doomed. If these events describe historical features of the life of Jesus [rather than being a post-resurrection theological development in the church] any thesis which purports to read into Jesus the view that he was unaware of his messianic role, or that he revealed it and then required people to be silent about it, is significantly circumscribed or compromised.

Nevertheless it remains the case that Jesus did not want his messiahship to be misunderstood. Brown refers us to the studies of Longenecker where in the Jewish thought frame of Jesus' day there would be a reticence to speak in such terms as messiah even though there would be an ultimate recognition of the validity of the ascription.

therapeuo	**12:22-28** Then they brought him a man who was possessed by a demon; he was blind and dumb, and Jesus *cured* him, restoring both speech and sight. The bystanders were all amazed, and the word went round: "Can this be the Son of
ekballo	David?" But when the Pharisees heard it they said, "It is only by Beelzebul prince of devils that this man *drives* the devils out." Knowing what was in their minds, he said to them, "Every kingdom divided against itself is laid waste;
ekballo	and no town or household that is divided against itself can stand. "And if it is Satan who *drives* out Satan, he is divided
ekballo	against himself; how then can his kingdom stand? If it is by
ekballo	Beelzebul that I *drive* out devils, by whom do your own people *drive* them out? If this is your argument they
ekballo	themselves will refute you. But if it is by the Spirit of God that I *drive* out the devils, then be sure the kingdom of God has already come upon you."

(The reference to 'restoring' in 12:22 is literally in the Greek "so that the deaf and dumb is able to speak and see".)

This passage leads us into an enormous range of issues each not without its own level of controversy. Patient exegesis and expository comment will seek to expose something of the depth of these verses.

First and foremost we note the efficiency with which Jesus carried out the healing. This sets the scene for the subsequent controversy. By whose authority did Jesus heal? The Pharisees drew the conclusion that Jesus healed the blindness and dumbness because he was in league with Beelzebul. But this perspective is the very opposite of Jesus' messianic intention. In that his ministry of healing encompassed the work of exorcism, it means that he released people from the power of the devil. One sometimes reads of people being released from the bondage of sin and evil. Indeed, we find the metaphor of the devil being himself tied up in 12:29. Jesus it would seem carried out his fight with the devil at the human level. It was a sign of his power over these demonic authorities that in his person and work the kingdom of God was a real presence.

The bystanders and the subsequent rumour which spread from them seemed to recognise in Jesus, the likely Son of David; "Could anyone with less authority do this?" we can imagine them saying. Such a term was a not uncommon messianic title from the century before the birth of Jesus. Echoes of its earlier presence are to be found in 2 Samuel 7:8-16 and Amos 9:11. Healing powers were not associated with the Davidic messiah but Matthew uses this motif with particular though not exclusive [cf. Mark 10:47f.] focus [cf. Matthew 9:27 and again at 15:22 where there is an apparent exorcism linked with the title 'Son of David']. What is also evident, not least from verse 24, is the fact that miracles in themselves even when widely attested were not sufficient proof of messiahship.

Colin Brown[23] offers concise commentary upon Jesus' own account of the success he found as an exorcist. He locates these in four or five controversy sayings, namely, Mark 3:22-29, Matthew 12:24-29 and its parallel Luke 11:15-23 [these last two being Q sayings]. All he proposes are given scholarly recognition as the *ipsissima verba* of Jesus. The crux of the position Jesus held is given that if it is by *the Spirit of God* that he drove out demons then *the kingdom of God* has come upon [them] - [italics mine]. The spirit of God was his authority; its activity through him was testimony of the kingdom of God in their midst. His kingdom rather than that of the devil [given his own domain in verse 26] would be that which would stand. Jesus contrasted his authority with that of others who exorcised by different means and by implication renders his the supreme manifestation of God's power. Thus, in him has the kingdom of God shown itself. This same self-understanding is implied in Mark 3:27.

Parallels in Mark 3:23-30 and Luke 11:17-23

> **12:43-45** "When an unclean spirit comes out of someone it wanders over the desert sands seeking a resting-place, and finds none. Then it says, 'I will go back to the home I left.' So it returns and finds the house unoccupied, swept clean, and tidy. It goes off and collects seven other spirits more wicked than itself, and they all come in and settle there; and in the end that person's plight is worse than before. That is how it will be with this wicked generation."

The same word for 'rest' *[anapauo]* applies equally to resting as the normal means of recuperation for normally day to day busyness, as well as to calming the disturbed person and to comfort and consolation as an expression of Christian love and support as in Philemon 7 and 20. As here 'the unclean spirit' also seeks its rest. The application here is metaphorical. The person who was originally left by the spirit has sought nothing to fill the consequent void. The returning spirit is thereby enabled to multiply unhindered. The metaphor applies not only to individuals but also to the nation. [This last is omitted in the Lucan parallel]. A spiritually bankrupt nation is one whose decline can only increase. A simple cleaning of the place of habitation is not sufficient. It requires renewing.

The desert as a place for the habitation of demons is graphically portrayed in the curiously enchanting exorcism in Tobit [see from chapter 6 onward to chapter 8:3]. In the sense of habitation the compound *katoikeo* means 'dwell' or in its transitive form 'inhabit'. In its literal application its meaning is straightforward but it also has figurative application in the habitation of people and places by demons. This contrasts with the teaching of Ephesians 3:17, "that through faith Christ may dwell in your hearts in love".

Parallel in Luke 11:24-26

13:14-15 The prophecy of Isaiah is being fulfilled in them: You may listen and listen, but you will never understand; you may look and look, but you will never see. For this people's mind has become dull; they have stopped their ears and shut their eyes. Otherwise, their eyes might see, their ears hear, and their mind understand, and then they might turn to me, and I would *heal* them.

iaomai

These two verses are a quotation of Isaiah 6:9-10. The same quotation appears in Acts 28:26-27 to which the reader should now refer. God's revelation and the life of faith as described in the New Testament echo in so many crucial ways material already familiar from the Old Testament. To select some instances, Deuteronomy 6:5 occurs in Mark 12:33 - the summary of the Law; Psalm 14:2-3 in Romans 3:11; Deuteronomy 32:21 in Romans 10:19; Isaiah 52:15 in Romans 15:21; Isaiah 29:14 in 1 Corinthians 1:19. Throughout these there is the recurring imputation of human reluctance to turn in faith to God. Those who show such reluctance are portrayed as 'hardened'. In the New Testament such a description would have applied equally to all those others whom Jesus variously castigated for their incapacity to see what God was unfolding before their eyes and ears if only they would look and listen. It seems that the prophetic tradition saw God as actually creating the conditions in which people would become hardened so that, all the more effectively, they might then overcome such limitations through an even greater commitment in faith.

This concept is to my mind worthy of a little more comment. It seems to me to be abhorrent that God might be considered as having deliberately created people whose hearts having been hardened might then be seen as more worthily praising him after change of mind. If I read the scriptures correctly it seems to me the case that what is being presented here is the human condition. Given the fallibility of humans the one thing that we can be relied upon to do constantly is choose the wrong course of action. In this vein it was not so much that God predestined Judas Iscariot to betray Jesus but rather that human being both could, and still can, be trusted to betray God. Accordingly, it was Judas. It was Peter. It could be any of us. When this apparent inevitability is resisted, in other words when human preference is subjugated to the divine will, then those who do this can all the more give glory to God.   **See also Acts 28:26-27**

> **13:57-58** So they turned against him. Jesus said to them, "A prophet never lacks honour, except in his home town and in his own family." And he did not do many miracles there, such was their want of faith.

The people took offence at Jesus, indeed much of the New Testament points to the way by which Jesus frequently scandalised those in his company both by what he said and by what he did. It would seem he did not conform to the peoples' expectations of him.

The Coptic version of the Gospel of Thomas [saying 31] and the Greek fragments in Papyrus Oxyrhynchus [lines 30-35] have an expanded form of Jesus' proverb. The latter reads, "Jesus said: A prophet is not acceptable in his own country, nor does a physician heal those who know him."[24]

Parallels in Luke 4:23 and Mark 6:4-6

> *therapeuo* **14:14** When he came ashore and saw a large crowd, his heart went out to them, and he *healed* those who were sick.

The reason for Jesus' compassion for the people is given in the parallel Mark 6:34, where the people are spoken of as being like sheep without a shepherd. There is in Mark, however, reference to Jesus being moved to teach the people rather than as here, healing. The compassion of Jesus is more than him simply feeling sorry for the people, rather it is a characteristic of his messianic activity in making God's kingdom real in the lives of people. Quite apart from the healings indicated here Jesus goes on to offer food to the people. So much more can be said about the table fellowship of Jesus as living the kingdom than is possible here.

Parallel in Mark 6:34 [a citation of Numbers 27:17; 1 Kings 22:17]

	14:30 But when [Peter] saw the strength of the gale he was afraid;
sozo	and beginning to sink, he cried, *"Save me, Lord!"*

The verse, and the passage of which it forms a part, is very reminiscent of the stilling of the storm in Matthew 8:17-27 not least because *sozo* is the verb used by Peter in 8:25 [Save us Lord] as well as here. At face value Peter's cry for help is a very definite call from someone who saw himself in mortal danger. But the cry for help has also a broader reference for it can be applied allegorically to the Matthean community from within which this narrative was framed as well as to readers of the narrative in later generations. Given this, *sozo* has both the immediate meaning of rescue from danger as well as from the 'storms of life' and ultimately salvation from the threat of eternal perishing. Followers of Jesus can achieve his mastery over the natural elements with faith for the task. But even when this falls short Jesus can still be relied upon to rescue. Ultimately all salvation is in and through him.

David Hill[25] once again, helpfully reflects on this. In the Marcan parallel the disciples more likely seemed to express their lack of understanding as a prelude to bringing the sick to Jesus for him to heal. In Matthew [which alone among the Gospels records Peter walking on water] the disciples' initial reaction was terror giving way ultimately to their messianic recognition of him as 'Son of God'.

David Hill cites verses 28-31 as a later Matthean insertion. A number of reasons are given. The word for 'the water' *thalassa* in 14:26, and *katapontizein* for 'sink' and *distazo* for 'doubt' are found only in Matthew [cf also 18:6 and 28:17]. Arguably the verses originate in a separate oral Petrine source. In that it indicates Peter's preeminence over the other disciples it also indicates quite clearly his weakness and fallibility.

Parallels in Mark 6:46-52 and John 6:15-21

	15:30-31 Crowds flocked to him, bringing with them the lame, blind, dumb, and crippled, and many other
therapeuo	sufferers; they put them down at his feet, and he *healed* them. Great was the amazement of the people when they saw the dumb speaking, the crippled made strong, the
blepo	lame walking, and the blind with *their sight restored*, and they gave praise to the God of Israel.

('with their sight restored' is literally 'being able to see')

These verses must be seen in the light of Isaiah's prophecies 35:5-6, 43:8, 61:1-2. In all likelihood the verses constitute the author's summary of the form and content of Jesus' ministry in and around Galilee. The restoration of sight to the blind was Jesus' acceptance that the kingdom of heaven is theirs as much as everyone else's. No longer was it to be considered a blemish and cultic barrier. In Jesus' life and work the messianic reality of the new age was being made real in front of people and for people. In this sense giving 'praise to the God of Israel' might be ambiguous. On the one hand it might point to the continuity between the God of their fathers and the God of Jesus the messiah. Equally it could be the confession of Gentiles who, having seen and experienced the mighty work of Jesus, 'gave praise to the God of Israel'.

17:14-18 When they returned to the crowd, a man came up to Jesus, fell on his knees before him, and said, "Have pity, sir, on my son: he is epileptic and has bad fits; he keeps falling into the fire or into the water. I brought [my son] to your disciples, but they could not *cure* him." Jesus answered, "What an unbelieving generation! How long must I be with you? Bring him here to me." Then Jesus spoke sternly to him; the demon left the boy, and from that moment he *was cured*.

therapeuo

therapeuo

This narrative is brief, especially when seen alongside its likely parent text in Mark. A significant difference in emphasis between the two is Matthew's focus upon the disciples', rather than the father's lack of faith.

From Matthew's description above we have it that the condition is given as epilepsy. The cure however was by means of exorcism. It is by no means uncommon for otherwise different causes to produce similar effects by way of describable symptoms. Although I have elsewhere warned against the too ready presumption of possession its likely reality in a number of scenarios cannot be ignored. In genuine possession the mind of the person is subsumed under the control of an evil influence. The stern word of Jesus is the appropriate form of exorcism even today.

The following little narrative from my pastoral practice may be appropriate at this point. A person once told me of her family life. It had been outwardly very normal but inwardly each had malfunctioned emotionally. Though nothing was said to me as such it was clear there had been much emotional abuse by an over domineering elderly male relative in the household. In course of time that elderly relative had become psychologically very ill due to a progressive psychosis. When visiting in hospital a few days before the relative died he was seen not to be his usual mentally and physically agitated self. The person then went on to describe being awakened later that evening and saw a ghostly grey/white figure standing at the foot of her bed. The response was to lift the bedside bible and tell 'it' to leave. The person described how 'it' drifted slowly towards the window then turned and moved from the room.

There is no reason for me to doubt this story. It was given me by someone whose judgment in all things I would trust. Neither am I necessarily making linkages between this and 'exorcism'. Any number of given causes can account for this experience. The ghostly form's movements were, it seemed, reminiscent of the elderly relative. The apparition need not have been 'evil' as no evidence exists for such an inference. Could it have been the relative's 'restless soul' seeking to return home? And again, how much was influenced by the person's subconscious and wishful thinking in the process of arising from sleep? This story arouses our interest for even though the apparition obeyed the command to leave in a manner not unlike exorcism there was no given description or sense of evil present in the room.

Parallels in Mark 9:14-27 and Luke 9:37-42

ekballo

17:19-21 Afterwards the disciples came to Jesus and asked him privately, "Why could we not *drive* it out?" He answered, "Your faith is too small. Truly I tell you: if you have faith no bigger than a mustard seed, you will say to this mountain, 'Move from here to there!' and it will move; nothing will be impossible for you."

Some MSS add:

ekballo

17:21 "But there is no means of *driving out* this sort but prayer and fasting."

The man's request to Jesus had been of the utmost urgency. His request to Jesus is for mercy. The mercy given will be compassion such that the grace of God flows into situations of human desperation through healing of illness and freeing from bondage. In this passage the demon possession of Luke's parallel is supplemented by more explicit reference to epilepsy. The addition of the title *Kyrios* 'Sir' or 'Lord' to the request for mercy gives a liturgical resonance to this passage.

The man's state of mind is changed because of the disciples' incapacity to effect the boy's healing. His confidence in Jesus' power to heal has to be absolute for there seems nowhere else to turn. God's healing through the word of Jesus is here shown to be unqualified. Faith in the healing power of Jesus' word is faith that stands in stark contrast to doubt, which in the context of this passage can be equated with faintheartedness. The situation is reminiscent of, though not identical to, that which existed Jesus' own home town. There, lack of faith was found to be an inhibiter upon Jesus' work. In this instance it was the disciples who lacked and could not heal. Jesus, nonetheless, can and does heal.

The notion of moving mountains is easily explained as a metaphor. It is a likely allusion to prophecy. Isaiah 54:10 reads, "Though the mountains may move and the hills shake, my love will be immovable and never fail, and my covenant promising peace will not be shaken...." All things on earth are temporary and transitory - even mighty mountains it seems. This contrasts powerfully with the love of God.

Parallels in Mark 9:14-27[28] and Luke 9:37-42

> **18:10-11** "See that you do not despise one of these little ones; I tell you, they have their angels in heaven, who look continually on the face of my heavenly Father."
> Some witnesses add:
> *sozo*   For the son of man came to *save* the lost.

Children, like the poor, have God's favoured attention. Verse 10 is helpfully seen in the context of 18:1-7. The Dead Sea Scrolls contain an angelology of worship to God.[26] Verse 11 in this passage is a likely insert from Luke 19:10.

> **19:1-2** When Jesus had finished this discourse he left Galilee and came into the region of Judaea on the other side of the
> *therapeuo*   Jordan. Great crowds followed him and he *healed* them there.

Matthew 19:1-2 is one of five summarising sentences in his gospel which round off the preceding portions of text. The others are 7:28, 11:1, 13:53 and 26:1.

> **20:29-34** As they were leaving Jericho [Jesus] was followed by a huge crowd. At the roadside sat two blind men. When they heard that Jesus was passing by they shouted, "Have pity on us, Son of David." People told them to be quiet, but they shouted all the more, "Sir, have pity on us; have pity on us, son of David." Jesus stopped and called the men. "What do you want for me to do for you?" he asked. "Sir," they answered, "open our eyes." Jesus was deeply moved, and touched their
> *anablepo*   eyes. At once they *recovered their sight* and followed him.

Matthew and Mark have the incident at Jesus' departure from Jericho; Luke at his arrival there. Only Mark names the single man in his narrative. Matthew has two men in the story - two were the required number of witnesses who might for example authenticate a miracle or, and as in this case, speak of the rising interest in Jesus' messiahship. Both men were to have direct experience of it through their healing. Jesus, moved with compassion, healed through touch. We are not told whether he said anything further. The action they took by following him implies immediate discipleship.

Not necessarily relevant to this section alone is the recognition that Jesus indicated some need for witnesses for his miracles. In John 5:31-34, "If I testify on my own behalf, that testimony is not valid. There is another who bears witness for me, and I know that his testimony about me is valid. You sent messengers to John and he has testified to the truth. Not that I rely on human testimony, but I remind you of it for your own salvation". Clearly Jesus is indicating here that his words and work are not validated by human authentication but he nevertheless is speaking within a tradition whereby authentication of miracles is not without significance. It is interesting in this regard to turn to a contemporary non-Christian source. Josephus, for example, in the *Jewish Antiquities* writes, "Put not trust in a single witness; but let there be three, or at the least two, whose evidence shall be accredited by their past lives".[27] Offensively, to our modern ears, Josephus excludes women as possible witnesses "because of the levity and temerity of their sex" along with slaves, "because of the baseness of their soul"!

A partial doublet is in Matthew 9:27-31. Parallels for 20:29-34 in Mark 10:46-52 and Luke 18:35-43

21:14 In the temple the blind and the crippled came to him, *therapeuo*   and he *healed* them.

In the New Testament the frequent reference to the blind and the lame being healed indicates something of Jesus' considerable compassion for them. In the temple precincts there would be no discrimination against them, as was the case elsewhere. The fact that they approached Jesus would therefore cause no scandal. What did irritate the temple authorities was Jesus healing them. After the heated exchange in the temple Jesus went across the Mount of Olives to Bethany, where [perhaps following his custom elsewhere] he spent the night in quiet [21:17].

27:39-42 The passers-by wagged their heads and jeered at [Jesus], crying, "So you are the man who was to pull down the temple and rebuild it in three days! If you really are the Son of God, *sozo*   *save* yourself and come down from the cross." The chief priests *sozo*   with the scribes and elders joined in the mockery: "He *saved* *sozo*   others," they said, "but he cannot *save* himself..."

The temple was the centre of the Jewish faith. Enormous effort and energy were required to build it with many of the lower temple wall stones being of colossal proportions. "How could anyone destroy such an enormous structure let alone rebuild it so quickly?" is the ironic question being asked.

See parallels in Mark 15:30-31 and Luke 23:35

Chapter 8 MARK

1:21-28 They came to Capernaum, and on the sabbath [Jesus] went to the synagogue and began to teach. The people were amazed at his teaching, for, unlike the scribes, he taught with a note of authority. Now there was a man in their synagogue possessed by an unclean spirit. He shrieked at him: "What do you want with us, Jesus of Nazareth? Have you come to destroy us? I know who you are - the Holy One of God."

phimoo

exerchomai

Jesus rebuked him: *"Be silent"*, he said, "and *come out* of him." The unclean spirit threw the man into convulsions and with a loud cry left him. They were all amazed and began to ask one another, "What is this? A new kind of teaching! He speaks with authority. When he gives orders, even the unclean spirits obey." His fame soon spread far and wide throughout Galilee.

The context for the exorcism is given by Jesus' manner. He taught with authority. In recognition of his authority the unclean spirit we are told 'shrieked', as if to challenge this authority. To this Jesus responded with the rebuke, "Be silent" and the order to depart. The same is found in Luke 4:35. In Deuteronomy 25:4 the same vocabulary is found and used in the sense of 'muzzling' an ox.

Jesus' world was one which viewed the devil to be responsible both for sin as well as for sickness. The devil was in opposition to God. With Jesus as the Word of God the devil is exorcised. Geza Vermes[1] identifies the origin for this in the period after the Babylonian exile during significant Iranian religious influence upon Judaism in the fifth and fourth centuries BC.

Mark draws a contrast between the teaching authority of Jesus and that of the scribes in their application of Rabbinic casuistry.[2] This contrasts with the Lucan parallel where there is no explicit mention of the scribes. That notwithstanding, however the frequent mention of scribes in the gospels is some indication of their likely influence upon Hebrew thinking of the day. This passage focuses concern upon the manner of Jesus teaching and the effect of both this and of his exorcisms upon those who heard him. The writer clearly wishes to point to the amazed reaction of the uncommitted onlookers. The authority of Jesus' word was backed up with deeds which had demonstrable power over demons.

Parallels in Matthew 7: 28-29 and Luke 4:31-37

1:29-31 On leaving the synagogue, they went straight to the house of Simon and Andrew; and James and John went with them. Simon's mother-in-law was in bed with a fever. As soon as they told him about her, Jesus went and took hold of her hand, and raised her to her feet. The fever left her, and she attended to their needs.

This is one of a number of gospel narratives where Jesus receives hospitality. The actions of Peter's mother after her healing are those of someone who serves at table. Table fellowship figures prominently in Jesus' parabolic teaching [implicitly in the parable of the Good Samaritan in Luke 10:34f., and in that of the friend who arrives during the night in 11:5ff.] and not least in his metaphor of the kingdom of heaven as a banquet [Luke 13:29 and 14:15ff.].[3]

Parallels in Matthew 8:14-15, Luke 4:38-39

therapeuo
ekballo

1:32-34 That evening after sunset they brought to him all who were ill or possessed by demons, and the whole town was there, gathered at the door. He *healed* many who suffered from various diseases, and *drove out* many demons. He would not let the demons speak, because they knew who he was.

The narrative continues Jesus' ministry in Capernaum. There is no distinction between the 'all' of v.32 and the 'many' of v.34. In the worldview of Jesus day 'many' also meant 'all'. The use of the word 'let' is figurative and indicates Jesus' control over the demons whom he would not permit to speak in the sense of giving them freedom to speak. This contrasts with Mark 5:9 where Jesus replies to the demons who speak to him by asking their name.

The inclusion of a significant number of exorcisms in the New Testament calls for consideration. The New Testament writers clearly viewed the illness of possessed people to be different from that of other named conditions. This accounts for its distinction from them. It may well be the case that New Testament understandings of demon possession might nowadays be ranged along a number of possible clinical disorders. Even given this, however, there remains the hermeneutical problem of explaining the speed by which Jesus 'exorcisms' effected a cure.

A clear distinction between illness and possession exists today. Illness is a description both of symptoms and the name of a condition. Possession is the identification of a [demonic] cause. A further category 'obsession' refers more to addictive practices, behaviour patterns and paranoia in its various forms.[4]

Parallels in Matthew 8:16-17 and Luke 4:40-41

1:39-44 So he went through the whole of Galilee, preaching *ekballo* in their synagogues and *driving out* demons. On one occasion he was approached by a leper, who knelt before him and begged for help. "If only you will," said the man, "you can *katharizo* *make* me *clean.*" Jesus was moved to anger; he stretched out *katharizo* his hand, touched him, and said, "I will; *be clean.*" The leprosy *katharizo* left him immediately, and he was *clean.* Then he dismissed him with this stern warning: "See that you tell nobody, but go and show yourself to the priest, and make the offering laid down by Moses for your cleansing; that will certify the cure."

Morna Hooker regards the narrative as relating to the cure of an illness otherwise considered incurable, perhaps therefore pointing to clinical leprosy in this situation.[5]

Many commentators prefer "moved to pity" rather than "moved to anger". Hooker argues for 'anger' as the correct reading, even if not the option preferred by the majority of MSS. The original highlights the sense of Jesus being moved to compassion from the very depths of his being. [Curiously perhaps, Matthew and Luke omit reference to Jesus' emotions.] If we are to retain anger as the correct interpretation we must appreciate the context. Given Jesus' compassion for the leper it is unlikely Jesus would be angry with him for any reason other than the man's imprisonment by impurity taboos which would forbid the leper human contact. Anger, rather than pity one could argue, is a more understandable response to destroying illness particularly when progressive degeneration caused by the illness is compounded by avoidable human prejudice.

Parallels in Luke 5:12-14[-16] and Matthew 8:2-4

2:1-12 After some days he returned to Capernaum, and news went round that he was at home; and such a crowd collected that there was no room for them even in the space outside the door. While he was proclaiming the message to them, a man was brought who was paralysed. Four men were carrying him, but because of the crowd they could not get him near. So they made an opening in the roof over the place where Jesus was, and when they had broken through they lowered the bed on which the paralysed man was lying. When he saw their faith, Jesus said to the man, "My son, *aphiemi* your sins *are forgiven*".

Now there were some scribes sitting there, thinking to themselves, "How can the fellow talk like that? It is blasphemy! Who but God can forgive sins?" Jesus knew at once what they were thinking, and said to them, "Why do you harbour such thoughts? Is it easier to say to this paralysed

111

man, 'Your sins are forgiven', or to say, 'Stand up, take your bed, and walk'? But to convince you that the Son of Man has authority on earth to forgive sins" - he turned to the paralysed man - "I say to you, stand up, take your bed and go home." And he got up, and at once took his bed and went out in full view of them all, so that they were astounded and praised God. "Never before", they said, "have we seen anything like this."

The sense of *aphiemi*, translated here as 'forgive', has a rich meaning which includes let go, set free, remit, dissolve, disband, take away.

In other locations I will speak of the relationship between sin and illness, and of the controversy Jesus caused in his claimed capacity to forgive sin as against only offering healing. The point I want to draw out now is the expository significance of the four stretcher bearers for those involved in the ministry of healing nowadays. In many ways those who brought the man to Jesus reflect the prayerful activity of people nowadays who, in prayer, carry people to Jesus for healing. They are exemplars perhaps of those who are involved in a general ministry of healing in the way I described in the earlier chapters of this book. Many people know the power and potential of Jesus' healing but find themselves unable to bring people close to him in any direct sense - conceivably because of obstruction caused either deliberately or in ignorance by local clerics.

Eager to find a way to Jesus, they opened the simple roof; a straightforward procedure as far as we can tell though it would create mayhem for those below. Jesus however saw the faith of the stretcher bearers [and presumably also the paralysed man] and reacted appropriately by firstly forgiving sin, secondly by rebutting the scribes and then thirdly by offering the man healing.

Sometimes in modern day thoughts about ministry we think both of Jesus and the disciples as appropriate icons upon whom to model our theory and practice. Perhaps we should also bring into view the stretcher bearers. Not without significance is the etymology of ambulance, 'the walking stretcher bearer'.

Parallels in Matthew 9:1-8 and Luke 5:17-26 [cf also John 9:1-5 and 1 Cor. 11:30]

xeraino	**3:1-5** On another occasion when he went to synagogue, there was a man in the congregation who had a *withered arm*; and they were watching to see whether Jesus *would heal* him on the sabbath so that they could bring a charge against him. He said to the man with the withered arm, "Come and stand out here." Then he turned to them: "Is it
cheir	
therapeuo	

<table>
<tr><td>*sozo*</td><td>permitted to do good or to do evil on the sabbath, *to save* life or to kill?" They had nothing to say; and looking round at them with anger and sorrow at their obstinate stupidity, he said to the man, "Stretch out your arm." He stretched it</td></tr>
<tr><td>*apokathistemi*</td><td>out and his arm *was restored.*</td></tr>
</table>

A number of features are present within these very rich verses. The context is the synagogue where it is clear that Jesus was an authority figure. His assumption of authority to question the Pharisees on points of law and the manner of his self-expression both demonstrate this. The manner in which Jesus questioned the Pharisees was perhaps designed to silence their expectation that he would seek to annul the Mosaic law.

Mark's use of the verb *xeraino* in reference to the withered arm is interesting. The same verb is used to describe the healing of the haemorrhage [Mark 5:29] and the rigid state of the boy in Mark 9:18. Additionally, *cheir* can indicate either hand or arm.

It would seem also that the attitude which Jesus shows in the narrative towards sabbath laws indicates considerable distance between him and the zealots and this in spite of Simon the Zealot [Mark 1:18] being one of the disciples.[6]

A second notable feature of this passage is Jesus' question concerning the legality of acting upon the sabbath to do good, save life or to do evil, kill. Is Jesus presupposing the validity of the law and by so doing defers to the Pharisees for opinion? Conversely, could he be adopting the technique of the apologist by situating his praxis upon ground otherwise held by an opponent? Perhaps more subtly Jesus is applying, by means of irony and rhetorical question, the teaching of the law in its function of offering salvation, wholeness, to the person through the action of healing. It is in this sense and for this reason that *therapeuo* is not used twice. Where the second reference to healing is made at verse 4 it is in connection with salvation and hence a change to *sozo.*

In its New Testament usage *apokathistemi* is found as a verb seven times and the cognate noun *apokatastasis* once, at Acts 3:21. The classical, secular, meaning of the verb is applied in this passage and its parallels to the healing of the sick. Classical reference from Xenophon meant restoration to a previous state and then later it came to mean more generally 'to restore'. An example of my own may illustrate the difference. When, for example, a painting is, in our terminology, 'restored' after wilful attack it can never be returned to its original state as though there never had been any damage. What happens in such cases of restoration is, if I understand the process correctly, the arresting and so far as is possible making good the effects of vandalism. Here Jesus restores the man's withered arm.[7] It has been suggested to me that something similar applies both after abuse as well as to the victims of other forms of physical attack.

Parallels in Matthew 12:9-14 and Luke 6:6-11

therapeuo	3:9-10 So he told his disciples to have a boat ready for him, to save him from being crushed by the crowd. For he *healed* so many that the sick all came crowding round to touch him.

Jesus' instruction was to have a boat available for his use, i.e. have one ready and waiting for him whenever he might need it. The boat would enable Jesus to teach the crowds onshore without him being crushed by the number of people who had gathered, see Mark 4:1.

In 3:10 the description of sickness *[mastix]* is that of a torment or suffering in the sense of an affliction. The literal meaning of *mastix* is 'lash' or 'flogging', i.e. what one would receive from a whip [the literal use is in Acts 22:24 and Hebrews 11:36]. In a figurative sense this means therefore some kind of affliction. This usage is rather like the figurative English use of 'scourge' - which also means literally a lashing or flogging. *Mastix* is also used of the haemorrhage in Mark 5:29 and 34. Luke 7:21 refers to healing people of illnesses *[nosos]* and afflictions *[mastix]* and evil spirits. It could be said that those who are blind and deaf do not necessarily have an illness but might however be said to have an affliction in the sense of *mastix*.

A person's affliction, seen in this way, would reinforce the contemporary view that disability *[mastix]* and sin are inevitably intertwined. Although Jesus recognised the contemporary connection between sin and illness [in healing the man in Capernaum in Mark 2:5, he said, "My son, your sins are forgiven"] Jesus nevertheless saw illness from a completely new perspective [cf. John 9:3] and removed the retributive interpretation of illness.

The force of Mark 3:10 makes it a natural prelude to the following verses where unclean spirits recognised Jesus.[8] It represents another image of the power of Jesus to heal when people with illness touched him. The fact that power to heal flowed from him was recognised both by the people in this story as well as by the woman who came up to him secretly to touch the hem of his garment [Matthew 9:20 and parallels].

Some interesting teaching points can be drawn from this story. Firstly Jesus clearly felt the hearing of his word had priority over the likely cultic following which would have developed had widespread healing happened to all who touched him, however faith-full their intentions. And secondly we do well to consider the place of 'touch' in the ministry of healing today. One person I know speaks movingly, and with obvious difficulty, that for substantial portions of her life touch in a ministry of healing would have made her recoil. Thankfully for her that emotional and physical situation is itself now healed but for many others it remains as acutely painful as ever.

In another situation a very traditional and correct Christian of lifelong standing whom I knew very well would only touch in the context of a handshake or other appropriate gesture. At what I wrongly interpreted to be his deathbed I took the view that his deep distress required the consoling effect of an embrace. Carefully moving some small items of bedside furniture I enabled this to take place. There were many tears from both of us. We moved on to discuss any anxieties that might be lingering in his mind and for the next visit I would, if he wished, anoint him. Two days later, his wellbeing was much improved. He considered anointing to be premature and proceeded to enter into a vigorous remission in which, though his illness remained, his health rejuvenated. I would not be so crass as to say that my embrace and prayers brought about this situation, but I would say that they, along with his medication, beneficially combined in a healing way.

ekballo	**3:14-15** He appointed twelve to be his companions, and to be sent out to proclaim the gospel, with authority to *drive out* demons.
therapeuo *ekballo*	[The *Authorised Version* reads: ...sent them forth to preach. And to have power to *heal* sicknesses, and to *cast out* devils....
	The words 'to heal sicknesses' are found in later manuscripts including the 5th Century *Codex Bezai*]
ekballo *ekballo*	**3:22** The scribes too, who had come down from Jerusalem, said, "He is possessed by Beelzebul" and, "He *drives out* demons by the prince of demons." So he summoned them and spoke to them in parables: "How can Satan *drive out* Satan? If a kingdom is divided against itself it cannot stand."

The Marcan narrative does not include the reference to the healing of the blind and dumb demoniac as a prelude to this narrative. We need not repeat the full parallel as sufficient comment upon it is included in the notes on Matthew 12:22-28. However one issue can attract us.

In Matthew it is the pharisees who are referred to, not the scribes. Sometimes the scribes are associated with pharisees, sometimes not. The scribes were more than writers. They were, it would seem [Acts 6:12] associated with the rulers and elders at the death of Stephen and with the difficulties encountered by Peter and John with the authorities [Acts 4:5]. Matthew 7:29 points to the scribes' teaching role with their authority being derived from scripture and tradition, the latter being used to offer source material supporting the scholarly teaching they sought to present. By comparison Jesus taught from the scriptures with the authority of his own name and with the conviction of his word, "Whoever hears these words of mine and acts on them is like the man who has the sense to build his house on a rock..." [Matthew 7:24] Little wonder the scribes [and pharisees] found much fault with Jesus' teaching and with his apparent adapting of the law and its traditions to suit his lifestyle and his choice of companions at table, to say nothing of his usurping of the authority of historic tradition in his own name. In Luke there is no reference either to scribes or to pharisees! Those critics who were present are described as "others".

Parallels in Matthew 12:22-28 and Luke 11:14-23

4:35-41 That day, in the evening, [Jesus] said to them, "Let us cross over to the other side of the lake." So they left the crowd and took him with them in the boat in which he had been sitting; and some other boats went with him. A fierce squall blew up and the waves broke over the boat until it was all but swamped. Now he was in the stern asleep on a cushion; they roused him and said, "Teacher, we are sinking! Do you not care?" He awoke and rebuked the wind, and said to the sea, "Silence! Be still!" The wind dropped and there was a dead calm. He said to them, "Why are you such cowards? Have you no faith even now?" They were awestruck and said to one another, "Who can this be? Even the wind and the sea obey him."

In the Matthean parallel I include notes on only two of the verse parallels. Much of the teaching around this passage involves Jesus' authority over natural elements. It is interesting to compare the three different ascriptions for Jesus:

Matthew	*kyrie*	Lord	also, *rabbi* teacher
Mark	*didaskale*	teacher	
Luke	*epistata*	teacher	

Parallels in Matthew 8:23-27 and Luke 8:22-25

5:1-17 So they came to the country of the Gerasenes on the other side of the lake. As [Jesus] stepped ashore, a man possessed by an unclean spirit came up to him from among the tombs where he had made his home. Nobody could control him any longer; even chains were useless, for he had often been fettered and chained up, but had snapped his chains and broken the fetters. No one was strong enough to master him. Unceasingly, night and day, he would cry aloud among the tombs and on the hillsides and gash himself with stones. When he saw Jesus in the distance, he ran up and flung himself down before him, shouting at the top of his voice, "What do you want with me,

Jesus, son of the Most High God? In God's name do not torment me." For Jesus was already saying to him, "Out, unclean spirit, come out of the man!" Jesus asked him, "What is your name?" "My name is Legion," he said, "there are so many of us." And he implored Jesus not to send them out of the district. There was a large herd of pigs nearby, feeding on the hillside, and the spirits begged him, "Send us among the pigs; let us go into *epitrepo* them." He *gave them leave*; and the unclean spirits came out and went into the pigs; and the herd, of about two thousand, rushed over the edge into the lake and were drowned.

The men in charge of them took to their heels and carried the news to the town and countryside; and the people came out to see what had happened. When they came to Jesus and saw the madman who had been possessed by the legion of demons, sitting there clothed and in his right mind, they were afraid. When eyewitnesses told them what had happened to the madman and what had become of the pigs, they begged Jesus to leave the district.

Epitrepo has the sense of 'giving permission', 'to yield them up', 'to suffer things'. In John 19:38 Pilate "gave leave to Joseph of Arimathea". In the Matthean parallel the translation may be given, "allow us to go away into the herd of swine".

The narrative then goes on to speak of the man's wish to go with Jesus. Jesus, however, instructs him to give the testimony of what had happened to him in his own home region. We are given to understand that the man did this. Along with sending the apostles out in pairs this constitutes a significant evangelistic injunction in the gospels, one sometimes overlooked. It is the conversation between Jesus and the man after his healing which underlines the man's cure [the reality of the cure is not mentioned by Matthew] and which leads Jesus to command to the man to 'tell his story' amongst his own people. The Decapolis [the 'ten cities'] was a grouping of ten Hellenistic cities east of the River Jordan under the Roman governor of Syria.

The demons recognise Jesus to be who he is, though their request that he not torment them does not have the same eschatological element as does Matthew's account of the same story. Matthew links this exorcism with the incoming of God's kingdom and the final judgment of those who have sought to torment others with their evil. Mark's demons seem merely to request a quiet life!

Conversation between Jesus and evil spirits could raise questions in the minds of many who are currently charged with the investigation of demonic signs and symptoms. Is conversation with an evil spirit giving the spirit a credibility it ought not to deserve? Mark 1:34 might lend support to this, though perhaps Jesus had another purpose in this particular verse [as also in 1:25], namely to keep his identity secret in his home country. Beyond Galilee he would be a stranger anyway and the same preference for secrecy would prevail less. Power over the spirits would be assured if Jesus knew their name for, having correctly identified who they were, he could then cast them out. The destruction of a herd of two thousand pigs seems wanton by modern standards. To Jesus and to those of Mark's readership who were Jews this would not have been so. The pig was unclean; the possessed man lived in graves themselves regarded as unclean and he sought to mutilate [and would have eventually destroyed] himself - as a result of the unclean spirits. The outcome for the pigs was therefore a natural outcome for Mark given the oral and other evidence upon which he has based this narrative. The man left his unclean home among the tombs, the unclean spirits were banished to unclean animals which in turn self-destructed. The man meanwhile dressed, recovered his faculties, and was given an evangelistic injunction based upon telling the story of what the Lord had done for him.

Parallels in Matthew 8:28-9:1 and Luke 8:26-40

5:21-24 As soon as Jesus had returned by boat to the other shore, a large crowd gathered round him. While he was by the lakeside, there came a synagogue president named Jairus; and when he saw him, he threw himself down at his feet and pleaded with him. "My little daughter is at death's door", he *epitithemi* said. "I beg you to come and *lay* your hands on her so that *sozo* her life may be *saved*." So Jesus went with him, accompanied by a great crowd which pressed round him.

5:25-34 Among them was a woman who had suffered from haemorrhages for twelve years; and in spite of long treatment by many doctors, on which she had spent all she had, she had become worse rather than better. She had heard about Jesus, and came up behind him in the crowd and touched his cloak; for she said, "If I touch even his clothes, I *sozo* shall be *healed*." And there and then the flow of blood dried *iaomai* up and she knew in herself that she was *cured* of her affliction. Aware at once that power had gone out of him, Jesus turned round in the crowd and asked, "Who touched my clothes?" His disciples said to him, "You see the crowd pressing round you and yet you ask, 'Who touched me?'" But he kept looking around to see who had done it. Then the woman trembling with fear because she knew what had happened to her, came and fell at his feet and told him the whole truth. *sozo* He said to her, "Daughter, your faith *has healed* you. Go in *hygies* peace, *free* from your affliction."

118

5:35-43 While he was still speaking, a message came from the president's house, "Your daughter has died; why trouble the teacher any more?" but Jesus, overhearing the message as it was delivered, said to the president of the synagogue, "Do not be afraid; simply have faith." Then he allowed no one to accompany him except Peter and James and James's brother John. They came to the president's house, where he found a great commotion, with loud crying and wailing. So he went in and said to them, "Why this crying and commotion? The child is not dead: she is asleep"; and they laughed at him. After turning everyone out, he took the child's father and mother and his own companions into the room where the child was. Taking hold of her hand, he said to her, "*Talitha cum*", which means, "Get up, my child." Immediately the girl got up and walked about - she was twelve years old. They were overcome with amazement; but he gave them strict instructions not to let anyone know about it, and told them to give her something to eat.

The long 'sandwiched' narrative of the woman with the haemorrhage is one of the famous examples where healing by Jesus is effected without either his conscious intention or direction, even though he was immediately aware of it. Colin Brown[9] sceptically reflects upon the interesting proposition that this might be an instance of the woman viewing Jesus as a healer working by practice of magic. It is conceivable that she considered touching Jesus clothes would be sufficient to bring about her healing and *prima facie* this might look like magical practice. But it is also the case that she had no alternative for her very condition made direct approach to Jesus out of the question. She was in Jewish Law unclean. Jesus' word of healing is also quite specific. It is the woman's faith which has saved her. There is no magical incantation. The story has none of the fantastical embroidery found for example in *The Infancy Gospel of Thomas*. It is clear simple and direct. Within the account she can do no other than 'tell the full truth' - such is the completion of her healing. Equally it follows that the 'long treatment' meant that for her Jesus was the likely final recourse.

The other healing narrative in this long passage is the revitalisation of Jairus' daughter. Some might say revivification; others resurrection. *Epitithemi*, notwithstanding what I say in the Matthean parallel, is given its place in the New Testament in connection with the laying on of hands for healing. It is a sign denoting God's power over anything which might seek to defeat his purpose and thereby is a sign of his kingdom. It would seem that the provision of food is the author's demonstration of the reality of the miracle.

Parallels in Matthew 9:18-26 and Luke 8:40-56

6:4-6 Jesus said to them, "A prophet never lacks honour except in his home town, among his relations and his own family." And he was unable to do any miracle there, except *therapeuo* that he put his hands on a few sick people and *healed* them; and he was astonished at their want [lack] of faith.

Jesus' use of teaching by proverb at v.4 is interesting insofar as it points to the clear self-understanding he had of himself as a divinely inspired prophet. Colin Brown[10] brings out the significance of this very clearly. In the Judaism of Jesus' day prophetic inspiration was regarded as given by the Spirit *[pneuma]*. Since rabbinic teaching held that the inspiration of the Spirit had been withdrawn from Israel at the time of Malachi only to be returned in the last days Jesus was therefore claiming to be a prophet in the last days before the eschaton. The context of the Lucan parallel brings forward this theme of fulfilment in prophecy very powerfully indeed.

Jesus' ministry in his home locality seems restricted to only a few individuals. The majority refused to believe the new teaching he was forming before them. Given that faith is a prerequisite for trust in God it seems little wonder that Jesus was therefore restricted because of the lack of it. It may be said that healing work, even that of Jesus, does not so much bring about faith as presuppose it. Jesus it would seem was astonished at this lack of faith amongst his home people.

The laying on of hands is not to be thought of as a quasi-magical or mystical action essential in the practice of healing. Rather, as in this verse, it denotes the dawn of the messianic age and the reality of the kingdom of God in Jesus. Those who are touched by his hands and by the hands of the apostles have the kingdom shared with them and brought to them in this very physical way.

Parallels in Matthew 13:57-58 and Luke 4: 23

6:12-13 So they set out and proclaimed the need for *ekballo, aleipho* repentance; they *drove* out many demons, and *anointed* *therapeuo* many sick people with oil and *cured* them.

The baptism of John the Baptist was one given to signify repentance and it would seem that the earliest Christian exhortations [not least verse 12 here] contain a call for repentance [cf also Acts 19:4 and 20:21].

The word for anointing used here is *aleipho*. Its other appearance specifically in the context of healing is in the important passage in James 5:14. Oil as a means of skin cleansing, and therefore giving rise to a heightened sense of well-being was widespread throughout the middle east as well as prior to the time of Jesus. It was equally a gesture of honour for a guest. Recall how the Pharisee did not anoint Jesus but the fallen woman did. In this context anointing is a sign to be associated with faith. However in Mark 6:13 it was, as elsewhere, associated with healing. Brunotte[11] hypothesises that the background to this might lie in exorcism.

Some additional thoughts however may be pertinent. The word for oil is *elaion*. The reference is to ordinary oil, freely available in most houses at the time. It had a wide range of medicinal, domestic and cleansing uses. The combination of *elaion* with *aleipho* indicates a routine domestic or home medicinal aid process. Had the word *chrio* been used in place of *aleipho* our interpretation would have pointed to the greater likelihood of a ritual or cultic practice. John Wilkinson offers the following observation:

> Our most complete information on medical practice at this time, albeit from a Roman source and giving an account of Greek medical practice, is the treatise *De Medicina* by Celsus. In the first four books... there are numerous references to the use of anointing with oil *[unctio]* in the treatment of different systemic diseases, and a general statement that "it is desirable that even in acute and recent diseases the body should be anointed."

Wilkinson's view is that the use of *aleipho* supports a medicinal practice both here and in James 5:14 rather than the cultic-sacramental application which, it seems to me, might perhaps come more readily to our own minds.[12]

Whatever the case, we are given here the evidence that Jesus extended his ministry of proclamation, exorcism and healing to his followers to whom he gave gifts specific for the work to be done. cf. Mark 3:14ff also.

	7:32-37 They brought to him a man who was deaf and had an impediment in his speech, and begged Jesus to lay his hand on him. He took him aside, away from the crowd; then he put his fingers in the man's ears, and touched his tongue with spittle. Looking up to heaven, he sighed, and
dianoigo	said to him, "Ephphatha", which means "Be *opened*." With
anoigo	that his hearing was *restored*, and at the same time the
luo	impediment was *removed* and he spoke clearly. Jesus forbade them to tell anyone; but the more he forbade them, the more they spread it abroad. Their astonishment knew no bounds: "All that he does, he does well", they said; "he even makes
akouo, laleo	the deaf *hear* and the dumb *speak*."

The translation of *ephphatha* is given from its Hebrew as *dianoichtheti*, with the associated *anoigo* in 7:35. The action of sighing is more than a simple expression of air. Its translation means in every sense 'be opened' [both the eyes and one's vision of God's kingdom] and 'be released' [from all that keeps one blind to the coming of God's kingdom]. Here in context it denotes deep inner emotion and feeling on the part of Jesus. As given with the onomatopoeic *ephphatha* its performative effect upon the onlookers [quite apart from the man healed] gave rise to significant astonishment if not fear.

As is the case with 8:22-25 this passage is fully patent of symbolic as well as literal interpretation. The people have been taught much [6:34], they have been urged to listen [7:14-16] but with even the disciples then failing to understand we now have a man incapable of hearing brought along whose ears are opened with Jesus uttering his sigh of exasperation as he does so. Although Jesus usually spoke the word of healing here he associates it with touch and with the application of spittle. Both were widespread in Jewish practice of the day and thoroughly familiar actions to all present.

Possible parallel in Mark 8:22-26
Other parallel in Matthew 15:29-31

8:22-25 They arrived at Bethsaida. There the people brought a blind man to Jesus and begged him to touch him. He took the blind man by the hand and led him out of the village. Then he spat on his eyes, laid his hands upon him, and asked whether he could see anything. The man's sight began to *anablepo* *come back*, and he said, "I can see people - they look like trees, but they are walking about." Jesus laid his hands on *apokathistemi* his eyes again; he looked hard, and now he was *cured* and could see everything clearly.

Apart from Mark 3:5 and its parallels [Matthew 12:13 and Luke 6:10] this is the remaining verse in the New Testament where *apokathistemi* is found in connection with the healing of the sick. *Anablepo* also translates 'he looked up'.

The action of Jesus in taking the man by the hand, *epilambano*, is both the term used to describe the scheming of Jesus' opponents and also his love as he turned to the ill and to the lost. In his letters Paul employs it as a word to describe the movement towards faith.

The 'laying on of hands' by Jesus, *epitheis tas cheiras*, is used through the New Testament [as here] in connection with healing miracles. The laying on of hands by Jesus for healing was a very visible sign of God's kingdom having come in him. The restoration of sight was both metaphorically and literally an indicator of this.

Possible parallel in Mark 7:32-37

122

9:14-27 When they came back to the disciples they saw a large crowd surrounding them and scribes arguing with them. As soon as they saw Jesus the whole crowd were overcome with awe and ran forward to welcome him. He asked them, "What is this argument about?" A man in the crowd spoke up: "Teacher, I brought my son for you to *cure*.* He is possessed by a spirit that makes him dumb. Whenever it attacks him, it flings him to the ground, and he foams at the mouth, grinds his teeth, and goes rigid. I asked your disciples to *drive* it out but they could not." Jesus answered: "What an unbelieving [a few quite early mss add, 'and perverse'] generation! How long shall I be with you? How long must I endure you? Bring him to me." So they brought the boy to him; and as soon as the spirit saw him it threw the boy into convulsions, and he fell on the ground and rolled about foaming at the mouth. Jesus asked his father, "How long has he been like this?" "From childhood", he replied; "it has often tried to destroy him by throwing him into the fire or into water. But if it is at all possible for you, take pity on us and help us." "If it is possible!" said Jesus. "Everything is possible to one who believes." At once the boy's father cried [some mss add, 'with tears']: "I believe; help my unbelief." When Jesus saw that the crowd was closing in on them he spoke sternly to the unclean spirit. "Deaf and dumb spirit", he said, "I command you to *come out* of him and never go back!" It shrieked aloud and threw the boy into repeated convulsions, and then came out, leaving him looking like a corpse; in fact many said, "He is dead." But Jesus took hold of his hand and raised him to his feet, and he stood up.

ekballo

exerchomai

It was seen earlier that Jesus was sometimes unable to effect cures, the reason being given as the peoples' [rather than his] lack of faith. The time Jesus was to spend with this 'faithless' generation should be read not so much as his annoyance at the people themselves but rather with what David Hill describes as "the prophetic exasperation of Jesus at the blindness of those who refuse to accept the presence and power of God."[13]

The contrast between the full [arguably over full] account of Mark compared to its parallel in Matthew is striking. At the very least it seems to be the case that Matthew is more concerned with teaching about the person and ministry of Jesus rather than dwelling upon the events involved as would appear to be Mark's emphasis.

---

* At verse 17 there is no word in the Greek for *cure*. The *Revised English Bible* is paraphrasing. More accurately perhaps the *Authorised Version* reads, "... I have brought unto thee my son, which hath...."

Exerchomai has a number of other connotations, hardly surprising as it is a very ordinary word for 'go out'. Forensically it refers to an accused person withdrawing from the country to avoid trial as well as being the end of a magistrate's term of office. A development of this meaning is found in the sense of a condition such as "When you go out you must never go back in". In the hippodrome *exerchomai* refers to the chariots leaving the starting point.

Parallels in Matthew 17:14-18 and Luke 9:37-43

	9:28-29 Then Jesus went indoors, and his disciples asked him
ekballo	privately, "Why could we not *drive* it out?" He said, "This
exerchomai	kind cannot be *driven* out except by prayer."
	Some witnesses add to end of verse 29, "... and fasting."

There seems no significance in the usage of *ekballo* and *exerchomai*. The former means literally 'throw out' and the latter 'come out' or 'go out'.

Mark has given us the fullest account of this incident: he alone mentions scribes in the crowd, he says more about actions and emotions, and in Mark the boy is not only epileptic but mute. The presence of an evil spirit as either the cause or occasion of the boy's condition is more explicit here than in either of the parallels.

The inability of the disciples to bring about a healing is worth comment. Even though Jesus had given them authority for this ministry it was clear, as this passage indicates, that their work was not equal to his. One can surmise that the authority of the word from him who was the Word incarnate has a level of authority which no human can ever match. But that having been said Jesus makes it quite clear that what is lacking in such situations is not so much God's authority as people's faith in it. How long, Jesus asks them, does he have to be with them for them to realise this? His rhetorical frustration in this comment is obvious. Faith is repeatedly given as the precondition for the reception of miraculous healing and conversely lack of faith is presented as an obstacle to it. This narrative continues in verse 28 in which context the healing which has preceded is placed in a reflective training conversation between Jesus and the disciples.

From a structural point of view the passage is interesting. A crowd moves forward twice [vv.14 &25], the child has his illness described twice [vv.18 & 22]. Has Mark conflated two original accounts [14-19,28 and 20-27] into one? There is some suspicion this might be the case, for of these two pericopes the former indicates the disciples' failure to bring about a healing and the second points out the father's desperate petitioning in faith. Both contrast with the linking theme of the two stories, namely the overarching authority of Jesus.

Parallels in Matthew 17:14-18,19-21 and Luke 9:37-42

ekballo 9:38-40 John said to him, "Teacher, we saw someone *driving out* demons in your name, and as he was not one of us, we tried to stop him." Jesus said, "Do not stop him, for no one who
dunamis performs a *miracle* in my name will be able the next moment to speak evil of me. He who is not against us is on our side."

The openness of Jesus in this passage is similar in kind to that of Moses in Numbers 11:26-30. In this story Eldad and Medad had been seized by the Spirit of God even though they had remained in the camp and had not gone into the tent along with the rest of the seventy. Joshua, like John in this New Testament passage, counselled that Eldad and Medad should have their ecstatic response to God curtailed. This debate still arises today. 'Institutional' churches argue that 'charismatic' churches should similarly be curtailed because they are 'ec-centric', 'extreme' or 'not like us' and so on. But more open minds must ask which is the more important - to be empowered by the Holy Spirit of God or to be in conformity with church order? Whilst automatically one might favour the former, the later epistles of the New Testament show up the deep significance of the latter. The church today lives with this tension, namely the ordered institution and the effervescent charismatic. In Acts 19:13ff. a similar story is outlined. In that location the disciples are warned against an exclusivist attitude.

Verse 40 is given the other way around in Matthew 12:30/Luke 11:23 and appears in this form in Cicero: "We have often heard you say that, while we considered all who were not with us as our enemies, you considered all who were not against you as your friends".[14]

The word *dynamis*, from which our own dynamite is derived, indicates something of the power [i.e. dynamism] at work in those who minister in the name of Jesus.

Parallel in Luke 9:49

10:46-52 They came to Jericho; and as he was leaving the town, with his disciples and a large crowd, Bartimaeus [that is, 'son of Timaeus'], a blind beggar, was seated at the roadside. Hearing that it was Jesus of Nazareth, he began to shout, "Son of David, Jesus, have pity on me!" Many of the people told him to hold his tongue; but he shouted all the more, "Son of David, have pity on me." Jesus stopped and said, "Call him"; so they called the blind man: "Take heart", they said. "Get up; he is calling you." At that he threw off his cloak, jumped to his feet, and came to Jesus. Jesus said to him, "What do you want me to do for you?" "Rabbi", the blind man answered, "I want my sight back." Jesus said to
sozo him, "Go; your faith has *healed* you." And at once he
anablepo *recovered his sight* and followed him on the road.

Jesus' action in requiring blind Bartimaeus to come to him was an instruction to lift him from his position of unseeing humiliation upon the ground. The people, recognising Jesus' authority seemed to adopt a different tone from that of moments earlier when they sought to silence him. Adopting a complete *volte face* they now encourage the man by repeating Jesus' instruction to him.

When Jesus was called 'Son of David' or one of the other messianic titles his response is neutral. It would seem that [by and large] he neither agreed with nor denied the charge. His response to Pilate about being 'King of the Jews' was, "The words are yours". At face value this also implies a neutral response, but if Jesus had used what for us is the more colloquial form, "You said it", our interpretation might be different. Apart from Peter at Caesarea Philippi the only others who addressed Jesus by messianic titles were evil spirits. That many perceived him in messianic role seems evident from the 'triumphal entry' into Jerusalem. In his actions it would seem that Jesus disappointed his public for though he lived and taught in the prophetic tradition he did not conform his words and deeds to popular understandings of messianic liberation. In this instance Jesus gave witness both to his power to heal as well as his capacity to offer God's saving work to those who would follow him in discipleship. As an actual curing, this is the final healing miracle in Mark's gospel.

Parallels in Matthew 20:29-34 and Luke 18:35-43

sozo	15:30-31 "...*Save* yourself and come down from the cross."
	The chief priests and the scribes joined in with one another:
sozo, sozo	"He *saved* others", they said, "but he cannot *save* himself."

If Jesus had saved himself he would not have saved others! This is the heart of the gospel. In the taunts there is irony in that the people seem to acknowledge Jesus' power and authority to have brought salvation to others.

Parallels in Matthew 27:42 and Luke 23:35

	16:16-18 Those who believe [the gospel] and receive baptism
sozo	will be *saved*; those who do not will be condemned. Faith
ekballo	will bring with it these miracles: believers *will drive out* demons in my name and speak in strange tongues; if they handle snakes or drink any deadly poison, they will come to no harm; and the sick on whom they lay their hands will
echo kalos	*recover*.

See my notes on Acts 28:1-6 and also my INforming FAITH, p.199, n.8 and also Chapter One above, 'Something for Everyone'.

Chapter 9   LUKE

Luke 4:18-19 "The spirit of the Lord is upon me because he has anointed me; he has sent me to announce good news to the poor, to proclaim *release* for prisoners and recovery of sight for the blind; to let the broken victims *go free*, to proclaim the year of the Lord's favour."

aphesis
aphesis

[*The Authorised Version* reads:] "The Spirit of the Lord is upon me, because he hath anointed me to preach the gospel to the poor; he hath sent me to *heal* the broken hearted, to preach *deliverance* to the captives, and recovery of sight to the blind, *to set at liberty* them that are bruised. To preach the acceptable year of the Lord."

iaomai
aphesis
aphesis

Aphesis occurs fifteen times in the New Testament where the meaning is the forgiveness of sins and two, including the passage here, where it relates to release from captivity. A literal translation of the clause which contains the second appearance of *aphesis* might be "to send away the crushed ones in release".[1]

Jesus' quotation of this passage from Isaiah 61 with its denouement, "Today ... in your hearing this text has come true", seems to indicate his clear acceptance that by his teaching or in his person, or both, Old Testament prophecy has been realised, albeit without the political connotations of liberation from enemies which would have been part of Isaiah's understanding.

The Authorised Version's extra clause is in some Greek manuscripts, but it seems the *Revised English Bible's* omission of it has more secure foundation. It would appear that a later scribe who knew of its presence in Isaiah 61:1 thought it ought to be added to Luke's text from which it had been previously left out.

This passage from Luke should also, however, be contrasted with John 7:8, "My time is not yet fulfilled". The passages are not incompatible. Although everything prophesied about Jesus was complete in him during his life there remained much for him to do. His dying words in John 19, "It is accomplished", constitute the final culmination of his work from birth to death.

Luke gives voice to Jesus' condemnation to the use of arms in any attempt to reconcile human with human, and human with God. Whilst captivity was utterly horrible [both for the Jews in Babylon as well as the Christians for their faith] God would on his judgment day free captives thereby winning on their behalf the final victory.

4:23 ...Jesus said, "No doubt you will quote to me the proverb,
therapeuo 'Physician *heal* yourself!' and say, 'We have heard of all your doings at Capernaum; do the same here in your own home town.'

The verse is part of the long preaching, teaching and healing ministry of Jesus in Galilee. There are only two locations in the New Testament where *therapeuo* denotes healing by medical processes; this one and Luke 8:43. *Therapeuo* otherwise refers to healing by Jesus and the disciples in the context of miracle accounts.

Parallels in Mark 6:4 and Matthew 13:57-58

4:27 ...in the time of the prophet Elisha there were many
katharizo lepers in Israel, and not one of them was *healed*, except Naaman, the Syrian.

Leprosy [in the biblical context a generic term for a wide range of skin conditions] was a condition held in abhorrence by the Hebrews.[2] Without modern day medication even conditions which we recognise as mild could take seriously disfiguring forms. Equally, leprosy sufferers were subject to ceremonial defilement rendering them unclean and for both reasons separated from contact with non sufferers. Leviticus 13 offers rules for given diagnoses and outlines in chapter 14 purification rites. In my comment on Matthew 8:2-3 I list various skin conditions which the generic term 'leprosy' would probably have included. [Actual clinical leprosy is known as Hansen's disease.]

In Luke 4:23-27 Jesus is linking his teaching to prophecy [he had just offered his personal messianic footnote to Isaiah 61:1-2] in the synagogue at Nazareth. Quite explicitly here he links his ministry with that first of Elijah and then of Elisha and indicates by way of barbed implication that the Nazarenes would not be those who would receive God's favour. It would go elsewhere, as it had in the past.

4:31-37 Coming down to Capernaum, a town in Galilee, he taught the people on the sabbath, and they were amazed at his teaching, for what he said had the note of authority. Now there was a man in the synagogue possessed by a demon, an unclean spirit. He shrieked at the top of his voice, "What do you want with us, Jesus of Nazareth? Have you come to destroy us? I know
epitimao who you are - the Holy One of God." Jesus *rebuked*
phimoo, exerchomai him: *"Be silent"*, he said, "and *come out* of him." Then the demon, after throwing the man down in front of the people, left him without doing him any injury. Amazement fell on them all and they said to one another: "What is there in this man's words? He gives orders to the
exerchomai unclean spirits with authority and power, and *they go*." So the news spread, and he was the talk of the whole district.

128

Morna Hooker in her commentary on Mark notes that the question "What do you want with us?" renders exactly the Hebrew of Judges 11:12 ["What quarrel had he with them?"] and 1 Kings 17:18 ["What made you interfere? "].[3] The demons [is there one voice or are we to consider the likelihood of multiple personality here?] address Jesus as 'Jesus of Nazareth' and as 'the holy one of God', and this indicates the writer's view that the demons knew the authority of Jesus. We can extrapolate from this and say that they recognised his authority as both man and as Word of God. It was the combination of the words themselves and the authority and power behind them which both effected the exorcism and gave rise to the peoples' sense of amazement. It is not without significance that Jesus did not accept the demons' recognition as mitigating circumstances to modify their fate. It seems Jesus used the authority they recognised as the basis for their expulsion.

The reference to Jesus, that he is holy, is uncommon in the New Testament. It is the [holy] Spirit of God which more usually has this epithet. That which is holy is that Spirit of God which has brought in the new age of God, fulfilling all that went before. In this sense the Holy Spirit of God may be seen in the prophetic tradition both emerging out of the Old Testament and arising in the New Testament and alive in the early church. The description 'the Holy one of God' is a title found in the Septuagint only twice; at Judges 13:7 and 16:17 where it means the bearer has been filled with the Holy Spirit. Insofar as it relates to Jesus in this verse it refers us back to the consecration of Jesus by the Holy Spirit at his baptism.

Parallels in Matthew 7:28-29 and Mark 1:21-28

	4:38-39 On leaving the synagogue [Jesus] went to Simon's house. Simon's mother-in-law was in the grip of a high fever; and they
epitimao	asked him to help her. He stood over her and *rebuked* the fever.
aphiemi	It *left* her, and she got up at once and attended to their needs.

From Luke we can gather that Jesus was regularly teaching in the temple [cf. Luke 20-21]. His place for teaching would be the outer courts, where in due course the earliest Christians would also have gathered for the same purpose. Similarly Luke, more than the other gospels, places Jesus in the local synagogues where he would have taught. Colin Brown indicates a continuity in this respect between Luke and Acts.[4]

The fever from which Peter's mother-in-law suffered is descriptively presented as a raised temperature rather than as a clinical diagnosis. The 'rebuke' to the fever *epitimao* is also found in exorcism formulae [Mark 1:25, 9:25] as well as in the stilling of the storm [Mark 4:39].

I am sure I cannot be alone in thinking that the richness of *diakonia* is only very limply expressed by the words "attended to their needs".

The more old-fashioned rendering of the *Authorised Version* "ministered unto them" has much more resonance and probably greater accuracy.

Parallels in Matthew 8:14-15, Mark 1:29-31

	4:40-41 At sunset all who had friends ill with diseases of one kind or another brought them to him; and he laid his hands
therapeuo	on them one by one and *healed* them. Demons also came out of many of them, shouting, "You are the Son of God."
epitimao	But he *rebuked* them and forbade them to speak, because they knew he was the Messiah.

There are over thirty references to demons, evil spirits and afflicting spirits in the synoptic gospels [Matthew, Mark and Luke] and eight in Acts whereas none are found in John's gospel. In this location the demons are seen to have inhabited many of those recorded as having been healed by Jesus. They are not seen, either here or anywhere else, as having a power equal to God. They are clearly under his jurisdiction.

Parallels in Matthew 8:16-17 and Mark 1:32-34

	5:12 [Jesus] was once in a certain town where there was a man covered with leprosy; when he saw Jesus, he threw himself to the ground and begged his help. "Sir", he said, "if
katharizo	only you will you can *make* me *clean*."

In this passage [5:12-14] the request to Jesus is definite and urgent. The word used is *deomai*. It is for a specific situation and the leper's dramatic body language indicates both deference to the person of Jesus as well as implicit submission to his ministry. The response of Jesus to the leper's recognition of his authority was also incontrovertible. Jesus stretched out his hand with an extravagance of gesture matching that of the leper's supplication. The impression given in 5:14 is that Jesus wished the priests to be informed of what had happened rather than for it first to become public knowledge.

The leper's request to be made clean raises interesting questions about 'purity'. *Katharos / katharizo* might refer to physical purity [Revelation 15:6], cultic purity [Matthew 8:2-4], spiritual purity [Matthew 5:8]. In New Testament usage the meaning of purity cannot be separated from the teaching of Jesus. In part this was formed in the context of his struggle with the Pharisees where the debated issue was external purity [Matthew 15:11, 16f and 23:25f]. Is it external influences which pollute and defile the person or is it that which comes from within a person which pollutes and defiles?

New Testament teaching radically transcended and rejected previously accepted obligatory concepts of ritual purity. According to Mosaic Law the leper was unclean, cut off from human contact and

Jesus in touching him risked not only leprous contagion but also, according to the law, personal uncleanness as a result of the contact. In the context of this healing Jesus is pronouncing the leper's freedom from cultic and physical impurity and in so doing effects a healing.[5] It is not so much that Jesus became unclean but rather, by asserting his own word and witness as superior to the law, made the man clean.

Jesus recognised the significance of his actions and following the direction of Leviticus 14 sends the man to the priest in whom resides the power to pronounce that a cleansing has taken place. Jesus' intention therefore has been threefold: [i] to pronounce the cleansing and assert his supremacy over the law, [ii] to effect the healing, [iii] thence to use the requirements of the law itself as a means of demonstrating [i] and [ii]. It is no doubt a sign of inevitably failed human response to Jesus that the cleansed leper, unable to contain his joy at the cure broadcasts what has happened far and wide.

Parallels for Luke 5:12-14[-16] in Matthew 8:2-4 and Mark 1:39-45

therapeuo **5:15** But the talk about him spread even wider, so that great crowds kept gathering to hear him and to be *cured* of their ailments.

The verse appears to follow naturally from the preceding healing of the leper. Even though Jesus enjoined silence upon the leper [at the very least until after ritual verification of the man s cleansing by the priest] news about Jesus spread rapidly. *Logos* has numerous New Testament meanings, appearing as it does some 331 times. It refers variously to utterance, question, command, discoursing, word of mouth, written word, words [seen in contrast to action or power], object, matter, words or scripture, words of warning, account, settlement of account, motive, proclamation, teaching, instruction, and perhaps most famously the word of God in the sense of the word of the Lord, word of promise, truth, of life, of Jesus and word of God in the person and work of Jesus. In this verse it has the reference of report, information and rumour.[6]

iaomai **5:17-20** One day as [Jesus] was teaching, Pharisees and teachers of the law were sitting round him. People had come from every village in Galilee and from Judaea and Jerusalem, and the power of the Lord was with him to *heal* the sick. Some men appeared carrying a paralysed man on a bed, and tried to bring him in and set him in front of Jesus. Finding no way to do so because of the crowd, they went up to the roof and let him down through the tiling, bed and all, into the middle of the company in front of Jesus. When Jesus saw their faith, he said to the man, "Your sins are forgiven you."

In Matthew 9:1-8 I considered Jesus' conflict with the scribes. This section of scripture is the backcloth for his enlarging dispute with the Pharisees. Along with the Pharisees are present *nomodidaskaloi*, meaning 'teachers of the law'. This is the only gospel use of the word indeed it is a term found only in Christian writings. As a description it indicates perhaps more fully than might otherwise be assumed the work of the scribes. Their role is far more than text copiers or writing clerks. Their teaching role is noted in Mark 1:22 and their place in the judiciary is indicated in Matthew 16:21.[7]

A friend, having lived previously in the Middle East, has described to me the relative ease in gaining roof access [if need be, across adjoining properties] from the street. Outside staircases were provided for the purpose, and flimsy but adequate roofing materials would still mean some commotion for those in the rooms below, but not necessarily the utter havoc one might more readily imagine. This is the only New Testament appearance of *keramos* meaning 'roof tile'.[8]

Parallels in Matthew 9:2-8 and Mark 2:1-12

	6:6-10 On another sabbath he had gone to the synagogue and was teaching. There was a man in the congregation whose right arm was withered; and the scribes and Pharisees were
therapeuo	on the watch to see whether Jesus would *heal* him on the sabbath, so that they could find a charge to bring against him. But he knew what was in their minds and said to the man with the withered arm, "Stand up and come out here." So he stood up and came out. Then Jesus said to them, "I
sozo	put this question to you: is it permitted to do good or to do evil on the sabbath, to *save* life or to destroy it?" He looked round at them all, and then he said to the man, "Stretch out
apokathistemi	your arm." He did so and his arm was *restored*.

The use of the three different Greek words is interesting from a structural perspective: [i] The expectation was that Jesus might cure [heal] the man of his condition; [ii] Jesus' reply was in terms of salvation/wholeness for the person in the context of Mosaic Law; [iii] the healing, when it did take place was a restoration which presupposed both [i] and [ii].

The scribes and Pharisees it would seem were almost 'lying in wait' *[paratereo]* to entrap Jesus. *Paratereo* means 'to watch suspiciously', to 'look with slit eyes'. The outcome of a charge against Jesus would have placed him answering his accusers before the local Sanhedrin. This narrative is one of three where a healing took place without Jesus touching the sick person. There is considerable significance in Jesus words of command, firstly, "Stand up and come out here", and then

132

most especially, "Stretch out your arm". Geza Vermes makes the important point that "Speech could not be construed as 'work' infringing the law governing the Jewish day of rest."[9]

This is the only healing account unanimously placed by all three synoptic gospels on the sabbath. There are echoes of 1 Kings 13:4-6 in this passage and its parallels though a direct link is unlikely.

Parallels in Mark 3:1-5 and Matthew 12:9-14

	6:17-19 [Jesus] came down the hill with them and stopped on some level ground where a large crowd of his disciples had gathered, and with them great numbers of people from Jerusalem and all Judaea and from the coastal region of Tyre
iaomai	and Sidon, who had come to listen to him, and to be *cured* of their diseases. Those who were troubled with unclean spirits
therapeuo	were *healed* and everyone in the crowd was trying to touch
iaomai	him, because power went out from him and *cured* them all.

The impact of Jesus was such that many came to him in the context of significant events and in dramatic form. The linking of this event with people who came not only from a number of regions near and far, but also and very importantly from Jerusalem further highlights the poignancy of this occasion. The motif of the catch of a great many fishes is an image of this event. Equally we can recall the woman with the haemorrhage secretly moved close so that even touching the hem of his cloak would enable power to flow from him. In this passage people pressed towards Jesus because, similarly, power "went out from him" to cure them all.

| | 7:3 Hearing about Jesus [a centurion] sent some Jewish elders to |
| diasozo | ask him to come and *save* his servant's life. They approached Jesus and made an urgent appeal to him. |

| | 7: 6-7 "Do not trouble further, sir; I am not worthy to have you come under my roof, and that is why I did not presume to approach |
| iaomai | you in person. But say the word and my servant will be *cured*." |

| | 7:10 When the messengers returned to the house, they found |
| hygiano | the servant *in good health*. |

A clear difference exists between this passage and its Matthean and Johannine parallels in that the centurion sends Jewish elders to petition Jesus. The force of this softens any anti-Jewish polemic which might be construed from Matthew's account as well as from 7:9.

Luke portrays the centurion as a benefactor to the synagogue and as someone who is a friend of the nation. It has to be said however that the centurion's messengers were clearly expecting an anti-Gentile response from Jesus - their apologetic implies it.

Luke's narrative also softens any expectation that Jews would automatically argue with Jesus. In Luke the centurion knew his place in society and recognised his personal deference to that society. Luke contrasts the centurion's position in this regard with the Jewish elders [distinguished presiding leaders of the local synagogue][10] who were employed as his mediators and thus deemed worthy to approach Jesus.

Because of his generosity to the synagogue it seems the centurion's mediators considered he merited Jesus' help. However it was not so much their petition which it seems moved Jesus as the centurion's faith in Jesus' authority.

Parallels in Matthew 8: 5-13, John 4: 46-53

7:18-23 When John was informed of all this by his disciples, he summoned two of them and sent them to the Lord with this question: "Are you the one who is to come, or are we to expect someone else?" The men made their way to Jesus and said, "John the Baptist has sent us to ask you, ` Are you the one who is to come, or are we to expect someone else?' *therapeuo* There and then he *healed* many sufferers from diseases, plagues and evil spirits, and on many blind people he bestowed sight. Then he gave them this answer: "Go and tell John what you have seen and *anablepo, peripateo,* heard: the blind *regain their sight*, the lame *walk*, *katharizo, akouo* lepers are made *clean*, the deaf *hear*, the dead *are egeiro, euangelizo* raised to life*, the poor are *brought good news*...*"

The Christmas stories[11] of the shepherds in the fields, popularly given nowadays as being to the east of Bethlehem and of the kings travelling from farther afield, need no repeating. The stories are well known. We are told that when both shepherds and kings found baby Jesus they knew him to be who he was even though they had never seen him before.

I want in what follows to reflect on someone else whose story is somewhat more enigmatic than that of either the shepherds or the kings. I'd like to ponder the relationship between John the Baptist and Jesus.

The respective mothers of John and Jesus knew each other. They were cousins. Luke documents Mary's visit to Elizabeth. Both women were pregnant. The visit lasted some three months. We may take it with some confidence that they knew each other well.

In due course John the Baptist began his work, his ministry of baptising in the river Jordan. This was clearly important work for all the gospels record it, though each stresses different traditions surrounding what he did. All four gospels recount the occasion when Jesus came to John to be baptised by him in the Jordan. Mark's description of Jesus' baptism is very brief though it is preceded by a more substantial narrative in which John speaks of the one who is to follow him, one much greater than he. As Jesus comes out of the water we are told that he saw the heavens open and the Spirit of God descending upon him like a dove.

Luke's gospel also records aspects of John's teaching. Some parts of Luke's record are clearly drawn from Mark's Gospel, other parts would appear to have their own independent origin. Luke's account of Jesus' baptism is described in very ordinary terms. Jesus it would seem is one of many having been baptised by John. Again the heavens opening and the descent of the Holy Spirit like a dove is described - though we are not told whether Jesus saw this. The possibility is presented that it was available for all to see.

Matthew also draws from Mark in his account of the baptismal teaching of John the Baptist as well as from the same separate sources as Luke. His account of the baptism of Jesus is more full, however, and seems to draw on material from a further tradition. An exchange between Jesus and an unwilling John is recounted. The diffident John is persuaded to baptise the Jesus whom he recognises as his superior. I will remark on the significance of this shortly. Once again the opening of the heavens and the descent of the Holy Spirit are described. It is given that Jesus saw this happening with the possibility that others witnessed it left open.

John's gospel has some similarities with the others but the historical tradition from which he drew has many unique features. Indeed it seems the case that John's narrative draws on two separate sources. In one [1:29-30] John recognises Jesus approaching and says, "There is the Lamb of God who takes away the sins of the world". In verse 33 we read almost by way of contradiction, "I did not know him [but I had been told] the man on whom you see the Spirit come down and rest is the one who ... is God's chosen one." [My paraphrase.]

In each Gospel then we have the account of John baptising Jesus. Each gospel draws on its own sources, some of these overlapping with other gospels, some of them independent.

The next significant accounts of John the Baptist in the Gospels record his imprisonment. The Gospel according to John identifies John the Baptist in dispute with the Jews. In only one line is John's imprisonment referred to. The other three gospels, however are much fuller in their record of John's time in jail before his execution. Mark's record, it has to be said, does not so much speak of John as of Herod and his daughter's wish to have John beheaded. Luke tells of John sending his own disciples to Jesus; presumably they had come to see

135

him in his cell, so that the question might be put, "Are you the one who is to come or are we to expect another?" [Luke 7:18-24] Luke's gospel has told us earlier that Herod had imprisoned John.

Matthew draws on the same tradition as Luke. John sends his disciples away from a prison visit to ask Jesus, "Are you the one who is to come, or are we to expect someone else?" Luke does not tell us whether John had or had not recognised Jesus at his baptism, though given the significant friendship between their mothers it would seem inconceivable that they did not know each other already. Matthew however is clear. John did know Jesus and knew Jesus' superiority to him. In prison John heard what Jesus was doing: the lame are enabled to walk, the blind to see and the poor to have the gospel preached to them. If John the Baptist knew who Jesus was as it seems he did, why then did he need to ask the question, "Are you the one who is to come?" What answer can be given?

Remember, John was in jail. He could no longer carry out the work he was called to do. If Jesus was the messiah then, in jail, John would know his work to have been complete. He would be needed to do no more. We are told that Jesus sent John's disciples back to report the signs they saw of Jesus living out the work he had come to do. Hearing this John would have been reassured.

For John, a man who knew Jesus well, there may have been the certainty of either the shepherd or of the wise man who recognised the Messiah in a baby they had never met before. But there was also the human need for reassurance that Jesus - his half-cousin - was actually the person he had previously known him to be; namely that he was the Messiah from God. John the Baptist was someone who, although he knew Jesus, wanted further or perhaps final affirmation that he was the Christ.

Christians today, as followers of Jesus, also know him albeit in a different sense. But we are in many other ways no different from John. We do not have the certainty of the shepherd or the wise man. Christians come in faith to worship at Christmas seeking reassurance, affirmation perhaps, by asking of the infant child that question for which they already have the answer: Are you the one? .

Parallel in Matthew 11: 2-6

7:48-50 [The woman living an immoral life anointed Jesus' feet with myrrh.] Then he said to her, "Your sins are forgiven." The other guests began to ask themselves, "Who is this that can forgive sins?" But he said to the woman, "Your *sozo* faith has *saved* you; go in peace."

Forgiveness with salvation [wholeness] is demonstrated here as elsewhere to be the supreme activity of Jesus, despite all objections to his carrying out such work. Clearly the word of forgiveness was understood by all who saw [and even questioned] his work as something which was effective. In modern, technical language Jesus' word of forgiveness was a 'performative utterance'. Namely it brought about the effect of which it spoke. This passage is but two verses in a section of teaching [verses 36-50] where Jesus engages his critics on the righteousness of sinners forgiven and by implication he criticises the righteous for being too blind to perceive their own unrighteousness.

cf. also Matthew 26:6-13, Mark 14:3-9, John 11:2 and 12:1-8

	8:1-2, 3 After this [Jesus] went journeying from town to town and village to village, proclaiming the good news of the kingdom of God. With him were the Twelve and a
therapeuo	number of women who had been *set free* from evil spirits and infirmities; Mary, known as Mary of Magdala, from
exerchomai	whom seven demons *had come out*... These women provided for them out of their own resources.

There are hints here of the common, and probably very simple life which Jesus and his disciples shared. It would seem that their freedom to move around meant they neither needed nor yet lacked material goods. This points to some basic financial stability in the twelve and the women at least as well as a likely further dependence upon characteristic middle eastern table generosity. It may be posited also that the euphoric Christian life depicted in the early chapters of the Acts of the Apostles was seen as an extension of the life of Jesus with his close circle of companions into the early church. Although Jesus called the twelve, and although this has especial resonances with the twelve tribes of Israel, the normal patriarchal structure of Hebrew life is disturbed in v.3 for the normal providers would not have been women but men.

There is a profound link here between the proclamation given in the teaching of Jesus and his healing miracles. It is the kingdom of God to which his word points in 8:1 and it is the kingdom which is being made real in the healing miracles. The traditional linking of Mary of Magdala's exorcism with her redemption of a life of prostitution is more steeped in legend than verifiable evidence. On this point Colin Brown writes, "... the way in which Mary is introduced in Luke 8:2 might well be Luke's modest and cryptic way of identifying Mary and of expressing the new beginning that she had found in Jesus. Her past was a nameless past; she had found a new identity. [12] Little more of her can be said with certainty. This passage is unique to Luke though see also Mark 15:40,41 and 16:9.

8:12 The seed along the footpath stands for those who hear it, and then the devil comes and carries off the word from their hearts for fear they should believe and be *saved*.

sozo

The context is the parable of the sower. Birds are given a bad press by implication in this short narrative. They are equated metaphorically with the action of the devil who removes the word of God from peoples' minds when it has not been recognised for what it is, or when it has not had chance to take root. Even this metaphorical alliteration however cannot mask the author's clear intention that 'something deliberately took off with the word'. The action of the devil is thereby personified.

Parallels in Matthew 13:1-23 and Mark 4:1-20

8:22-24 One day [Jesus] got into a boat with his disciples and said to them, "Let us cross over to the other side of the lake." So they put out; and as they sailed along he fell asleep. Then a heavy squall struck the lake; they began to ship water and were in grave danger. They came and roused him: "Master, Master, we are sinking!" they cried. He awoke, and rebuked the wind and the turbulent waters. The storm subsided and there was calm. "Where is your faith?" he asked. In fear and astonishment they said to one another, "Who can this be? He gives his orders to the wind and the waves, and they obey him."

It could be argued that inclusion of the nature miracles in these study notes on healing miracles is a departure from the direction I have intended. In part this is a correct comment. But by way of defence I would contend that the nature miracles, of which this and its parallels are one of comparatively few, show direct similarities where Jesus in fulfilment of his divine commission has lordship over sin, sickness, evil and natural forces, thereby rendering him Lord of all creation.

Parallels in Matthew 8:18; 8:23-27 and Mark 4:35-41

8:26-39 So they landed in the country of the Gerasenes, which is opposite Galilee. As [Jesus] stepped ashore he was met by a man from the town who was possessed by demons. For a long time he had neither worn clothes nor lived in a house, but stayed among the tombs. When he saw Jesus he cried out, and fell at his feet. "What do you want with me, Jesus, son of the Most High God?" he shouted. "I implore you, do not torment me." For Jesus was already ordering the unclean spirit to come out of the man. Many a time it had seized him, and then, for safety's sake, they would secure him with chains and fetters; but each time he broke loose and was driven by the demon out into the wilds.

Jesus asked him, "What is your name?" "Legion", he replied. This was because so many demons had taken possession of him. And they begged him not to banish them to the abyss.

There was a large herd of pigs nearby, feeding on the hillside; and the demons begged him to let them go into these pigs. He gave them leave; the demon came out of the man and went into the pigs, and the herd rushed over the edge into the lake and were drowned.

When the men in charge of them saw what had happened, they took to their heels and carried the news to the town and countryside; and the people came out to see what had happened. When they came to Jesus, and found the man from whom the demons had gone out sitting at his feet clothed and in his right mind, they were afraid. Eyewitnesses told them how the madman *sozo* had been *cured*. Then the whole population of the Gerasene district was overcome by fear and asked Jesus to go away. So he got into the boat and went away. The man from whom the demons had gone out begged to go with him; but Jesus sent him away: "Go back home", he said, "and tell them what God has done for you." The man went all over the town proclaiming what Jesus had done for him.

The text most closely resembles the Marcan parallel, though with some textual tidying and adjustment.

The witnesses it would seem recognised not only an exorcism but also a fuller healing of the madman [indicated by Luke's use of *sozo*]. The man's encounter with Jesus and what happened to him is sufficient in itself to generate his evangelistic fervour. In this narrative 'telling the story' of the grace and healing of God becomes proclamation in its own right. Perhaps it might also be the case that since Jesus could not remain in the area he employed the man's thirst for discipleship by using him for locally based evangelism in the area Jesus had to leave.

Parallels in Matthew 8:28-9:1 and Mark 5:1-20

8:40-56 When Jesus returned, the people welcomed him, for they were all expecting him. Then a man appeared - Jairus was his name and he was president of the synagogue. Throwing himself down at Jesus's feet he begged him to come to his house, because his only daughter, who was about twelve years old, was dying.

8:42b-48 While Jesus was on his way he could hardly breathe for the crowds. Among [the crowds] was a woman who had suffered from haemorrhages for twelve years; and [some witnesses add at this point: "though she had spent all she had on doctors"] nobody had been able to *therapeuo* *cure* her.

She came up from behind and touched the edge of his cloak, and at once her haemorrhage stopped. Jesus said, "Who was it who touched me?" All disclaimed it, and Peter said, "Master, the crowds are hemming you in and pressing upon you!" But Jesus said, "Someone did touch me, for I felt that power had gone out from me." Then the woman, seeing that she was detected, came trembling and fell at his feet. Before all the people she explained why she had touched *iaomai* him and how she had been *cured* instantly. He said to her, *sozo* Daughter, your faith has *healed* you. Go in peace."

8:49-56 While he was still speaking, a man came from the president's house with the message, "Your daughter is dead; do not trouble the teacher any more." But Jesus heard, and said, "Do not be afraid; simply have faith and she will be well again." When he arrived at the house he allowed no one to go in with him except Peter, John, and James, and the child's father and mother. Everyone was weeping and lamenting for her. He said, "Stop your weeping; she is not dead: she is asleep"; and they laughed at him, well knowing that she was dead. But Jesus took hold of her hand and called *egeiro* to her: *"Get up*, my child." Her spirit returned, she stood up immediately, and he told them to give her something to eat. Her parents were astounded; but he forbade them to tell anyone what had happened.

Colin Brown writes,

There are occasional cases where those regarded by the doctors as dead are reported as brought back to life by Jesus. He took the hand of Jairus' daughter and caused her to get up and walk [Mark 5:41]. According to the Matthew 9:25, Mark 5:4 and Luke 8:54f it was his touch and kingly command that gave the child back her life. The command was expressed by the imperative *egeire*. The Synoptics and John each indicate that death can set no bounds to Jesus' activity, but that the life which proceeded from him stripped death of its power, i.e. the otherwise immutable frontier of death and time had been broken through or leaped over. The spectators' laughter at such a statement [Mk.5:40] serves best to stress the extraordinary and incomprehensible nature of this life-giving power. What the Jews expected, apart from their belief in eschatological resurrection [Jn 11:24; Martha], was that someone should be preserved from death... But now God, the Lord over life and death, stood in person before them.[13]

I have spoken elsewhere of the relationship between faith and healing. It is not a person's faith, nor yet the faith of others which brings about a healing. Rather however, faith is the precondition for healing to take place. In his commentary on the Matthean parallel David Hill says this, "The faith that made her well is the expectant admission, by reason of her presence and action, that only Jesus can deal with her condition. This confidence is the ground on which Jesus authoritatively banishes her illness. It is the word of Jesus which heals, not the woman's action or faith".[14]

The combination of these two miracle stories is a highly plausible narrative device. The age of the daughter mirrors the length of the woman's condition. Each has its differing, but complementary aspect of faith; that shown outwardly by the president of the synagogue and the attempted privacy of the woman. Luke does not have the same contrasting resurrection-hope vocabulary as does Mark 5:23 in the use of 'save' and 'live', *sozo* and *zao*. This motif is not lost in v.52 when the contrast is between being dead and being asleep, *apothnesko* and *katheudo*. The instruction *egeire* has overtones of resurrection and the mocking laughter of v.53 will find its echoes in the passion narratives.

Parallels in Matthew 9:18-26 and Mark 5:21-43

therapeuo
iaomai

9:1-2 Calling the Twelve together [Jesus] gave them power and authority to overcome all demons and to *cure* diseases and sent them out to proclaim the kingdom of God and to *heal* the sick.

A literal translation might read, "... authority over all demons and to cure diseases..." These first two verses of Luke 9 along with the longer ending of Mark and the great commission in Matthew are crucial for the church's approach to evangelism in any age. If Jesus had not commanded people to go and teach, baptise, pronounce forgiveness and heal in his name Christianity would have been deprived of much of its essential core. Each of these activities points to an aspect of God's kingdom becoming real. In these Jesus shared his work with his followers. Their task was to teach all he had commanded them to teach and also, crucially, they were to perform the same tasks which they had shared with him in their time with him. In the healing ministry they [and we after them] instance the active presence of the risen and exalted Lord within the life of the church. In the expository notes on Paul we shall see that the tasks and gifts given to the apostles are equally available [and arguably more so] in the church which becomes the visible body of Christ on earth.

Parallels in Matthew 10:1-2 and Mark 6:13

therapeuo

9:6 So [the twelve] set out and travelled from village to village and everywhere they announced the good news and *healed* the sick.

Here the proclamation of the gospel by the disciples is explicitly linked to a healing ministry. The teaching of Jesus is given direct application by the disciples in 'works' which accompany the word.

Parallels in Matthew 10:7-8, Mark 6:12, Luke 10:9

therapeuo *iaomai*	9:11 ...but crowds found out and followed. He welcomed them, and spoke to them about the kingdom of God, and *cured* those who were in need of *healing*.

The structure of this verse mirrors, almost exactly, that of 9:6. In him proclamation and healing are linked as the kingdom of God made real in him.

sozo *sozo*	9:24 Whoever wants to *save* his life will lose it, but whoever loses his life for my sake will *save* it.

The understanding of Christian discipleship as complete renunciation of the world is part of the very heart of the teaching of Jesus. This should not be taken as meaning the world should be despised but rather that salvation [wholeness] cannot be attained by means of the world. For its first readers this teaching would resonate loudly with echoes of martyrdom.

This verse hinges around the use of paradox in Christian interpretation. The human instinct for self-preservation will always result in a near inevitable preference to avoid death. But seeking the kingdom of God and being prepared for martyrdom will both bring the kingdom closer on earth and lead one to salvation by the surrender of one's life for the sake of Jesus. A recent author, Ian Bradley, has written movingly of the sacrifice which is part of the very web of reality. He is seeking to restore the concept of 'sacrifice' back to its rightful place in the centre of Christian thinking. Bradley's message is very timely.[15]

Parallels in Matthew 10:39, Luke 17:33, John 12:25

	9:37-43 Next day when they came down from the mountain a large crowd came to meet him. A man in the crowd called out: "Teacher, I implore you to look at my son, my only child. From time to time a spirit seizes him and with a sudden scream throws him into convulsions so that he foams at the mouth; it keeps on tormenting him and can hardly be made to let him go. I begged
ekballo	your disciples *to drive it out*, but they could not." Jesus answered, "What an unbelieving and perverse generation! How long shall I be with you and endure you? Bring your son here." But before the boy could reach him the demon dashed him to the ground and threw him into convulsions. Jesus spoke sternly to the
iaomai	unclean spirit, *cured* the boy, and gave him back to his father. And they were all struck with awe at the greatness of God.

The son's likely condition is a form of epilepsy. The Matthean parallel is clear about this though Mark is insistent that the presence of a spirit is the root cause of the son's problem. The crowd which met Jesus at the foot of the Mount of Transfiguration stands in deliberate contrast to the intensity of isolation that had accompanied the dramatic happenings on the mountain. Jesus' use of mountains and hills both in Galilee and also the Mount of Olives near Jerusalem as a refuge from crowds and as a retreat for prayer is well attested throughout the gospels.

The reference to an "unbelieving and perverse generation" is a likely citation from Deuteronomy 32:5. It signals the peoples' lack of recognition that the kingdom of God was coming in Jesus himself and draws echoes of the unbelief Jesus saw in his own home district where, consequently, he was unable to minister in word and deed. His following words, "How long..." express Jesus' sense of exasperation at people's unbelief more than they express any direct criticism of them.

The man's request to Jesus for healing is quite specific. The word used is *deomai* and has a fully religious connotation of beseeching God [in the person of Jesus] for real help to meet his own and his son's need with the expectation that the petition will result in an unambiguously satisfactory outcome.

Parallels in Matthew 17:14-18 [19-20,21] and Mark 9:14-27[28]

ekballo	9:49-50 "Master", said John, "we saw someone *driving out* demons in your name, but as he is not one of us we tried to stop him." Jesus said to him, "Do not stop him for he who is not against you is on your side."

The New Testament contains an extensive demonology. Common throughout however is the subordination of demons to the authority of Jesus and of his power in the early church. In a number of situations they cause illness, but by no means is all illness demon-caused. In some New Testament accounts demons had taken over the personality of people. By his embodiment of God's kingdom Jesus had authority over demons. Most, if not all references to demons in the New Testament, are in the context of Jesus' lordship over them.

The 'detached exorcist' referred to in this passage is I would suggest someone who, rather than travelling with Jesus, elected to remain at home even if nevertheless a believer.

Parallel in Mark 9:38-39

therapeuo	10:8-9 When you enter a town and you are made welcome, eat the food provided for you; *heal* the sick there and say, "The kingdom of God has come."

There is an important sequence of teaching in the ministry of Jesus which can be drawn out from Luke. In Luke 4:16 Jesus' teaching begins in his home district of Galilee. It then extends throughout Galilee [Chapters 5-8] and comes to the commissioning of the twelve in 9:1. He gives them his authority to carry his word and work further. This is extended to a commissioning of "a further seventy two" in 10:1. Throughout there is a developing extension of his mission both in terms of territory covered and in terms of sharing the work with an increasing number of others. These two verses form part of this last extended commission.

As expressed within verse 9, the coming of the kingdom within the disciples' teaching will have carried resonances both of physical closeness of the kingdom as well as a reverential closeness more proper to an atmosphere of worship. This latter perspective speaks of the transcendent coming close in immanence. God's promise of his coming, given in former days in prophetic teaching, is realised in the person and work of Jesus. This promise is to be proclaimed as real by the twelve.

ekballo	11:14-20 [Jesus] was *driving out* a demon which was dumb; and when the demon had come out, the dumb man began to speak. The people were astonished, but some of them said, "It
ekballo	is by Beelzebul prince of demons that he *drives* the demons *out*." Others, by way of a test, demanded of him a sign from heaven. But he knew what was in their minds, and said, "Every kingdom divided against itself is laid waste, and a divided household falls. And if Satan is divided against himself, how
ekballo	can his kingdom stand - since, as you claim, I *drive out* the
ekballo	demons by Beelzebul. If it is by Beelzebul that I *drive out*
ekballo	demons, by whom do your own people *drive* them *out*? If this is your argument, they themselves will refute you. But if it is
ekballo	by the finger of God that I *drive out* the demons, then be sure the kingdom of God has already come upon you."

In the Matthean parallel the demon is both blind and dumb, rather than as here only dumb. There is no reference to either condition in Mark. Luke 11:24-27 outlines with some care the dispatching of demons to a distant lonely place following the 'cleaning of the house' where once there was lodging. Mark 5:10 speaks also of the banishing of demons; such action being a clear indication of their defeat. The obverse of this is the local habitation of demons whether in people or places. Lucan demonology is uncompromising. The disciples were given power over demons and, apparently authenticating their claim Jesus himself claims to have seen "Satan fall, like lightening, from heaven". [Luke 10:17-18].

Concerning the casting out of demons some reference to terminology is relevant. *Diabolos*, devil, is always singular in the New Testament Greek and refers only to Satan. Only in Luke 22:3 and John 13:27 is Satan recorded as having entered a human being [Judas Iscariot]. *Daimon*, demon, has both singular and plural usage and is linked in general terms with unclean spirits.

Jesus' power is "the finger of God" [Luke 11:20], likewise the "Spirit of God" [Matthew 12:28]. The manner of exorcism was simple and straightforward; in his name Jesus commanded the evil spirits to "go", or "come out". Violence and defiance is reported to have accompanied the departure of demons [cf. Mark 1:26]. Although the healing ministry is carried out today with increasingly widespread acceptance, and although it is firmly based within the ministry of Jesus, we are well advised not to move into the area of exorcism without substantial caution. This is particularly the case given that first century cosmology was so different from that of today.

Parallels in Matthew 12:22-28 and Mark 3:23-30

> **11:24-26** "When an unclean spirit comes out of someone it wanders over the desert sands seeking a resting place; and if it finds none, it says, 'I will go back to the home I left.' So it returns and finds the house swept clean and tidy. It goes off and collects seven other spirits more wicked than itself, and they all come in and settle there; and in the end that person's plight is worse than before."

This passage is substantially the same as its parallel and my expository notes in that section apply equally here. The context is the same, namely conflict between Jesus and the Pharisees though here we find the added warning for individuals in the crowd who heard him. Verse 23 reads, "He who is not with me is against me..." In Luke, reference to the nation [the "generation" of verse 29] is separated from the narrative above by other incidents. One can imagine the spirit saying to itself, "This place is empty [Matthew], has been swept tidy [Matthew and Luke], I need some friends to help me effect entry and inhibit further removal." Accordingly he collects seven friends. In this sense, whether individual or national, the outcome is significantly worse than before.

Parallel in Matthew 12:43-45

> **13:10-13** [Jesus] was teaching in one of the synagogues on the sabbath, and there was a woman there possessed by a spirit that had crippled her for eighteen years. She was bent double and quite unable to stand up straight. When Jesus saw her he called
>
> *apoluo* her and said, "You are *rid* of your trouble", and he laid his hands on her. Immediately she straightened up and began to praise God.

Apoluo in the New Testament is used both in its classical sense of releasing prisoners [as in Mark 15:6-15], acquitting from a charge [Luke 6:37], dispatching people [Mark 6:36], dismissing crowds [Matthew 14:15], releasing people from obligations - debt [Matthew 18:27], life [Luke 2:29], as well as of divorce [Matthew 1:19]. Here its sense is also in the classical tradition, namely being set free from illness.

The references to Jesus laying his hands upon people in connection with the action of healing are few: Matthew 9:18 [parallel Mark 5:23], Mark 6:5, 7:32, 8:23 and here in Luke 13:13. Elsewhere the laying on of hands forms the action of blessing in that it symbolises a mutual sharing in the kingdom of God by one person with another.

The woman's illness is worthy of mention also. Clearly she was perceived to have a very definite spirit identifiable through its effect upon her; she was bound by it into a state of paralysis. Anthony Thiselton in his essay 'Word' in Colin Brown[16] argues that we cannot in the cultural and linguistic translation between New Testament times and our own ignore the fact that people of the day actually considered spirits like this one to have personal reality. Thiselton says, Probably few would follow J.B. Phillips in regarding "ill from some psychological disease" as a correct translation of "possessed by an evil spirit". The reasons for this, he tells us, lie in the very nature of language itself.

	13:14 ... the president of the synagogue, indignant with Jesus
therapeuo	for *healing* on the sabbath, intervened and said to the
therapeuo	congregation, "There are six working days; come and be *cured* on one of them and not on the sabbath."

In his healing on the sabbath Jesus was expressing an imperative will of God to heal [that is, save people] whatever the day. For this reason his sharp exchanges with the president of the synagogue in front of the congregation will have revolved around Jesus' claim [implicit or explicit] to be following God's will rather than that of rabbinical tradition as it perceived God's will.

	13:15-17 The Lord gave him this answer: "What hypocrites you
luo	are!" he said. "Is there a single one of you who does not *loose* his ox or his donkey from its stall and take it out to water on the sabbath? And here is this woman, a daughter of Abraham, who *has been*
deo	*bound* by Satan for eighteen long years: was it not right for her *to*
luo	*be loosed* from her bonds on the sabbath?" At these words all his opponents were covered with confusion, while the mass of the people were delighted at the wonderful things he was doing.

Significant here is the word-play used in near mocking tones by Jesus in the synagogue debate. It was perfectly permissible within Mosaic law to *untie* an animal to water it. Here Jesus was confronted by a woman *bound* in her paralysis by Satan for eighteen years. Should she not be *untied* from this bondage? His question was rhetorical and therefore all the more effective for being so.

	13:32 [Jesus replied] "Go and tell that fox, 'Listen today
ekballo	and tomorrow I shall be *driving out* demons and working
iasis	*cures*; on the third day I reach my goal'."

In the context of rabbinic thought [and not least that of our own day as well] the reference to the fox would mean slyness and in Herod's case a man of no consequence. Clearly Jesus was not to be defeated by Herod for on the third day he will have achieved that salvation of which his work today and tomorrow is the present outworking. With hindsight this can be seen as a resurrection motif though for his first hearers the meaning of the passage would have been a puzzle.

	14:2-4 ... in front of [Jesus] was a man suffering from dropsy,
	and Jesus asked the lawyers and the Pharisees: "Is it permitted
therapeuo	to *heal* people on the sabbath or not?" The Pharisees said
iaomai	nothing. So he took the man, *cured* him, and sent him away.

Once again we find Jesus confronting the established religious leaders of his day in his presentation of the word of God. He did this not only in the manner of someone who spoke in the prophetic tradition but as someone who in himself embodied God's word. As the Son of the Father no one knew the Father as did he, and no one could reveal the Father's will as he could [cf. Matthew 11:27, John 12:49-50].

The connotations of the silence which fell upon the Pharisees when they 'said nothing' was such as to indicate they had been defeated [quietened, *hesychazo*] by an opponent.

	17:12-19 As [Jesus] was entering a village he was met by ten
	men with leprosy. They stood some way off and called out
	to him, "Jesus, Master, take pity on us." When he saw them
	he said, "Go and show yourselves to the priests", and while
katharizo	they were on their way they *were made clean*. One of them,
iaomai	finding himself *cured*, turned back with shouts of praise to
	God. He threw himself down at Jesus's feet and thanked
	him. And he was a Samaritan. At this Jesus said: "Were not
katharizo	all ten *made clean*? The other nine, where are they? Was no
	one found returning to give praise to God except this
	foreigner?" And he said to the man, "Stand up and go on
sozo	your way; your faith has *cured* you."

| | [in the *Authorised Version* it reads: "Thy faith hath made |
| | thee whole".] |

147

Jesus not only felt sorry for the lepers, but offered them the full compassion of God. His actions not only healed [cleansed] their condition but restored to them full ritual purity and, in requirement of the Law, referral was made to the priest who was empowered to pronounce such purity. In the teaching resulting from his healing work the reference to 'being clean', 'pure' *[katharizo]* came to have broader reference - thus, clean, spotless, unsoiled, pure hearts, clean hands and so on. It is the same word which is also in Acts 10:15 and 11:9. Its application to cultic uncleanness is also developed through various connotations of unrighteousness etc. cf. also 2 Cor 7:1, Eph. 5:26, James 4:8, 1 John 1:7, 1:9.

The reference, by Jesus, to the man being a foreigner [the only New Testament use of the word *allogenes*] is interesting. A Samaritan is an Israelite though in Jewish eyes an apostate or heretical Israelite - therefore not a foreigner of another race. He observed Mosaic purity rules, but Jews would suspect him of not observing them properly and, most importantly, would not be in a position to get rid of corpse impurity [the most contagious kind] in the Jerusalem temple [the only way Jews thought one could get rid of corpse impurity, something contracted by everyone whenever they had to deal with a death].[17]

The use of *sozo* can be seen as having the sense of healing the whole person; not only the leprous condition, but also the cultic and religious uncleanness and to add to that the bridging of the barrier of national division. The man was the only one to come [back] to Jesus to give thanks. In this sense *sozo* can mean everything from curing to cleansing to purifying to redeeming and saving. Whether what I am saying here will stand the test of linguistic scrutiny remains for others to test. My purpose in offering this interpretation of the passage is to help widen our appreciation of what healing might mean. I will return to this in a moment.

> **18:35-43** As [Jesus] approached Jericho a blind man sat at the roadside begging. Hearing a crowd going past, he asked what was happening, and was told that Jesus of Nazareth was passing by. Then he called out, "Jesus, Son of David, have pity on me." The people in front of him told him to hold his tongue; but he shouted all the more, "Son of David, have pity on me." Jesus stopped and ordered the man to be brought to him. When he came up Jesus asked him, "What do you want me to do for you?" "Sir, I want my sight back", he answered. Jesus said to him, "Have back your sight; your faith has *healed* you." He recovered his sight instantly and followed Jesus praising God.

sozo

148

Once again the use of *sozo* I would suggest indicates more than the simple healing of a physical complaint. That said, Richard Bauckham has written in correspondence with me, "I must confess I'm not sure what the verbal link between healing and salvation is. It *could* be [eg] that *sozo* in healing miracles means the physical cure, but that the word is meant to encourage the reader to see it as a *sign* of more than just physical cure." And then Bauckham adds, "But I'm not sure."

Parallels in Matthew 20:29-34 in Mark 10:46-52

iaomai   **22:51** But Jesus answered, "Stop! No more of that!" Then he touched the man's ear and *healed* him.

This narrative occurs significantly apart from the main body of healing accounts in Luke's Gospel. Graber and Müller indicate this story is one of those embellished by later addition of detail though recognise that the simplicity of the New Testament accounts contrast with the 'romantically embellished stories' in for example the *Infancy Gospel of Thomas* or in the apocryphal *Acts of the Apostles*.[18]

sozo, sozo   **23:35** The people stood looking on, and their rulers jeered at him: "He *saved* others: now let him *save* himself, if this is God's messiah."

As in 23:37 the context enshrines the paradoxical taunt that if he was the Messiah he ought to be able to effect the saving act which the occasion, *prima facie*, seemed to require. It is the touchstone of Christian faith however that in dying Jesus actually did bring about the saving deed asked for others even if not for himself.

Parallels in Matthew 27:42 and Mark 15:30-31

sozo   **23:39** One of the criminals hanging there taunted him: "Are not you the messiah? *Save* yourself, and us."

Jesus' messianic claims were being questioned on account of his humiliation by death through crucifixion. The use of *sozo* in this verse might refer to healing people - if Jesus could save [in the sense of heal] himself in this situation it would be an ultimate demonstration of the peoples' and rulers' mistaken understanding of his messiahship. Equally *sozo* could refer back to the nature miracles and the saving of the disciples in a storm. Whether the onlookers actually believed that Jesus had saved people in an eschatological sense is dubious, though their taunts could have been in irony. This is the likely context of the taunt by the criminal in 23:39. In any event Jesus did not perform any miracles which would have removed him from the fate of the cross.

Chapter 10 JOHN

3:17 It was not to judge the world that God sent his Son into
sozo   the world, but that through him the world might be *saved*.

As was the case with the first text we considered in Matthew the word *sozo* comes into its own. Although not a healing narrative in the strict sense Jesus' mission, his 'gospel , is to bring salvation to all people. Within this orbit the kingdom of God becomes real for people and healing is known and experienced. cf. also 12:47

4:47-53 When [an officer in the royal service] heard that Jesus had come from Judaea into Galilee, he went to him and
iaomai   begged him to go down and *cure* his son, who was at the point of death. Jesus said to him, "Will none of you ever believe without seeing signs and portents?" The officer pleaded with him, "Sir, come down before my boy dies." "Return
zao   home," said Jesus; "your son *will live*." The man believed what Jesus said and started for home. While he was on his way down his servants met him with the news that his child
zao, echo   was going *to live*. So he asked them at what time he *had begun*
kompsoteron   *to recover*, and they told him, "It was at one o clock yesterday afternoon that the fever left him." The father realised that this was the time at which Jesus had said to him, your son
zao   *will live*, and he and all his household became believers.

It seems there is within this passage an ascending process of faith. Firstly the officer, clearly anxious about his son, begs Jesus to cure him. This is the instinctive cry of a parent on behalf of a sick child. It is, one could say, a 'first level' faith. It arises from the heart at a crisis. Jesus persists and asks why signs are demanded for faith. Such discourse only serves to make the officer more urgent in his entreaties. Upon hearing Jesus' word of healing the officer's faith rises to a second level. He trusts what Jesus says and turns for home. Whilst travelling homeward servants, meeting the officer, confirm that the boy's recovery began at the time Jesus spoke the word of healing. A third level of faith then came about as the officer and his household believed. Implicit in the narrative is the officer's testimony of Jesus' words and actions as well as the family's experience of the cure.

    This is the second of the seven Johannine signs by means of which Jesus revealed his glory. The first was the 'nature miracle' whereby it is recorded that Jesus turned water into wine.

Parallels in Matthew 8:5-13, Luke 7:1-10

5:1-9 Some time later, Jesus went up to Jerusalem for one of the Jewish festivals. Now at the Sheep Gate in Jerusalem there is a pool whose Hebrew name is Bethesda. It has five colonnades and in them lay a great number of sick people, blind, lame, and paralysed. Among them was a man who had been crippled for thirty-eight years. Jesus saw him lying there, and knowing that

hygies   he had been ill a long time he asked him, "Do you want *to get well?*" "Sir," he replied, "I have no one to put me in the pool when the water is disturbed; while I am getting there, someone else steps into the pool before me." Jesus answered, "Stand up,

hygies   take your bed and walk." The man *recovered* instantly; he took up his bed, and began to walk.

At 5:3 some MSS add: "... waiting for the disturbance of the water." Other MSS also add: "... for from time to time an angel came down into the pool and stirred up the water. The first to

hygies   plunge in after this disturbance *recovered* from whatever disease [the sense is presented as 'unwholesome affliction'] had afflicted him."

Chapter Five of John's Gospel contains a fleet of healing narratives with conversation and teaching. These are heralded by the words of 5:1, "Some time later, Jesus went up ..." and closed at 6:1, "Some time later, Jesus withdrew ..." Alone amongst the Gospels John seems to have Jesus as a periodic visitor to Jerusalem [cf also, 2:13ff, 7:10ff and 12:12ff].

We are told in Nehemiah 3:1 that the Sheep Gate, on the east side of the city, was rebuilt by "Eliashib the high priest and his fellow priests". Modern day excavations reveal this to be between 165-220 feet wide and 315 feet long. With a depth throughout of sixteen metres a lame person would have needed assistance not only to get in the pool but to remain safe once in it. Four porticoes [arched walkways] bordered the pool on each side and a central portico divided the two basins of the pool. The basins were for male/female use respectively. At the time of the events to which this narrative refers the porticoes would be quite new having only relatively recently been added by Herod. Access to the pool would be by the corner stairs. It would appear the water had healing powers; hence the presence of the sick in seemingly substantial numbers. H. Müller offers the view that the pool would likely have been disturbed in the way described here by an intermittent spring. Whilst there was in fact no spring at the pool pipework leading to it has been found. If the story is taken at face value it is given that an illness of thirty eight years is reversed by immediate action.

therapeuo   **5:10-15** So the Jews said to the man who had been *cured* "it is the sabbath. It is against the law for you to carry your

hygies   bed." He answered, "The man who *cured* me, he told me,

151

'Take up your bed and walk'." They asked him, "Who is this man who told you to take it up and walk?" But the man *iaomai* who had been *cured* did not know who it was; for the place was crowded and Jesus had slipped away. A little later Jesus found him in the temple and said to him, "Now that you are *hygies* *well*, give up your sinful ways, or something worse may happen to you." The man went off and told the Jews that it *hygies* was Jesus who had *cured* him.

The literal interpretation of the Mosaic Law as given by the *halachah* [legal interpretation] is offered here as the normative stance of the Jews who spoke to the man who had been healed by the pool of Bethesda. Jeremiah 17:21-22 gives content to the Deuteronomic law of Exodus 20:8-11 [cf Deuteronomy 5:12-15]. On the Sabbath a person should not be carrying his bed around. However, by healing on the sabbath and by telling the man to stand, take his bed and walk, Jesus is quite explicitly placing the authority of his own teaching above that of the Jewish custom. It is this authority to which the man appeals by way of defence against accusation of breaking the sabbath. Jesus' own defence revolved around the continuing work of his Father in whose work he is an obedient Son.

Jesus tells the man to give up his sinful ways now he has been made well. In doing this Jesus is breaking any given necessary link between sin and health. Clearly the man has been made well even though it would seem his sin remains. However it would also seem that the healing could be undone by the man who, if he does not stop sinning, will court further and worse calamity.

5:25 In very truth I tell you, the time is coming, indeed it is already here, when the dead shall hear the voice of the Son *zao* of God, and those who hear *shall come to life*.

Notice how the two verb tenses interrelate. The time *is* already here when the dead *shall* hear, and those who hear *shall* come to life. Charles Talbert, in his commentary lists the locations in John's Gospel where emphasis is on the present possession of eternal life and the assurance of future salvation in the context of present response.[2] For John this is the beginning of the Christian life not its completion. Only in final victory over death [cf. verses 28-29] is this completion made real.

6:1-2 Some time later Jesus withdrew to the farther shore of the sea of Galilee [or Tiberias], and a large crowd of people followed him *astheneo* because they had seen the signs he performed in *healing* the sick.

Following this narrative are two significant nature miracles - the feeding of the crowd with five loaves and two fish and Jesus' walking on the water. The verses combine both to close the preceding narrative and set the scene for the succeeding one. Those whom Jesus healed are given as lacking in strength.

> **9:1-5** As he went on his way Jesus saw a man who had been blind from birth. His disciples asked him "Rabbi, why was this man born blind? Who sinned, this man or his parents?" "It is not that he or his parents sinned," Jesus answered; "he was born blind so that God's power might be displayed in curing him. While daylight lasts we must carry on the work of him who sent me; night is coming, when no one can work. While I am in the world I am the light of the world."

Thus begins the longest healing narrative [if one includes the associated interrogations] not only of the comparatively few which there are in John's Gospel but also of the four gospels. I will deal with it here in sections relevant to the teaching each contains.

Following Mosaic teaching [Exodus 20:5 and Deuteronomy 5:9, also 2 Kings 5:27] the disciples asked whether the parents of this man had sinned in such a way as to cause his blindness. If it was not they who had sinned then it would seem the only alternative open to view that it was the man himself who, since the blindness had been from birth, would have therefore sinned before birth. Jesus, in reply, rejects sin as the cause of his blindness though the text could be read as saying God caused the blindness, thus "he was born blind so that God's power might be displayed". However, whatever reading might be construed the condition is present as a given, an unavoidable fact. It therefore is a situation in which the glory of God can be displayed. In this regard John 11:4 might also be considered. Jesus had turned the question around from, "Why is this man blind?" to "What is the purpose of his blindness?"

> **9:6-7** With these words he spat on the ground and made a paste with the spittle; he spread it on the man's eyes, and said to him, "Go and wash in the pool of Siloam." [The name means 'Sent'.] The man went off and washed and came back able to see.

An intriguing metaphorical interpretation can be made of the application of clay to the eyes of a blind man for healing. One can imagine few substances more opaque than wet clay yet by using it as a poultice over unseeing eyes the man is able to see and so God's glory is revealed. Jesus is performing no strange action here. W.L. Lane[3] cites the admixture of spittle and the laying on of hands as widespread healing practice in the Jewish world of Jesus. Jesus, as light of the world [verse 5] gives light to the darkened eyes of the man born blind.

9:8-12 His neighbours and those who were accustomed to see him begging said, "Is not this the man who used to sit and beg?" some said, "Yes, it is." Others said, "No, but it is someone like him." He himself said, "I am the man". They asked him, "How were your eyes opened?" He replied, "The man called Jesus made a paste and smeared my eyes with it, and told me to go to Siloam and wash. So I went and washed," and found I could see. "Where is he?" they asked. "I do not know", he said.

John's gospel uses the word 'see' in three senses. First, the simple and quite ordinary usage here in verse 8 applies to ordinary sense perception. John the Baptist's vision of the descent of the dove [1:32] is the second sense and may well be interpreted in as physical a form as the first. The third sense is denoted by for example the seeing which comes from faith. Thus the glory of Jesus is revealed to those in faith by means of signs and wonders [1:14 and 2:11].[4] The significance of the narrative which is to follow is heightened by a reminder of the man's humiliating posture when begging. When one was at table in Jesus day the verb would be 'to recline'. The word for 'opened' has the further connotation of gaining access to God.

9:13-17 The man who had been blind was brought before the Pharisees. As it was a sabbath day when Jesus made the paste and opened his eyes, the Pharisees too asked him how he had gained his sight. The man told them, "He spread a paste on my eyes; then I washed, and now I can see." Some of the Pharisees said, "This man cannot be from God; he does not keep the sabbath." Others said, "How could such signs come from a sinful man?" So they took different sides. Then they continued to question him: "What have you to say about him? It was your eyes he opened." He answered, "He is a prophet."

The questioning of John 9:15 stands in marked contrast to the disciples' request of 9:2. Verse 2 stands as the only occurrence in John of the disciples asking something of Jesus by way of standard inquiry. Otherwise *erotao*, has implications of doubting, sceptical interrogation. It would seem the Pharisees were divided about the authority of Jesus. Such was his ambiguity.

9:18-23 The Jews would not believe that the man had been blind and had gained his sight, until they had summoned his parents and questioned them: "Is this your son? Do you say that he was born blind? How is it that he can see now?" The parents replied, "We know that he is our son, and that he was born blind. But how it is that he can now see, or who opened his eyes, we do not know. Ask him; he is of age; let him speak for himself." His parents gave this answer because they were afraid of the Jews;

for the Jewish authorities had already agreed that anyone who acknowledged Jesus as Messiah should be banned from the synagogue. That is why the parents said, he is of age; ask him.

In contrast to the given divergence of Pharisaic opinion about the authority of Jesus in 13-17 the Jews it seems now turn their disbelief to the man who was the subject of the healing. It seems also to be the case that even though the parents could vouch for both the blindness from birth and the healing, their fear of some form of retributive action by the Pharisees was great. The use of the word *anablepo*, meaning to see again, is slightly confusing in that having been born blind the man had not seen before. In this context it has messianic connotations for *anablepo* is associated also with, for example, the opening of the eyes of Saul of Tarsus and again in the message Jesus gave to John the Baptist concerning his messianic work [cf. Matthew 11:5, Luke 7:22]. God's investiture of Eliakim promised in Isaiah 22:22 is significant here. The key of David's palace was to be placed on his shoulder symbolising Eliakim's authority to open and shut as the agent of God. Matthew 16:19 echoes this as does Revelation 5:2-9. John gives the earthly Jesus the authority to open. This factor [known only too well by the Pharisees and probably the parents] gives clear poignancy to their interrogation.

> **9:24-29** So for the second time they summoned the man who had been blind, and said, "Speak the truth before God. We know that this man is a sinner." "Whether or not he is a sinner, I do not know," the man replied. "All I know is this: I was blind and now I can see." "What did he do to you?" "I have told you already," he retorted, "but you took no notice. Why do you want to hear it again? Do you also want to become his disciples?" Then they became abusive. "You are that man's disciple," they said, "but we are disciples of Moses. We know that God spoke to Moses, but as for this man, we do not know where he comes from."

The significance for faith of having one's eyes opened begins to emerge in this narrative. After demanding of the man that he speak the truth he seeks to respond fairly and honestly. How could he know whether or not Jesus is a sinner? But for him the fact of his healing is undeniable. With the healing has come the opening of his eyes in the sense of a commitment to be a disciple of Jesus. With mischievous irony the man asks if the repetition of his testimony will bring them to discipleship of Jesus. At the background of all this is of course the question of Jesus' authority. The Pharisees appealed to the authority of Moses as the source of the revelation of God which they articulate. The challenge before them is a healing miracle which attests Jesus as someone in their own day whose word and work is the Word of God. It was to this that the man's eyes were opened and to this vision he now challenges the Pharisees. Verse 30 indicates his clear astonishment of their failure to recognise the implications of the miraculous cure which has come to him.

> **9:30-34** The man replied, "How extraordinary! Here is a man who has opened my eyes, yet you do not know where he comes from! We know that God does not listen to sinners; he listens to anyone who is devout and obeys his will. To open the eyes of a man born blind - that is unheard of since time began. If this man was not from God he could do nothing." "Who are you to lecture us?" they retorted. "You were born and bred in sin." Then they turned him out.

The eviction from the synagogue in v.34 was the very fate feared by the man's parents in v.22. The word used for turning the man out of the synagogue is *ekballo*, a word which we have found to have theological significance when used in the New Testament for the expulsion of demons. The picture of turning the man out of the synagogue was such as to ensure he would not be seeking to return.

> **9:35-38** Hearing that they had turned him out, Jesus found him and asked, "Have you faith in the Son of Man?" The man answered, "Tell me who he is, sir, that I may put my faith in him." "You have seen him," said Jesus; "indeed, it is he who is speaking to you." "Lord, I believe," he said, and fell on his knees before him.

The man's response to Jesus in v.36 is arguably rhetorical. It seems closely parallel to the question of John the Baptist conveyed to Jesus, "Are you the one or are we to expect another?" The chapter goes on to relate the judgment of Jesus in the context of those who are blind and to those who are not. There are strong echoes of the encounter of the risen Jesus with Thomas in John 20:24-29.

> **11:1-44** There was a man named Lazarus who had fallen ill. His home was at Bethany, the village of Mary and her sister Martha. This Mary, whose brother Lazarus had fallen ill, was the woman who anointed the Lord with ointment and wiped his feet with her hair. The sisters sent a message to him: "Sir, you should know that your friend lies ill." When Jesus heard this he said, "This illness is not to end in death; through it God's glory is to be revealed and the Son of God glorified." Therefore, though he loved Martha and her sister and Lazarus, he stayed where he was for two days after hearing of Lazarus' illness.
>
> He then said to his disciples, "Let us go back to Judaea." 'Rabbi," his disciples said, "it is not long since the Jews there were wanting to stone you. Are you going there again?" Jesus replied, "Are there not twelve hours of daylight? Anyone can walk in the daytime without

stumbling, because he has this world's light to see by. But if he walks after nightfall he stumbles, because the light fails him."

After saying this he added, "Our friend Lazarus has fallen asleep, but I shall go and wake him." The disciples said, "Master, if he is sleeping he will recover." Jesus had been speaking of Lazarus' death, but they thought that he meant natural sleep. Then Jesus told them plainly: "Lazarus is dead. I am glad for your sake that I was not there; for it will lead you to believe. But let us go to him." Thomas, called 'the Twin', said to his fellow disciples, "Let us also go and die with him."

On his arrival Jesus found that Lazarus had already been four days in the tomb. Bethany was just under two miles from Jerusalem, and many of the Jews had come from the city to visit Martha and Mary and condole with them about their brother. As soon as Martha heard that Jesus was on his way, she went to meet him, and left Mary sitting at home.

Martha said to Jesus, "Lord, if you had been here my brother would not have died. Even now I know that God will grant you whatever you ask of him." Jesus said, "Your brother will rise again." "I know that he will rise again", said Martha, "at the resurrection on the last day." Jesus said, "I am the resurrection and the life. Whoever has faith in me shall live, even though he dies; and no one who lives and has faith in me shall ever die. Do you believe this?" "I do, Lord," she answered; "I believe that you are the Messiah, the son of God who was to come into the world."

So saying she went to call her sister Mary and, taking her aside, she said, "The Master is here and is asking for you." As soon as Mary heard this she rose and went to him. Jesus had not yet entered the village, but was still at the place where Martha had met him. When the Jews who were in the house condoling with Mary saw her hurry out, they went after her, assuming that she was going to the tomb to weep there.

Mary came to the place where Jesus was, and as soon as she saw him she fell at his feet and said, "Lord, if you had been here my brother would not have died." When Jesus saw her weeping and the Jews who had come with her weeping, he was moved with indignation and deeply distressed. "Where have you laid him?" he asked. They replied, "Come and see." Jesus wept. The Jews said, "How dearly he must have loved him!" But some of them said, "Could not this man, who opened the blind man's eyes, have done something to keep Lazarus from dying?"

Jesus, again deeply moved, went to the tomb. It was a cave, with a stone placed against it. Jesus said, "Take away the stone." Martha, the dead man's sister, said to him, "Sir, by now there will be a stench; he has been there four days." Jesus said, "Did I not tell you that if you have faith you will see the glory of God?" Then they removed the stone.

Jesus looked upwards and said, "Father, I thank you for hearing me. I know that you always hear me, but I have spoken for the sake of the people standing round, that they may believe it was you who sent me."

deuro exo   Then he raised his voice in a great cry: "Lazarus, *come*
exerchomai   *out.*" The dead man *came* out, his hands and feet bound with linen bandages, his face wrapped in a cloth. Jesus said,
luo, aphiemi   "*Loose him; let him go.*"

The passage then goes on to point how some witnesses placed their faith in Jesus whilst others reported the incident to the aggrieved chief priests and Pharisees. The passage should also be seen in context with the following two passages from John 12:1-2, 17-19.

Charles Talbert has a fascinating commentary on this passage. What follows draws heavily though not exclusively on Talbert's commentary. In context this resuscitation narrative is not dissimilar to others in Jewish history [1 Kings 17:17-24], 2 Kings 4:8-37; 13:20-21], to narratives in non-biblical sources as well as to others in the Gospels [Matthew 9:18-26 and the parallels in Mark 5:21-43 and Luke 8:40-56; Luke 7:11-17; Acts 9:36-43; 20:7-12]. There is no common theme linking any or all of these [excepting of course the parallels] except that they explicitly speak of the death of someone and his or her subsequent resuscitation. The person will ultimately have to face death a second time and this time, presumably, its reality will be permanent. It could well be the case that there is a resurrection motif operating in this narrative - a 'from death to life story', and it could well be the case that the story is a metaphor of the resurrection. Such an interpretation however would pose for us the problem of how to interpret the very physical nature of the narrative's form. Remaining true to the text may well require us to wrestle with the issue of its facticity and of its presentation as an event in the life of the Word made flesh. When, in prayer, Jesus brings Lazarus back to this life he does so as one in constant communion with the Father not (as in our case) as a petition interrupting the normal flux and flow of life. From this perspective we should not offer our own non-experience of the resuscitation of a corpse as the base-line from which to make an assessment of the historical nature of the work of Jesus. If Jesus did raise Lazarus from the dead he did so because he was the Word made flesh. There is no other reason. By way of aside we might ponder how fearful most people in history have been of death. It could be that by subjecting Lazarus to a second experience of the same event Jesus did not, as we might crudely put it, do him any favours!

The purpose of the resuscitation is clearly given; it is for "the glory of God". Its function, as verses 17-19 of chapter 12 indicates is declaratory and evangelistic. Jesus' behaviour, his actions, have all the outward appearances of self-centredness when judged by a 20th/21st century yardstick. He does not race immediately to the home of Martha and Mary either to offer solace nor yet to rescue Lazarus from his grave. By modern standards hardly an action filled with pastoral tact. I remember once hearing the atheist philosopher Anthony Flew give a paper in which he compared episodes such as this [also the disciples selfishness in leaving their livelihood to follow Jesus] with those who seek and join modern day cults leaving home and family in order to do so. Flew's thesis was based on the view that if modern day cult followers are deemed wrong by Christians, Christians have no biblical authority upon which to found their judgment. The considered Christian perspective sees Jesus encourage others to follow his own example of putting the demands of God first before even family, friends and their livelihoods. The theory is exemplary but the practice difficult if not impossible. One is reminded of the camel and the needle's eye.

Talbert gives the structure of the passage: firstly the problem is stated [vv. 1-3], then there is Jesus' response [vv. 4-16]. The miracle narrative flows in two consecutive cycles which Talbert cites respectively as the Martha and Mary cycles,[5] thus:

Martha Cycle	Mary Cycle
Occasion: Jesus comes [vv.17,20a]	Occasion: Jesus calls [v.28]
Mourners [vv.18-19]	Mourners [vv. 30-31]
Martha goes to meet him [v.20b]	Mary goes to him [vv.29, 32a]
Martha says: "Lord, if you had been here" [vv.21-22]	Mary says: Lord, if you had been here" [v.32]
Dialogue [vv.23-27]	Dialogue and action [vv.34-44]

In her dialogue with Jesus Martha affirms belief in the resurrection as per Pharisaic teaching, not that of the Sadducees, and in distinction from the Essenes' teaching of the immortality of the soul. Jesus' promise is not just for new life in a general resurrection of the dead as Martha is attesting but the specific resuscitation of Lazarus' corpse. Mary is however more demanding in her approach to Jesus. In response Jesus is very deeply moved with a mix of emotions in which the translation can equally well mean 'angered'. Jesus' weeping [which must always be distinguished from the wailing of hired mourners] generates the mixed response of some being moved by his sadness and pity whilst others saw it as an excuse to taunt.

The soul was given as residing near the body until the third day. Therefore by the fourth day the likelihood of its repossession would have vanished totally. Such was the emphasis of Jesus upon his power in response to his mission as Word made flesh.

egeiro | **12:1-2** Six days before the Passover festival Jesus came to Bethany, the home of Lazarus whom he had *raised* from the dead. They gave a supper in his honour, at which Martha served, and Lazarus was among the guests with Jesus.

Amongst other motifs we have here the recognition that Jesus is Lord of all life, both of the living and of those who have died seen here in the person of Lazarus who though once dead is so no longer. Tests such as this are seen as part of the fulfilment of the prophetic promise of Isaiah 35:5ff and 61:1ff. With the raising of the dead we are given also the miracles of healing and the exorcism of evil spirits. If my own understanding of the passages holds true we may take it that a ministry of healing is a normal and natural part of the work of the church. Exorcism follows as a rare but periodically necessary ministry. The revivification of corpses has no such place in our ministry except perhaps in clinical treatment and prayer with those near death.

phoneo | **12:17-19** The people who were present when he *called* Lazarus out of the tomb and raised him from the dead kept telling what they had seen and heard. That is why the crowd went to meet him: they had heard of this sign that he had performed. The Pharisees said to one another, "You can see we are getting nowhere; all the world has gone after him!"

The effect of the raising of Lazarus is only too plain to Jesus' critics. There are a number of advocates who would wish to propose the resuscitation of corpses is legitimate work today. Against this I would argue that given the assurance of life after death offered by Jesus we have no business seeking to remove those who now enjoy this state back to the frailty and finitude of life within the 'mortal coil'. What I say here however is good theory for those accounts given in the life of Jesus situated before the crucifixion and resurrection. My words are tested somewhat by the revivification accounts involving corpses in Acts.

iaomai | **12:40** "He has blinded their eyes and dulled their minds, lest they should see with their eyes and perceive with their minds, and turn to me and *heal* them."

This verse is based on Isaiah 6:10. The consequence of not accepting ['hearing'] the message of Jesus is a hardening of the heart. A 'turning' [in this case *epistrepho*] will effect the necessary healing of such hardening. The Hebrew for heal is *rapha*.

Parallels: Matthew 13:10-15, Mark 4:10ff., Luke 8:9f., Acts 28:26-27

sozo | **12:47** But if anyone hears my words and disregards them, I am not his judge; I have come not to judge the world, but to *save* the world.
See my comment on John 3:17.

Chapter 11   THE ACTS OF THE APOSTLES

3:1-10   One day at three in the afternoon, the hour of prayer, Peter and John were on their way up to the temple. Now a man who had been a cripple from birth used to be carried there and laid every day by the temple gate called Beautiful to beg from people as they went in. When he saw Peter and John on their way into the temple, he asked for alms. They both fixed their eyes on him, and Peter said, "Look at us." Expecting a gift from them the man was all attention. Peter said, "I have no silver or gold; but what I have I give you: in the name of Jesus Christ of Nazareth, get up and walk." Then, grasping him by the right hand he helped him up; and at once his feet and ankles grew strong; he sprang to his feet, and started to walk. He entered the temple with them, leaping and praising God as he went. Everyone saw him walking and praising God, and when they recognized him as the man who used to sit begging at Beautiful Gate they were filled with wonder and amazement at what had happened to him.

The John being referred to is John, son of Zebedee. Both he and Peter were within the inner circle of Jesus' disciples during his life time and were leaders in the Jerusalem Christian community after Jesus' resurrection. It is in Jerusalem, indeed in the Temple itself, where the historical life and work of Jesus now begins to find expression in the work and teaching of the disciples who accompanied him. Jesus' continuing work was beginning from Jerusalem [cf Luke 24:47] as Jesus had indicated it should. In accordance with much that we found in the gospels a healing miracle is here accompanied by the authoritative word of teaching. It is maybe significant that Peter's actions indicate perhaps his foremost wish that the man should beg no longer but rather that he should be raised from his lowly state. When Peter acts he does so "in the name of Jesus Christ of Nazareth". So must we. The man's response is seemingly one of ecstatic praise and thanksgiving.

Josephus tells us that the given times for sacrificial offering in the temple were "in the morning and at the ninth hour", this last being around 3pm, the time varying throughout the year depending on times of dawn and sunset.[1] This reflects the early Christian ritual attendance in the temple as they followed the duties and practices related to the observance of purification and holiness principles.

The intensity of the gazing is indicated by the use of the word *atenizo*. Three times in the Acts of the Apostles the word is used in connection with miracles, here as well as in 14:9. The other location is 13:9 where it is linked to Paul's curse.

> **3:11** While he still clung to Peter and John all the people came running in astonishment towards them in Solomon's Portico, as it is called.

iaomi
> [The *Authorised Version* reads: And as the lame man which was *healed* held Peter and John ...

The verse and those following relate to the healing of the cripple in 3: 1-10. Solomon's Portico was a great colonnade of pillars along one side of the court of the Gentiles in the Temple. This portico was a principal locus for teaching. The sense of 'clung to' *[krateo]* is metaphorical. It means he did not leave them; he 'stuck' to them.

This healing gave the occasion for Peter's address in the Temple and the questioning of him and the authority upon which he acted. The preaching was a crucial [and, if we are to follow C.H. Dodd, an 'obscure'] part of the apostolic kerygma.

The *Authorised Version* translated the [so-called] Received Text which follows at this point a very inferior manuscript reading. The *Revised English Bible* in common with others since the *Revised Version* has not used this form of the Greek text.[2] It was issued in 1550 for the New Testament by Stephanus and based on late texts from the Byzantine era.

holokleria
> **3:16** The name of Jesus, by awakening faith, has given strength to this man whom you see and know, and this faith has made him *completely well* as you can all see.

The problems of this text surround principally the translation of complex material. In the last clause the meaning could be either 'the faith that is through him [Jesus]' or 'the faith that is through it [his name]'. Though the adjective *holokleros* occurs in 1 Thessalonians 5:23 and James 1:4, the noun *holokleria* is a New Testament *hapax legomenon*, that is it occurs once in the New Testament. *Holokleria* translates as wholeness, completeness.

sozo

hygies
> **4:9-10** [Peter to the rulers and elders] "... if it is about help given to a sick man that we are being questioned today, and the means by which he was *cured*, this is our answer to all of you and to all the people of Israel: it was by the name of Jesus Christ of Nazareth, whom you crucified, and whom God raised from the dead; through him this man stands here before you *fit and well*.

In September 1995 I was privileged to lead a pilgrimage from Saint Andrew's Church, St Andrews to the Holy Land. During one of the excursions our Israeli guide turned to me and quite spontaneously asked if I knew anything about the crucifixion. My immediate thought was to answer in terms of its theological significance - why Jesus had to die and so on. But the guide's question it turned out was much more basic.[3]

He wanted to know what I knew about the history and method of crucifixion. It has to be said that I hadn't thought of these before. He went on to detail how Hannibal had brought crucifixion as a ritual form of capital punishment into the Roman Empire from North Africa. How, as a punishment, it also carried with it particular connotations of insult and abhorrence. Those who were to be crucified were the lowest of the low of the scum of the earth. Cicero, for example, is at a loss to find any word in the Roman language which could describe the total sense of outrage which would accompany the crucifixion of a Roman citizen.

The person who was hanged on a tree, the person who was crucified, was accursed in the Jewish teaching of the Old Testament as well. These words come from Deuteronomy 21:22, "When someone is convicted of a capital offence and is put to death, and you hang him on a gibbet, his body must not remain there overnight; it must be buried on the same day. Anyone hanged is accursed in the sight of God, and the land which the Lord your God is giving you as your holding must not be polluted."

Since returning from that Holy Land Pilgrimage I have discovered that the introduction of crucifixion into the Roman Empire was more complicated than our guide explained. But he was correct when he pointed me towards the total sense of shame and curse that crucifixion had as a punishment. It wasn't only that crucifixion was a cruel death - it was a socially abhorrent death.

Now, we know that Jesus was crucified. In other words he took to his death the increasing social sense that he was a pariah, an outcast from the depths of society. And yet in spite of the socially insulting manner of his death, the Christian believers in the early church took the manner of Jesus' death to be a blessing upon them. They turned upside down the very shame of crucifixion and made it their greatest glory.

Galatians 3:13 says, "Christ bought us freedom from the curse of the law by coming under the curse for our sake; for Scripture says, 'Cursed is everyone who is hanged on a gibbet'." And then also from Hebrews 12:2, "For the sake of the joy that lay ahead of him, he endured the cross, ignoring its disgrace, and has taken his seat at the right hand of the throne of God." But perhaps most famously of all we have these words from Paul, in 1 Corinthians 2:3, "I resolved that while I was with you I would not claim to know anything but Jesus Christ - Christ nailed to the cross."

Not for Jesus the calm of a Socratic draught of hemlock, or even the speed of stoning. But the ritual humiliation of capital punishment reserved for the lowest of the low.

What a scene change, what a transformation therefore in the minds of the believers in the very earliest church that they should begin to acknowledge this worst form of punishment as totally fitting for the Messiah.

Something of their attitude has come down to us today - I have often given to girls, as a confirmation gift, a gold cross. The gold cross is a sanitised version of that ancient blood-encrusted stake and cross-piece so abhorred by Cicero and yet so gloriously adopted by the early church. Nicky Gumbel in his ALPHA course draws attention to the paradox that whilst we are prepared to wear a cross we would not so readily wear an electric chair about our necks.

Another relatively recent example comes to mind from the Sheffield Diocese of the Church of England. Originally the Nine O'Clock service had been part of a highly commendable process of growth within the church of St. Thomas, Crookes. In due course the service moved from its parent church, and with its own leadership set up its base within a local community centre albeit still under the overall jurisdiction of the Diocese. What emerged in the 1990's was an ultra-modern [often described as post-modern] liturgy called the Planetary Mass. Very sadly, what had begun as a real visionary growth point came to lose its direction. The Planetary Mass, with God's creation as the explicit intention for the eucharist, was exploited and given a legitimising vocabulary to justify any amount of abuse and manipulation within the Nine O'Clock Service leadership.

It seems to me that clergy go off the rails, and take other people with them, when they forget that at the heart of the Christian faith is the ritual humiliation of the cross. Christ died to rescue us from our sins. He did not die to excuse our sinfulness.

That lesson is a hard one for many to hear for the road to sinfulness is a fast track whereas the redemption from sin requires the response of personal discipline and open acceptance of what Jesus has done for each of us, you, me, all of us.

His death was no ordinary death. As a believing Jew Jesus knew the curse which death on a cross carried with it. Small wonder he is recorded as having shouted, "My God, My God why have you forsaken me?" His sense of being abandoned was real, and his total estrangement from God was real. It had to be. Nothing else would enable him to plummet to our depths and then by those self-same tortured arms lift us with him to the Father's glory.

therapeuo   **4:14** ... with the man who had been *cured* standing in full view beside [Peter and John] they had nothing to say in reply.

The context for this verse is the healing in 3:1-10. With the recipient of the healing and the ready testimony of the apostles to hand, the boldness of Peter and John could not be gainsaid.

iasis   **4:22** The man upon whom this miracle of *healing* had been performed was over forty years old.

Except perhaps to remark that the man's illness had been significantly longstanding there is nothing noteworthy here to attract commentary.

eis iasin   **4:30** Stretch out your hand *to heal* and cause signs and portents to be done through the name of your holy servant Jesus.

The context here is a prayer of thanksgiving supplication to God after the release of Peter and John from the temple authorities. This verse is taken from the prayer which was offered to God in this way. Interesting perhaps is the comparison between Peter reaching out his hands to lift the lame man forward in healing and the petition to God to stretch out his hand to heal and effect signs and portents in the name of Jesus.

5:15-16 ... the sick were carried out into the streets and laid there on beds and stretchers, so that at least Peter's shadow might fall on one or another as he passed by; and the people from the towns round Jerusalem flocked in, bringing those

therapeuo   who were ill or harassed by unclean spirits, and all were *cured*.

The potential for artefacts to be seen as having healing effects is seen also in Acts 19:12. The word 'overshadow' *[episkiazo]* finds its place elsewhere in the New Testament with especial reference to God's glory being present. The locations are Matthew 17:5, Mark 9:7, Luke 9:34 [the Transfiguration parallels] and fourthly at Luke 1:35. Here in Acts as in the other locations God's *shekinah*, his overshadowing power and majesty, is placed in a particular locus at a particular time for a particular purpose.[4]

Colin Brown[5] identifies the eschatology of Luke [and therefore of Acts] to be within a two stage manifestation of God's kingdom as present and future. This is linked with the activity of God's Holy Spirit. This is also seen in the following narrative beginning at 8:7 and running up to verse 29. By way of comparison he sees Matthew's eschatological understanding as coupled with the church.

8:7 In many cases of possession the unclean spirits came out *therapeuo* with a loud cry, and many paralysed and crippled folk were *cured.*

The context of this verse is the spread of the gospel to Samaritan territory where, as elsewhere in Acts, exorcisms and the healing of lame and paralysed people figure prominently.

The account in Acts 8:9-13 which I am choosing not to include here is interesting in that [along with Acts 19:13-20] the power of the Holy Spirit is being compared and contrasted with spiritual power implicitly given as from other sources than God. Even though in the Acts 19 passage the name of Jesus is used it would seem that the invocation is used falsely claiming to have special skills.

9:12 "[Saul] has had a vision of a man named Ananias coming *anablepo* in and laying hands on him to *restore his sight.*"

Significant in this verse is our appreciation of Saul's vision. *Horama* refers to Saul's inner sight that Ananias would come to him with healing. *Horama* gives the impression of having some transcendent, transfiguring or supernatural effect. At one level this relates to the healing of his temporary blindness but at another level, as circumstances were to unfold, it also was the occasion of the sealing of Saul's commissioning as an apostle. There is nothing in the New Testament which speaks of visions of the risen Christ in dreams though the gospels have instances of the visions of angels in connection with, for example, the coming of Jesus [Luke 2:11] and the temptations in the desert [Matthew 4:11]. There are however other accounts of visions given by God at Acts 9:10 and 10:3. Another may be found at 2 Corinthians 12:1 where the word used is *optasia*, rather than *horama* as here in Acts.

9:17-19 So Ananias went and, on entering the house, laid his hands on him and said, "Saul, my brother, the Lord Jesus, who appeared to you on your way here, has sent me to you so *anablepo* that you may *recover your sight* and be filled with the Holy Spirit." Immediately it was as if scales had fallen from his eyes, *anablepo* and he *regained his sight*. He got up and was baptised...

The general application to all Christians of being filled with the Holy Spirit is applied here to Saul as a particular individual. This gives emphasis to much of what I said in earlier chapters when I argued that whilst the gift of healing is something granted to all Christians it is nevertheless a specific gift given to some in particular. There is no contradiction in this, both are part of God's given reality.

Epitithemi tas cheiras refers to the action of laying on of hands in connection with healing [Matthew 9:18, Mark 5:23, 6:5, 7:32, 8:23, Luke 13:13 and Acts 28:8]. The phrase is also used in the blessing of children in Matthew 19:13 and 15. In the context of Acts 9:17 it relates to the bestowing of the Holy Spirit upon which Saul was baptised forthwith.

iaomai
anistemi
anistemi
epistrepho

9:33-35 [At Lydda Peter] found a man named Aeneas who had been bedridden with paralysis for eight years. Peter said to him, "Aeneas, Jesus Christ *cures* you; *get up* and make your bed!" and immediately he *stood up*. All who lived in Lydda and Sharon saw him; and they *turned* to the Lord.

The man's condition was clearly chronic and in all likelihood progressively debilitating. The healing is carried out by Peter but the source of the healing is explicitly given to be in the presence of Jesus Christ. *Anistemi* is a weak form of reference which may relate not only to resurrection but also in other contexts to the raising of the offspring of a dead relative. *Epistrepho* is not infrequently used to describe the outcome of evangelistic endeavour and demonstrates a once and for all turning to the Lord.

Though not relevant to these verses I must record the constant encouragement I find in 9:31 that whilst the church was left in peace it built up its strength and grew in numbers under the tutelage of the Holy Spirit.

9:36-42 In Joppa there was a disciple named Tabitha [in Greek, Dorcas, meaning 'Gazelle'], who filled her days with acts of kindness and charity. At that time she fell ill and died; and they washed her body and laid it in a room upstairs. As Lydda was near Joppa, the disciples, who had heard that Peter was there, sent two men to him with the urgent request, "Please come over to us without delay." At once Peter went off with them. When he arrived he was taken up to the room, and all the widows came and stood round him in tears, showing him the shirts and coats that Dorcas used to make while she was with them. Peter sent them all outside, and knelt down and prayed; then, turning towards the body, he

anistemi

said, "Tabitha, *get up*." She opened her eyes, saw Peter, and sat up. He gave her his hand and helped her to her feet. Then he called together the members of the church and the

zao

widows and showed her to them *alive*. News of it spread all over Joppa, and many came to believe in the Lord.

The work of Jesus in the resuscitation of corpses puts him in the succession of Elijah. Here we see Peter exercising the command of Jesus over death in the work of the early - post-resurrection - church. In his first commission to his disciples in which he sent them out in pairs we find a threefold imperative to go, preach and heal. In the final commission, for which there is no common biblical tradition [Matthew 28:18-20, Mark 16:15-16, Luke 24:45-49, Acts 1:8, John 20:21-23], there is no explicit injunction to heal as was the case in the first. To determine how the early church interpreted Jesus' final commission to go into all the world, preach the gospel of repentance and forgiveness of sins we need to look to the Acts of the Apostles and to the Letters. Within the longer [i.e. later] ending of Mark there is specific reference to healing where it is placed in the context of prophetic utterance concerning the actions in healing, removal of evil and bravery in face of danger by the people of faith. In Acts 10:42 Peter indicates the manner of Jesus' commission to his faithful followers. How is it put into practice? We find in Acts accounts of physical healing involving both individuals and groups, an exorcism and two revivifications of corpses. In other words all that was found in the gospels is in Acts too. It is against this scenario that we must allow church tradition and reason, rather than straightforward biblical text, to inform post-apostolic practice of the non-resuscitation of corpses.

| | **10:38** You know how God anointed Jesus of Nazareth with the Holy Spirit and with power. Because God was with him *iaomai* he went about doing good and *healing* all who were oppressed by the devil. |

As is given on three other occasions God anointed [blessed] Jesus with the Holy Spirit by this means indicating his commission to be with the power of God.[6] Such testimony points to the consistent presentation in the New Testament of Jesus as God's Messiah. The disciples firstly, and then subsequent believers sharing in this work, continue the messianic work of Jesus "in his name and in the power of the spirit". The Acts of the Apostles presents the powerful and transforming activity of the Holy Spirit as one of its most persistent themes. The work of the Holy Spirit in the early church is present in three ways: in the process of conversion to Christian faith, in prophecy - something which causes awkwardness in our day - and third, in the provocation for mission. In this last sense note how frequently the healing narratives in Acts are set in a missionary and evangelistic context in which the power of the Holy Spirit is openly acknowledged and testified.

14:9-10 [the cripple from Lystra] sat listening to Paul as he spoke. Paul fixed his eyes on him and, seeing that he had the *sozo* faith to be *cured*, said in a loud voice, "Stand up straight on your feet"; and he sprang up and began to walk.

This passage echoes a number of the themes from 3:2-8 very clearly though a significant difference here is the presence of faith within the person being healed. When it is used in this way the word *sozo* points to the deliberate redeeming healing action of God upon the whole person.

16:18 [a slave girl possessed by a spirit of divination had been obsessively following Paul and the others ...] She did this day after day, until, in exasperation, Paul rounded on the spirit. "I command you in the name of Jesus Christ *to* *exerchomai* *come out* of her," he said, and it came out instantly.

The girl it would seem from the text had been declaring Paul, Silas and the others to be the bringers of the news of God's salvation. What seems to have provoked Paul to effect the exorcism was not so much what the girl said as the obsessively compulsive manner of her attendance with the apostles.

I recall listening to a talk being given by Ian Cowie formerly of the Christian Fellowship of Healing in Edinburgh. A questioner quizzed him upon the place or relevance of exorcism in late twentieth century culture. He responded by saying that if a malign spirit could be perceived in someone then the appropriate action was exorcism. With appropriate prayer and the command to depart the exorcism need take but only a short time. If however, in the same subject a more therapeutic process of counselling [and maybe clinical intervention] was offered the benefits might take weeks to unfold. Cowie left us to ponder which might be the better.

I have expressed elsewhere my own reservations about the hasty road to exorcism and am not easily persuaded that Cowie's alternative is credible. On this subject I am grateful to Naomi Higham for offering me the logic that if someone is possessed by a malign spirit that spirit cannot be counselled out of them. If the person isn't possessed then exorcism isn't appropriate and ought not to be practised. Only one particular action is appropriate in either circumstance.

A thoughtful letter appeared in *The Times* in December 1996 from retired psychiatrist Derek Anton-Stephens. The letter is worth quoting at length:

... in the course of a career in psychiatry I have had dealings with three would-be exorcists, whose excitable and undisciplined attempts to dislodge supposedly possessing agents resulted in the deaths of the allegedly possessed victims. In the wrong hands, exorcism can be ... dangerous; and even in good ones there is need for vigilance and authoritative oversight.

I myself am not convinced that the primary cause of all instances of alleged demonic possession can automatically be attributed to psychiatric disorder, but it would be reprehensible in the extreme of anyone to act on the assumption that psychiatry can supply none of the answers.

There is a case for regarding some behavioural problems and mood alterations as the result of the operation of a motivating force or energy the nature of which we do not fully understand, but which does not always and necessarily arise solely from within the personality of the person concerned. Such a concept does not, however, in any way absolve those contemplating exorcism from the responsibility of ensuring that the clinical status of the 'possessed' person is fully explored before deliverance techniques are employed.

In making this point, I have in mind an attempt to exorcise a 'demon' held to be responsible for the depression, altered behaviour and severe headaches of a woman who had an operable tumour within her skull.

I do not want to be thought of as criticising Ian Cowie *per se* for what I heard him to say in a conference plenary when, quite probably, his position was actually more subtle than I remember it to be. My principal criticism is levelled at those who see society as demon-infested and employ varieties of inappropriate stratagems involving exorcism-like procedures very often upon deeply vulnerable people for whom, as with Anton-Stephens' example, other therapy is necessary. Only greater damage can result from such naivete and ignorance however well intentioned.

therapeuo	**17:25** It is not because he lacks anything that he accepts service at our hands, for he is himself the universal giver of life and breath - indeed of anything.

See Brown II, p.616; There is a likely echo of Isaiah's thought in 42:5 here at verses 24-25. Acts 17:25 is the only place in the NT where the classical use of *therapeuo* referring to service/serving is used. In this classical usage service refers to the service offered to a superior and, in its cultic sense, means to venerate the gods. Likewise the word *prosdeomai* only occurs in this verse, where it indicates that God being self-sufficient and independent in himself lacks nothing and therefore

170

our response to him in worship is not given because of any deficiency on his part. Indeed it is he who gives everything there is to his creation.

19:11-12 God worked extraordinary miracles through Paul: when handkerchiefs and scarves which had been in contact *apallasso* with his skin were carried to the sick, they were *cured* of *ekporeuo* their diseases, and the evil spirits *came out* of them.

N.B. I offer brief comment on Acts 19:13-20 in 8:7 above.

As in eight other locations in Acts and in some thirty in the synoptic gospels the proximation of evil spirits with illness is made. See also for comparison Luke 8:44 and Acts 5:15.[7]

28:1-6 Once we had made our way to safety, we identified the island as Malta. The natives treated us with uncommon kindness: because it had started to rain and was cold they lit a bonfire and made us all welcome. Paul had got together an armful of sticks and put them on the fire, when a viper, driven out by the heat, fastened on his hand. The natives, seeing the snake hanging on to his hand, said to one another, "The man must be a murderer; he may have escaped from the sea, but divine justice would not let him live." Paul, however, shook off the snake into the fire and was none the worse. They still expected him to swell up or suddenly drop down dead, but after waiting a long time without seeing anything out of the way happen to him, they changed their minds and said, "He is a god."

The Maltese locals would have spoken a Punic or Phoenician dialect which would be 'Barbarian' to a Greek. There may have been poisonous snakes in Malta then, though there are none now. Equally Luke may have thought a snake such as the *Coronella Austriaca* to be poisonous. An exactly similar incident is recorded as having happened to Bishop Philip Strong of Papua New Guinea in recent years.[8] It is the case that non-poisonous snakes may bite in exactly the same way as non-poisonous lizards. Viewed in such a light the account becomes rationally plausible.[9]

28:8-9 It so happened that [Publius'] father was in bed suffering from recurrent bouts of fever and dysentery. Paul *iaomai* visited him and, after prayer, laid his hands on him and *healed* him; whereupon the other sick people on the island came *therapeuo* and were *cured*.

In contrast to those occasions where the spoken word of authority "in the name of Jesus" or by Jesus himself is the sufficient means of healing this is one of the relatively few where we find hands being laid upon someone for healing. Whilst such a practice is commonplace nowadays practitioners of the ministry of healing should be aware that the action of the imposition of hands is psychologically very powerful even to the extent of being domineering or dominating. In this sense it is a practice easily open to abuse. More concretely I have considerable anxiety about the practice of laying hands upon the affected part of the body. There is no scriptural warranty for this. At one level it seems to me there is no need beyond that which cannot be brought into force by prayer and supplication for healing 'in the name of Jesus' which demands the requirement to lay on hands.

For some, however, there is an emotional need for touch, for an embrace. In these situations the powerful psychological 'force' of touch is something that can be creatively harnessed within the ministry of healing. What is required of those practising the ministry is deep and careful concern for the person who has come to them to ensure that whatever is done is done with the person's permission and does not exploit vulnerability and weakness.

> **28:26-27** For this people's mind has become dull; they have stopped their ears and closed their eyes. Otherwise, their eyes might see, their ears hear, and their mind understand, and then they might turn again, and I would *heal* them.

iaomai

The passage is quoted from Isaiah 6:9-10 and 43: 8 and occurs also in Matthew 13:14-15, Mark 4:10ff., Luke 8:9ff. and John 12:39ff. Simple hearing of the word of Christ is the precondition of understanding its implications for faith. Hearing the word and rejecting it leads to what Isaiah calls hardening. In the New Testament this attitude of hardening is not infrequently ascribed to the Jewish people. It can be interpreted that Jewish resistance in turning to God in Christ is not so much the result of Jesus' ministry but rather is the precondition for it. The early Christians seemed to view this opposition as given by God in advance to maximise the effect of turning to him in the light of the new covenant inaugurated by Jesus. I make no further comment upon this except, with the advantage of hindsight, to ponder with some remorse the formative influence this might have had upon centuries of historic anti-semitism.

Parallel passages are Matthew 13: 10-15, Mark 4:10ff. Luke 8:9f. and John 12:39ff.

Chapter 12   THE EPISTLES and REVELATION

1 Corinthians

iama

12:9 Another, by the same Spirit, is granted faith; another, by the one Spirit, gifts of *healing*.

In the Epistles, as distinct from the Gospels and Acts, narratives which refer to healing function in a different [albeit complementary] fashion. In the Gospels and Acts the narratives have a historical function as a record of events. In addition they have a teaching function in demonstrating something of crucial importance in the life and work of Jesus. Both the historical and teaching functions operate within an evangelistic framework in which God's kingdom could be seen through the healing work of Jesus. In the epistles all this was a given. For the early church however the issue was understanding how the healing work of God, effected by Jesus, was part and parcel of their own work.

For Paul the multiplicity of gifts bestowed by God through the power of the Holy Spirit is part of the ordering of the church in the unity for which Jesus prayed and which should be lived out in its practice.

iama

iama

12:28-30 Within our community God has appointed in the first place apostles, in the second place prophets, thirdly teachers; then miracle workers, then those who have gifts of *healing*, or ability to help others or power to guide them, or the gift of tongues of various kinds. Are all apostles? All prophets? All teachers? Do all work miracles? Do all have gifts of *healing*? Do all speak in tongues of ecstasy? Can all interpret them?

Paul, it seems to me, considered all Christians have some gift or other given them by God as part of their calling. The gift is not to be buried in a field [to use a gospel allusion] but is rather to be used in building up, in re-membering, the body of Christ seen in the unity of the church. In this sense I wholeheartedly endorse what Ian Bradley says in his timely volume *The Power of Sacrifice* that remembering in this sense is the opposite of dismembering, and not the opposite of forgetting.

Some may have more than one gift, rightly so. But each should use his or her gift in response to the grace given them by God. There is no room for rivalry or competition in any of this. In our own day the word 'charismatic' has true biblical authenticity denoting God's gracious bestowal of gifts upon all those of faith in him. It is a word more believers should readily accept for themselves and be pleased to own openly.

Hebrews

12:13 ... and keep to a straight path; and then the weakened
iaomai   limb will not be put out of joint, but *will regain its former powers.*

[The *Authorised Version* reads: and make straight paths for your
feet, lest that which is lame be turned out of the way; but let it
rather be *healed.*]

One has to ask the question whether the author of Hebrews is speaking
to a particular person or situation in his address to the wider group.
His metaphor of the 'weakened limb' perhaps indicates this.
Responsibility for this weakened limb rests upon the shoulders of the
wider group who are enjoined to "keep to a straight path" as the means
of giving strength and direction to the weaker member. The Greek
ektrape could read 'be turned aside' [as per the *Authorised Version*] but
continuing the medical metaphor [implied by the use of *iaomai*] seems
a better rendering. Accordingly the *REB* more appropriately adopts
the sense of 'dislocation' with its wording "put out of joint".

Notwithstanding all this the verse stands as an exhortation to a
church [citing Proverbs 4:26] not to become weary. An implicit
comparison may be made with the wandering people being led by
Moses through the desert. Keeping sight of the promise ahead gives
direction for the path and confidence against falling along the way.

James

5:13-16 Is anyone among you in trouble? Let him pray. Is
anyone in good heart? Let him sing praises. Is one of you ill?
Let him send for the elders of the church to pray over him
and anoint him with oil in the name of the Lord;... the prayer
sozo   offered in faith will *heal* the sick man, the Lord *will restore*
egeiro   him to health, and if he has committed sins they will be
forgiven. Therefore confess your sins to one another, and
iaomai   pray for one another, that you *may be healed.*

Along with 5:20 these are important verses. Warnings in James 1:14-
15 and 4:17 form part of the backcloth to the instruction given in
these verses. But they are not the end of the story for God's gracious
restoration through a healing of the whole sinful person will come.
Furthermore it will do so in the context of the prayers of faithful
people. The restoration [as forgiveness, healing, making whole] comes
as a normal part of the church's proclamation in general as well as the
individual ministry of one Christian to another. A free gift of grace is
given in these situations and for these situations. Whilst no one would
ever deny the desperate prayer of anyone, the sustained prayers of

those who are in a continuing and dynamic relation to God are more genuinely those which recognised God's love for the world. In this sense the prayers of the righteous person are especially real.

Confession of sin in the presence of illness has become significant in the pastoral practice of the Christian church.

My comments on Mark 6:13 on the use of oil are relevant for this passage also. I agree with John Wilkinson[1] that James' teaching refers to the [by his day] regular and given practice of using normal medicinal processes and practices "in the name of the Lord" though the case [particularly with respect to exorcism] that cultic procedures can be excluded still remains to be concluded. Perhaps one can say that had the context been cultic one might well have expected more material here and elsewhere on the methodology and principles involved. As with Mark 6:13 the verb for anointing is *aleipho*. The verb's usage in the gospels in six locations is in for non-cultic purposes. [Matthew 6:17; Luke 7:38, 46; John 11:2; 12:3; and in honour of the dead, Mark 16:1.

sozo   **5:20** ... you may be sure of this: the one who brings a sinner back from his erring ways will be *rescuing* a soul from death and cancelling a multitude of sins.

It is the love of God which rescues a sinner and which is seen in the life of a church faithful to its vocation. Perhaps this verse echoes something of Proverbs 10:12, Hate is always picking a quarrel, but "love overlooks every offence". God's love can cancel sin, rather than accumulate a ledger-list of them.

There is an apparent harshness in this verse which is worth some comment. Eternal death is that which is not enjoyed by those who have eternal life. Bringing people to eternal life is the purpose of Christ's work in salvation. It is his will that not one one should be lost to eternal death but that through him all should be saved.

3 John

hygiano   **2** Dear friend, above all I pray that things go well with you, and that *you may enjoy good health*. I know it is well with your soul.

Clearly there is much affection between the writer and his friend. The greeting is for health, prosperity and that all may go well. All this is framed in a prayerfully generous expression.

The verse raises, however, interesting questions. In correspondence with me about these expository notes Professor Richard Bauckham has written, "... People in the ancient world didn't try to 'keep healthy' in the sense of doing anything such as we might like take exercise,

vitamins etc. Unless they became ill they never thought about health..."
People didn't think about being healthy the way we do. Healthy was
just what one ordinarily is, and one paid no attention to the question
until one became ill, when something had to be done about it .

This understanding can be amplified from Stephen Smalley's
comment on 3 John 2 where a wish for good health is to be found,
"The presbyter continues with the personal and warm-hearted prescript
of his letter to Gaius with a health-wish typical of secular letters at this
time ..."[2] Whilst he adds a note that, possibly his friend was not in the
best of health physically he nevertheless underscores what he is saying
with the further comment, "A health-wish of this kind would have
been conventional in letters of this period".[3] Accordingly, whilst
keeping healthy was not idolised in New Testament times in the way
it is nowadays people were, for obvious reasons, concerned about health
and well-being.

Revelation of John the Divine

13:3 One of the heads seemed to have been given a death
therapeuo   blow, yet its mortal wound was *healed...*

The heads belong to a great sea monster - a dragon for which the given
Greek is *drakon*, a word found only in the Revelation of John with
the monster being a symbol of Satan. Its multifaceted features make it
recognisable easily as the state or any other secular authority who
with their multiple manifestations seek the adherence of subjects and
the elimination of alternative authority voices. In July 1944 an attempt
on the life of Hitler failed. A plan to inflict upon him a mortal blow
had come to naught. The capacity of the antichrist to be delivered
from that which would otherwise fell them should never be
underestimated. And yet in the longer term God's victory is secure.

13:12 [Another beast] wielded all the authority of the first
beast in its presence, and made the earth and its inhabitants
sozo   worship the first beast, whose mortal wound had been *healed.*

It is not without significance that those who seek to supplant the
authority of God work miracles and seek to secure worship. For this
reason at least miraculous powers and even signs are not in themselves
sufficient indicators of the presence and power of God. Neither is the
capacity to survive attack and even be healed. Such are the depths and
ways of evil.

21:24 By its light shall the nations walk, and to it the kings of the earth shall bring their splendour.

sozo

[The *Authorised Version* reads: "And the nations of them which are *saved* shall walk in the light of it: and the kings of the earth do bring their glory and honour into it."]

A comparison of these REB and AV texts points up an immediate problem in the narrative. Why did the editors or redactors of Revelation include the reference to "them which are saved"? As far as I am aware this phrase is found only in one very late Greek manuscript. Arguably some scribe must have thought it necessary to explain that these are not the nations who worshipped the beast and are damned.

The 'nations' are those who having trampled the Holy City underfoot and been seduced by the whore were finally conquered by Christ's forces [cf. 11:2,18; 18:3,23; 19:15]. The kings of the earth are those who are now under God's rule, having wrought great suffering upon faithful believers. Though once vindictive in this new era they bring of their glory to beautify the City of God [see in this respect, 6:15; 17:2,18; 18:3,9]. All earthly wealth and peoples can be transfigured and transformed in the new Jerusalem of the people of God. Nothing is irredeemably profane except that which is totally alien to the character of God [cf. 21:27]. It seems also that the unrepentant who choose the way of unholiness and sinfulness will by their own actions deny the election that God nevertheless offers.

22:2 On either side of the river stood a tree of life, which yields twelve crops of fruit, one for each month of the year. The leaves of the trees are for the *healing* of the nations.

therapeia

Important Old Testament images are brought forward in this verse, Ezekiel 47:1-12, Genesis 2:9-10 and Psalm 46:4.

The image, or motif, indicated by *karpos*, fruit, is deeply significant. Flowing from the new Jerusalem is a river passing downhill almost four thousand feet to the barren and bromide-laden Dead Sea. The tree of life points to the all-encompassing, healing, presence of God through all seasons in this new and redeemed world, the instantiation of his kingdom. It is this eschatological vision to which all the healing narratives in the New Testament have been pointing.

Arguably there is no better point than this with which to finish my sweep of New Testament healing narratives.

CHAPTER NOTES

Chapter One

1 M. Maddocks, *The Christian Healing Ministry*, SPCK, 1990.
2 Stephen Pattison, *Alive and Kicking, Towards a Practical Theology of Illness and Healing*, SCM Press, 1989. [The author has told me that his misleading title caused its relative obscurity!]
3 J. Cameron Peddie, *The Forgotten Talent*, Arthur James, 1985, p.13.
4 p.42.   5 p.14.
6 I repeat this from my own *A Way for Healing*, Handsel Press, 1995, p.29.
7 Morna D. Hooker, *The Gospel According to St. Mark*, A. & C. Black, 1991, p.390.
8 1 Cor. 12:4-11, 27-13:3; Rom. 12:6-21; Eph. 4:11-13.

Chapter Two

1 Maddocks, *op. cit.*, pp.192ff.
2 Mark 9:2-9; Matthew 17:1-9; Luke 9:28-36.
3 Alan Alerck, 'What is Counselling?' in *Marriage Guidance* [January 1967] quoted by Maddocks, pp.167-168.
4 page 1, British Association for Counselling, Leaflet, 'Counselling: Definition of terms in use'.

Chapter Three

1 Peddie, *op. cit.*, pp121ff.
2 p.18.   3 p.105.
4 I am taking much of this from *Alive and Kicking*, Chapter 2.
5 A member of the St Andrew's, St Andrews congregation once acerbically commented that the only subjects upon which I preached were holiness and nationalism. [I am in favour of the former and opposed to the latter!] And again, I am not a golfer but I once put myself in the lion's den when preaching at the annual St Andrews golf service in 1994 by taking the St Andrews golfing community to task for some very unsavoury mutual hostility revolving around the running of the golf links and beginning to attract the world's press. I have also used Grampian Television's 'God Slot' *Reflections* to talk about both personal holiness and politics.
6 Calvin, J. *Institutes of the Christian Religion*, trans. Henry Beveridge in two vols, James Clarke & Co. Ltd., London, 1962. The section here is taken from Vol. One, Book III, Chapter IV; pp.532-570.
7 p.540
8 p.541, quoting Chrysostom.
9 p.545.
10 Paul Ricoeur, 'Guilt, Ethics and Religion', in *Talk of God, being the Royal Institute of Philosophy Lectures*, Volume 2, 1967/8, Macmillan and Co. Ltd., London, 1970, pp.100-117
11 pp.100-101.
12 p.101.
13 p.104.
14 Quoted, and adapted slightly, with permission. Higham refers the reader to Imbers and Jonker, *Christianity and Incest*, Burns and Oates, 1992, p.113.

15 Most helpful material on the market comes from secular sources and is directed towards a secularised readership. Whilst I add my appreciation to a great deal of this I distance myself from much of the current Christian writing on the subject of abuse and particularly sexual abuse for I find it flows from a prescriptive and nearly always fundamentalistic stable and which, it seems to me, simply compounds the effects of the abuse it claims to help. Dan B. Allender's *The Wounded Heart*, CWR, Farnham, Surrey, 1991 [especially his Chapter Two] is in this latter category.

16 A conversation with Alison Naylor has helped my thoughts crystalise upon this.

Chapter Four

1 K. Stendahl, *Peake's Commentary*, ed. Matthew Black and H.H. Rowley, Nelson, London, 1972, para 683f.

2 Morna Hooker, op. cit, pp.156, 157. And cf. also David Hill, *The Gospel of Matthew*, Marshall Morgan & Scott, London, 1981, p.186.

3 J.N.D. Kelly, *The Pastoral Epistles: I & II Timothy, Titus*, A. & C. Black, 1986, p.129.

4 John Wilkinson, *Health and Healing; Studies in New Testament Principles and Practice*, Handsel Press, Edinburgh, 1980, p.109.

5 John Calvin, *The First Epistle of Paul the Apostle to the Corinthians*, Oliver and Boyd, Edinburgh, 1960, trans J.W. Fraser, p.262.

6 Alan Richardson ed., *A Dictionary of Christian Theology*, SCM Press, London, 1969, p.328.

7 Edward Schillebeeckx, Jesus; *An Experiment in Christology*, Collins, London, 1983, especially pp.180ff.

8 pp.199-201.

Chapter Five

1 C.S. Lewis, *The Problem of Pain*, Fount, London, 1977.

2 For this I am indebted to Dr Keith Birkinshaw of Queen Margaret Hospital, Dunfermline.

3 A superb discussion, which gives substance to my own brief comment here, can be found in 'Emotional Aspects of Pain' by Kenneth D. Craig, in Patrick D. Wall and Ronald Melzack, *Textbook of Pain*, [3rd edition], Churchill Livingstone, Edinburgh, 1994, pp.261-274.

4 Let me note in passing that in general, where there is real pathology underlying the condition, acupuncture only gives temporary relief for a day or two.

5 Patrick D. Wall, 'Intro. to the edition after this one', in Wall and Melzack, *op cit.*, p.1.

6 2 Corinthians 12:7-9.

7 I have spent considerable periods of my ministry counselling survivors of sexual abuse and one particularly helpful tool which releases the imprisonment of silence which some survivors of abuse feel unable to overcome is to encourage them to write when speech is an impossibility. The quotation which is included in the text comes from someone who was writing at the time of experiencing intense abdominal pains. She then forwarded me these notes so that we might discuss them at our next meeting.

179

8   Wilkinson, *op. cit.*, p.141.
9   Galatians 6:14.
10   Donald Baillie, *The Sense of the Presence of God*, Oxford University Press, 1962.
11   Peddie, *op. cit.*, pp.45-46.
12   Morris Maddocks, *The Vision of Dorothy Kerin*, Hodder and Stoughton, London 1991 is an excellent documentation of Kerin's mystical pilgrimage.
13   p.57.   14   p.60.
15   pp.68,69.
16   Brian Sibley, *Shadowlands; The True Story of C.S.Lewis and Joy Davidman*, Hodder and Stoughton, 1994, London, p.155.

Chapter Six

1   ed. Colin Brown, *The New International Dictionary of New Testament Theology*, The Paternoster Press, Carlisle, 1986 edn.
2   ed. Gerhard Kittel, *Theological Dictionary of the New Testament*, trans. Geoffrey W. Bromiley, Eerdmans, Grand Rapids, 1979.
3   Paul is also alluding here to Isaiah 42:5.
4   Beyer in Gerhard Kittel [ed], Vol. III, 1979, p.129.
5   Numbers 12:7 and cf also Galatians 4:1.
6   cf. the Hippocratic Oath.
7   Oepke in Kittel, *op cit.*, p198 gives illustrations.
8   p.201.
9   Luck in Kittel, *op. cit.*, Vol. VIII, p.308.
10   p.312.
11   I Timothy, 1:10, 6:3; 2 Timothy 1:13, 4:3; Titus 1:9, 2:1, 2:8.
12   Oepke in Kittel, *op. cit.*, Vol. I, p.387.
13   H.G. Link in Colin Brown, *op. cit.*, Vol. 3. p.146.

14   cf. in this respect Genesis 23:16, 29:3, 41:13, Exodus 14:26ff.
15   H. Bietenard in Colin Brown, *op. cit.*, Vol. 1, p.453.
16   Hauck in Kittel, *op. cit.*, Vol. I, p.528 offers illustrations.
17   Kittel, *op. cit.*, Vol. VII, pp.964-1024.

BIBLICAL STUDY NOTES

Matthew

1   George Anderson, *The History and Religion of Israel*, Oxford University Press, Oxford, 1966, p.32, n1.
2   David Hill, *op. cit.*, pp.106-107.
3   Didache 11: 8, cited from J. Stevenson, *A New Eusebius: Documents illustrating the history of the Church to AD337*, SPCK, Revised W.H.C. Frend, 1987, p.11.
4   J. Jeremias, *New Testament Theology, The Proclamation of Jesus*, p.77 Volume 1, SCM Press, London, 1971.
5   see Colin Brown, ed., 'Leprosy' in *op. cit.*, The Paternoster Press, Exeter, Volume 2, 1976, pp.463ff.
6   Colin Brown, *op. cit.*, Vol. 2, pp.168-169. Although Brown does not specify to which of the Gospels of Thomas he is referring he must mean the 'Infancy' Gospel as the other, the 'Coptic' Gospel carries no miracle stories.
7   Colin Brown *op. cit.*, Vol. 3, p.1059.
8   David Hill, *op. cit.*, p.166 followed by Colin Brown, *op. cit.*, Vol. 3, p.211 recognises that Matthew may not only be recounting a story of Jesus here but

also addressing himself to the early Matthean Christian community.

9 Josephus *Antiquities*, viii, 48. English Translation by H.St. J. Thackeray and Ralph Marcus, Harvard University Press and William Heinemmann, reprinted 1988 in the Loeb Classical Library.

10 David Hill, *op. cit.*, p.167.

11 Morna Hooker, *op. cit.*, p.144.

12 I continue to draw extensively from David Hill's *The Gospel of Matthew*, pp.69-72.

13 Robert A. Gillies, *op. cit.*, pp.75.

14 Colin Brown, *op. cit.*, Vol. 1, p.219. In private conversation with me Richard Bauckham has questioned this.

15 Matthew more than the other Gospels lays emphasis upon the Davidic descent of Jesus.

16 Colin Brown, *op. cit.*, vol.2, p.57.

17 Isaiah 29:18f, 35:5f, 61:1f.

18 Colin Brown, *op. cit.*, Vol. 2, p.631.

19 *Ibid.*, citing Karl Barth, *Evangelical Theology: An Introduction*, Wm. B Eerdmans, Grand Rapids, 1963 p.68. I have deliberately not repeated Brown's full citation of Barth, since Barth continues, if I interpret him correctly, to imply that because Jesus' miracles were "isolated and temporary" there would be no extension of his ministry to us within a contemporary ministry of healing. If this is Barth's position it is, of course, something I would seriously question. In the context of Barth's chapter in *Evangelical Theology* his reference to miracles is upon their pre-eschatological significance as "radically helpful and saving" and as "promises and intimations, anticipations of a redeemed nature, of a state of freedom..." [p.68]. Perhaps therefore the inference I am drawing is away from Barth's main focus. Nonetheless I feel my comments are relevant.

20 William Wrede, *The Messianic Secret*, [English translation from the German by J.C.G Greig], J. Clarke, Cambridge, 1971.

21 His own essay in *Dictionary of New Testament Theology*, Vol. 3, pp.506-511. My own reflections draw heavily upon Brown's helpful essay.

22 J.D.G. Dunn, 'The Messianic Secret in Mark', *Tyndale Bulletin*, 1970, pp.92-117.

23 Colin Brown, *op. cit.*, Vol. 3, p.696.

24 I am indebted to Richard Bauckham for this.

25 David Hill, *op. cit.*, pp.247-248.

26 *Songs for the Holocaust of the Sabbath*, 4Q400-407 and 11Q5-6. The discovery of some of these fragments in the final stronghold of the Essenes at Masada might be an indication [there can be no stronger inference than this] that when deserting Qumran the Essenes thought it fit to take them with them rather than leave them hidden in the caves. Perhaps they considered them of especial importance in the face of the likely emerging resistance that was to lead to their extinction. See Geza Vermes, *The Dead Sea Scrolls in English*, 4th edn, Penguin Books, London, pp. 254ff.

27 Josephus, *Jewish Antiquities*, Book 4, viii:15. [para 219].

Mark

1 Geza Vermes, *Jesus the Jew*, Fontana / Collins, Glasgow, 1976, pp.61ff.

2 See Colin Brown, *op. cit.*, Vol. 2, p.671.

3 I owe many of my own first insights into the significance of table fellowship and God's kingdom to James P. Mackey, *Jesus, The Man and the Myth*, SCM Press, 1979, Chap. 4.

4 A fuller description of possession and associated material is in my *A Way for Healing*, pp.49-62.

5 Morna Hooker, *op. cit.*, p.78ff.

6 I say this in disagreement with S.G.F. Brandon, *Jesus and the Zealots; A Study of the Political Factors in Primitive Christianity*, Manchester University Press, 1967; cf. Brandon, 'Zealots' in *Encyclopaedia Judaica*, Vol. 16, p.947.

7 See Colin Brown, *op. cit.*, Vol. 3, pp.147f. for other uses of *apokathistemi*, not least in political messianism and the hope of a redeemer who will "restore all things" for the chosen people of the Hebrews. It has also an interesting application in the military command, "As you were!"

8 I am indebted to Richard Bauckham for this information.

9 Colin Brown, *op. cit.*, Vol. 2, p.560.

10 Vol. 3, p.696.

11 W. Brunotte, in Colin Brown, *op. cit.*, Vol. 1, pp.120-121.

12 John Wilkinson, *Health and Healing, Studies in New Testament Principles and Practice*, Handsel Press, Edinburgh, 1980, pp.152-153.

13 David Hill, *op. cit.*, p.270.

14 Cicero, *Oratio pro Ligario*, XI, cited from Morna Hooker, *The Gospel According to St. Mark*, p.230.

Luke

1 I am indebted to Richard Bauckham for this translation.

2 I am drawing from Colin Brown, *op. cit.*, Vol. 2, pp.463ff.

3 Morna D. Hooker, *op. cit.*, p.64.

4 Colin Brown, *op. cit.*, Vol. 3, p.785.

5 I have drawn on a number of texts here, esp. Colin Brown, *op. cit.*, Vols.1,2 & 3 and Kittel, *op. cit.*, Vol. 3, especially pp.413-429.

6 My list here is drawn from Colin Brown, *op. cit.*, Vol. 3, p.1106.

7 Two contributors in Colin Brown, *op. cit.*, Vol. 3 seem to disagree on the reference of *nomodidaskalos*. Wegenast [p.768] refers it to the Pharisees and Hillyer [p.480] to the scribes.

8 Colin Brown, *op. cit.*, Vol. 3, p.912 refers to other instances of people being lowered through openings in the roof.

9 Vermes, *Jesus the Jew*, p.25.

10 Colin Brown, *op. cit.*, Vol. 1, pp. 196-197, 199.

11 Adapted from a sermon I preached at Saint Andrew's Episcopal Church, St. Andrews at the Midnight Liturgy of Christmas, 1995.

12 Colin Brown, *op. cit.*, Vol. 3, pp.1059-1060.

13 *op. cit.*, p.280.

14 David Hill, *op. cit.*, p.179.

15 Ian Bradley, *The Power of Sacrifice*, Darton, Longman and Todd, London, 1995.

16 Colin Brown, *op. cit.*, Volume 3, p.1142.

17 see H. Bietenhard, in Colin Brown, *op. cit.*, Vol. 1, p.685 and article 'Samaritan' in Vol. 2.

18 F. Graber and D. Müller in Colin Brown, *op. cit.*, Vol. 2, p.168.

John

1   H. Müller in Colin Brown, *op. cit.*, Vol. 3, p.709.
2   Charles Talbert, *Reading John*, SPCK, London, 1992, p.126.
3   W.L. Lane in Colin Brown, *op. cit.*, Vol. 3, pp.916-7. A typographical error in Brown [five lines up] should be corrected to John 2:
4   Rudolf Bultmann, *The Gospel of John*, (English translation from the German by G.R. Beasley-Murray) Blackwell, Oxford, 1971, p.69, n.2.
5   For this and other references in this exegesis see Charles H. Talbert, *op. cit.*, pp.171-176.

The Acts of the Apostles

1   Josephus, *Antiquities*, XIV, 4.3.
2   I am indebted to Professor Richard Bauckham for this detail.
3   This narrative is based on a talk I gave in St Andrew's Episcopal Church, St. Andrews during an ALPHA course in Advent 1995.

4   I recounted this in a broadcast on Grampian Television on July 3rd 1996. See also my *INforming FAITH*, Handsel Press, 1996, p.168.
5   Colin Brown, *op. cit.*, Vol , p.921.
6   cf. Luke 4:18 [quoting Isaiah 61:1], Acts 4:27 and Hebrews 1:9 [quoting Psalm 45:7].
7   See also my *A Way for Healing*, pp.80-81 where further comment on Acts 19:10-12 and Acts 19:13-17 is given.
8   cf. C.S.C. Williams, *The Acts of the Apostles*, A. & C. Black, London, 1985, p.275.
9   This comment is taken from my *A Way for Healing*, p.73.

The Epistles and Revelation

1   John Wilkinson, *op. cit.*, p.153.
2   Stephen S. Smalley, *Word Biblical Commentary; 1,2,3 John*, Word Publishing, Milton Keynes, p.345.
3   *op. cit.*, p.346.

BIBLIOGRAPHY

Anderson, George, *The History and Religion of Israel*, Oxford University Press, Oxford, 1966

Barrett, C.K., *The First Epistle to the Corinthians*, A. & C. Black, London, 1987

Bauckham, Richard, *The Theology of the Book of Revelation*, Cambridge Univ. Press, 1993

Best, Ernest, *The First and Second Epistles to the Thessalonians*, A. & C. Black, London, 1986

Bradley, Ian, *The Power of Sacrifice*, Darton, Longman and Todd, London 1995

ed. Brown, Colin, *The New International Dictionary of New Testament Theology*, The Paternoster Press, Exeter. Volume 1, Volume 2 [1976], Volume 3 [1978], Volume 4 [1986]

Caird, G.B., *The Revelation of St. John the Divine*, A. & C. Black, London, 1966

Calvin, J., *Institutes of the Christian Religion*, trans Henry Beveridge in two volumes, James Clarke & Co. Ltd., London, 1962.

Hill, David, *The Gospel of Matthew*, New Century Bible Commentary, Marshall, Morgan & Scott Ltd., London, 1981

Hooker, Morna D., *The Gospel According to St. Mark*, A. & C. Black, London, 1991

Josephus Flavius, *Jewish Antiquities*, in the Loeb Classical Library, Harvard University Press

Keele, K.D., *Anatomies of Pain*, C.C. Thomas, Springfield, Illinois, 1957

Kelly, J.N.D., *The Pastoral Epistles: I & II Timothy, Titus*, A. & C. Black, 1986

Melzack, R. & Casey, K.L., 'Sensory, motivational and central control determinants of pain: a new conceptual model' in D.L. Kenshalo [ed] *The Skin Senses*, C.C. Thomas, Springfield, Illinois [particularly p.423]

ed. Kittel, Gerhard trans. Geoffrey W. Bromiley, *Theological Dictionary of the New Testament*, Eerdmans, Volumes 1 [1979], 2, [1980], 3 [1979], 7 [1971], 8 [1980]

Maddocks, Morris, *The Christian Healing Ministry*, SPCK, London, 1990

Maddocks, Morris, *The Vision of Dorothy Kerin*, Hodder and Stoughton, London, 1991

Montefiore, H.W., *A Commentary on The Epistle to the Hebrews*, A. & C. Black, London, 1987

Pattison, Stephen, *Alive and Kicking*, SCM, London, 1989

Peake's Commentary, ed. Matthew Black and H.H. Rowley, Nelson, London, 1972, para 683f.

Peddie, J. Cameron, *The Forgotten Talent*, Arthur James, 1985

Ricoeur Paul, 'Guilt, Ethics and Religion', in *Talk of God*, being the Royal Institute of Philosophy Lectures, Volume 2, 1967/8, Macmillan and Co. Ltd., London, 1970, pp.100-117

Schillebeeckx, Edward, *Jesus; An Experiment in Christology*, Collins, London, 1983, especially pp.180ff

Sibley, Brian, *Shadowlands; The True Story of C.S. Lewis and Joy Davidman*, Hodder and Stoughton, London, 1994

Smalley, Stephen S., *1,2,3 John*; Word Biblical Commentary, Vol 51, Word Publishing, Dallas, 1991

Stevenson J., *A New Eusebius: Documents illustrating the history of the Church to AD337*, SPCK, Revised W.H.C. Frend, 1987

Talbert, Charles H., *Reading John*, SPCK, London, 1992

Vermes, Geza, *Jesus the Jew*, Fontana / Collins, Glasgow, 1976

Wall, Patrick D. and Melzack, Ronald, *Textbook of Pain*, [3rd edn], Churchill Livingstone, Edinburgh, 1994

Wilkinson, John, *Health and Healing, Studies in New Testament Principles and Practice*, Handsel Press, Edinburgh, 1980

Wilkinson, John, *The Bible and Healing: a Medical and Theological Commentary*, Handsel Press, Edinburgh, 1998

Williams, C.S.C., *The Acts of the Apostles*, A. & C. Black, London, 1985